# Social Justice under Islam

# Social Justice Under Islam

**A. Mannan**

Reference Press

4831/24, Ansari Road
Darya Ganj
New Delhi-110 002
Phone: 51563444
Fax: 51563334
*E-mail: info@essessreference.com*
*url: http://www.essessreference.com*

First Published 2005

ISBN: 81-88583-84-7

Rs.750/-



Published by:
**Reference Press**
4831/24, Ansari Road, Darya Ganj,
New Delhi-110 002.
Phone: 51563444
Fax: 51563334
*E-mail: info@essessreference.com*
*url: http://www.essessreference.com*

Printed in India at:
Mehra Offset Press, New Delhi

# Contents

*Preface* *vii*

1. **Basic Concept** 1
Fundamental Elements • The Roots • Various Issues

2. **Social Justice** 33
Basic Issues • Judicial Perception • No Discrimination • Various Angles

3. **Basic Freedom** 91
Freedom of being Safe • The Protection • Different Free Acts

4. **Rights in Islam** 165
Human Relations • Universal Laws • Ideals in Islam • The Perception

5. **Protection by Law** 257
Rights Guaranteed by Law • Individual Liberties • Religious Liberties • Basic Rights • Special Rights

6. **Natural Rights** 277
Basic Rights • Equality for All • Slavery Condemned

7. **Law and Social Justice** 313
The Jurisprudence • Cultivation and Evolution • Laws in Force • Laws of Society • Great Contributions

*Bibliography* 341

# Preface

Social Justice in Islam is a much talked about subject. Still the high-profile debates on this area of high concern are persisting in the socio-religious and intellectual spheres of our society. However, some major issues and problems in Islamic society are very often left unaddressed. As the debates go on, and books being published are from political or ideological points of view, very often, this turns out to be biased and ambiguous. So now a major chunk of people is left in dark with regards to the Social Justice under Islam. Only a succinct academic work on this contentious issue may help scholars and students to have a clear-vision about Social Justice in Islam. I write fastidiously about this subject and has left no stone unturned in addressing all the issues including those areas unaddressed so far.

To begin with, the author lays stress on the basic concepts in Islam, which include fundamental issues, the roots and various issues connected with this. With a machine-like precision, I dig out the very issues and problems linked with the social justice in Islamic society like basic issues, judicial perception, non-discriminatory attitude and various other aspects.

Next, I have touched upon an area, which has not been addresed so far, in a judicious manner. Of the basic freedoms author elaborates the interesting areas such as freedom of being safe the protection and different free acts. As for the rights in Islam, basic factors of this area like human relations, universal laws and ideals in Islam are elaborated. The protection given to the community members is convincingly explained in the book by pinpointing the constitutionally guaranteed rights, like individual liberties, religious liberties, basic rights and special rights. The book also speaks of the area of natural rights, which comprises basic rights, equality for all and condemnation of slavery. Lastly this author puts his thoughts on law and social justice in the book, covering the jurisprudence, cultivation and evolution of laws in force and laws of society.

Considering the areas dealt with and the style, which this book is completed in, should fetch a large number of readers and also change the whole perception of social justice in Islam in the minds of people.

**Author**

# 1

# Basic Concept

The man is sociable by nature. His herd instinct urges him on to live together with fellow beings. Right from his birth until death he stands severely in need of the attention, aid and support of innumerable individuals. Not only to meet the needs of his upbringing, food, clothing, lodging and education and training, but also for the development and blossoming of his natural capabilities and their practical demonstration, he is compelled to lead, and participate in collective life. This corporate life binds up a vast fabric of relationships around him, the small and big spheres of relationships of the family, brotherhood, locality, town, country and humanity as a whole, determine his rights and obligations. He has certain obligations in the various capacities of mother, father, son, pupil, teacher, the employer, employee, trader, customer, citizen and the ruler, and as against all these obligations, he is entitled to certain definite rights.

Among these rights some are of a moral nature, for instance, the right of respect for the elders, the right of affection and consideration for the youngsters, the right of help for the needy, the right of the guest to be entertained, and so on. And some have a legal protection and support, for example, the right of ownership, the right of wages (for work done), the right of obtaining dower (mahr), and the right of compensation and the like. These are the rights of a nature related to some interests, and the law of the land recognizing such interests makes them realizable through the judiciary. These rights are known as Legal Rights or Positive Rights.

There is yet another sphere of the rights of the individual concerning his relations with the state. In this sphere the rights given to an individual in relation to a state with vast powers and resources, are called Fundamental Rights. They are also sometimes termed Basic Human Rights and Birth Rights of man. These rights are guaranteed to him under the highest law of the land, the "Constitution" instead of the ordinary laws obtaining in a country. They are called "Fundamental Rights" because none of the various arms of the state, executive or legislature can violate them. These rights are enjoyed by the individual not as the citizen of a state but as a member of the universal brotherhood of mankind. They transcend all distinctions of colour, race, territory, language and the rest, and man is entitled to them as human being. They have not been conferred on him as a result of legislation by any state legislature, or as the outcome of a covenant, but naturally enjoyed by him and forming an integral part of his existence. In case of a state failing to recognize or enforce them, it is considered guilty of usurping the rights of man conferred on him by nature, since they are inalienable and irrevocable. The state has no power even to amend, abridge or hold them in abeyance temporarily on some pretext, not to speak of revoking them, save in case of the sovereign or the people all having conferred those powers on it with definite limits and conditions expressly mentioned in the constitution. And even this scope has been provided in the western constitutions. The Islamic constitution does not allow any individual, institution or even the Muslim Ummah as a whole to revoke, abridge or suspend the fundamental rights in any form whatsoever.

It was only three or three centuries and a half ago that this term fundamental rights came to be introduced in Europe. In fact it is just another name for the "Natural Rights" first used by the Greek thinker, Zeno, and later explained in legal and constitutional language by the Roman legislator, Cicero. W. Friedman thus:

> But the conception of a society based on definite rights of the individual citizen is a relatively modern one, developed in reaction, first against the medieval order of society and secondly, against the absolutist

> government of the modern state, in the seventeenth and eighteenth centuries. It finds expression in the legal philosophy of Locke, the French Declaration of the Rights of Man, and the American Constitution.

Gaines Ezejiofor defines fundamental rights thus:

> Human or fundamental rights is the modern name for what have been traditionally known as natural rights, and these may be defined as moral rights which every human being, everywhere, at all times, ought to have simply because of the fact that, in contradistinction with other beings, he is rational and moral. No man may be deprived of these rights without grave affront to justice.

Elucidating the nature of Fundamental Rights Justice Jackson says:

> One's right to life, liberty, and property, to free speech and a free press, freedom of worship and assembly, and other fundamental rights may not be submitted to vote; they depend on the outcome of no elections.

## Fundamental Elements

The concept of fundamental rights has two aspects. One of them is moral, according to which man must occupy a respectable and dignified position in the society. Man as such is worthy of respect, and like other members of the society this respect for him must come from the rulers as well. Those who happen to deal with them in authority, should not forget that they themselves are men (like all other men) and as regards human dignity and honour, the fact of their holding any office of authority does not bring to them any superiority or supremacy. The other aspect of the fundamental rights is their legal aspect, according to which these rights must be recognized legally and must be given protection by the highest law of the land. From the angle of practical enforcement this aspect comprises three factors:

(1) Fundamental Rights get human dignity recognized and furnish guiding principles for legal and administrative procedures.

(2) These rights provide a person protection against tyranny and oppression. The limits prescribed by them, which cannot be violated, safeguard him against the discriminatory treatment of the law, and officers of the executive and the judiciary, since well defined sections are provided for the law relating to these rights.

(3) Fundamental rights bring into existence an institution which guarantees the enforcement of these rights against all other individuals and the rulers. This institution is the Judiciary.

Inclusion of the Fundamental Rights in the constitution of a country aims at demarcating the sphere of legislative powers of the state, and also limits its activities through the judiciary within the limits and protections provided by the constitution, so that the rulers may not usurp the fundamental rights of the people and take to the dictatorial pattern of rule. The real motive behind the recognition of these rights is to offer protection to man's honour and greatness and his dignity and respect against the high-handedness of dictatorship or cruel collectivism, to furnish it with guarantee of leading a respectable life, and provide him opportunities to develop his personal capabilities and to be benefited by the prints of these capabilities, and to maintain a certain sphere of the freedom of thought and action which may be immune from the interference of other individuals of the society. The term fundamental rights has emerged in the peculiar historical background of Europe. A civil war extending over a thousand years, the despotism of the monarchs, the exploitation of the feudal order, the unbearably tight hold of the Church on the individual, the blood-shed due to the differences of the creed, nationalism and the hunger for expansionism created by it, and taking over countries by the sword, and the way, it injured the self-respect of man, and ruthlessly trampled his life, property and honour and dignity, and rendered him powerless and totally helpless against the tyrannical state.

This roused the conscience of those left with any feeling for humanity and compelled them to ponder over the measures to protect man against degradation and debasement and to restore the respect and honour due to him, and to show the despots and dictators the way humanity should be respected. It was under these conditions that the theory of natural rights during the course of its attaining the state of practical application, was transformed into Fundamental Rights, and the movement for definite rights for the individual and constitutional safeguards, started gathering momentum. When the entire globe got converted into a smouldering hell due to the tyranny of the days of colonialism and the use of fire arms and atom bomb in the two world wars and its flames engulfed the entire human race, the din made by the echoes of "Fundamental Rights" in Europe became a world-wide demand, as a result of which the charter of the United Nations, and the charter of Human Rights came into existence. In this way the technical term which had emerged in an atmosphere of tyranny and oppression, reached every nook and corner of the world.

Since the Islamic concept of rights does not have the background which gave birth to the European concept of basic rights, it is totally different from it. We shall deal with it at length later on.

## The Roots

Before taking up the Islamic concept of man's fundamental right and their determination and protection, it will be in the fitness of things to take stock of the history of human rights, the various theories of the Westerners regarding the source and origin of these rights as also the protective measure provided by them for their preservation. Let us see how far is man, in the west and in the rest of the world, following them is the recipient of the bounties of the protection of the life and property, establishment of an order of justice and equity, safety of his honour and dignity, freedom of action, and independence of thought; how far are his fundamental rights inalienable, and what have been his chances of leading a life of peace and safety, and honour and dignity as a result of the continuous struggle during the past three or four centuries for the determination and acquisition of these rights.

The Westerners commence the evolutionary history of the concept of the Fundamental Human Rights, from Greece of the Fifth century B.C., and then linking their political thought with the degenerate Roman Empire of the Fifth century A.D., they take a big leap into the eleventh century, thus leaving a wide gap of five hundred years from the sixth to the tenth century A.D., in the history put together by them. And, pray, why is it so? Most probably for the reason that this is the Islamic period (to which the Christian West has ever been most allergic- Tr.).

Undoubtedly the Greek philosophers have laid great stress on the rule of law and (meting out) justice and equity, and have written books on its need and importance with great erudity. But the concept of human equality is conspicuous by its absence there. They divide men into different classes very much like the water tight compartments into which Brahmins (the ruling class and religious leaders), Kshatriyas (reserved for military services), Vaisya (the traders and the cultivators) and the Shudras (performing menial services for the other three classes, and their slaves), were placed in ancient India, and where they are very much there even today. Exactly like that of Manu-Shashtra they (the ancient Greeks,) too had these four classes. Plato, in his book *The Republic* grants the right to rule only to the philosophers, and divides the remaining population into soldiers (fighting men), cultivators and slaves. He says:

> Citizens, you are brothers, yet God has framed you differently. Some of you have the power of command, and these he has composed of gold: others of silver, to be auxiliaries: others again who are to be farmers and craftsmen he has made of brass and iron.

And here is Plato's concept of justice:

> I proclaim justice is nothing else than the interest of the stronger. Everywhere there is one principle of justice, which is the interest of the stronger.

And let us see what he has to say in his further elucidation of Justice:

> Justice is the art which gives good to friends and evil to enemies.

According to Plato, the greatest weakness of democracy is that it grants equal status to all citizens.

Democracy is a charming form of government, full of disorder and dispensing a sort of equality to equals and unequals alike.

Elucidating the objective of law, Plato says:

> The object of laws is to make those who use them happy. Plato does not believe in equality in the matter of dispensing justice. He is in favour of separate laws for every class. About slaves he writes in his book *Laws*:

Slaves ought to be punished as they deserve, and not admonished as if they were freemen, which will make them only conceited.

He is tolerant of equality between man and woman. He says:

> Women's nature is inferior to that of men in capacity of virtue.

Like his teacher, Plato, Aristotle too stands for a society divided into various strata or classes. He too is embarrassed at the idea of equality. In his book *The State* pointing out democracy as the worst form of government he says:

> A democracy is a government in the hands of men of low birth, poverty, and vulgar employments.

The last and worst form is that which gives a share to every citizen.

Aristotle's concept of justice, too, is near about the same as that of his teacher, Plato. He says:

> Now justice is the virtue by which each has his own as the law prescribes.

Here, introducing the condition of position he strikes at the very roots of justice. His views about slavery are very well defined:

> It is clear that some are free by nature, and others are slaves, and that in the case of the latter the lot of slavery is both advantageous and just.

He grants the free and "noble" men the right to divide this large number of slaves among themselves, put them to work the worst type of drudgery Tr.) and look after their food and clothing. It is in his *The State* that he writes:

the award of this charter, the parliament started a campaign for the enhancement of its powers. In 1188 the principal of Habeas corpus was recognized by King Alphonso IX under compelling circumstances. On 15th June, 1215, "Magna Carta" was issued which was declared by Voltair as the Charter of freedom Undoubtedly Magna Carta is the most important document of fundamental rights that has made history in England. But it interpreted as much later. At the time of its issuance it was sort of a covenant between the barons and king John of England, in which the rights of the feudal lords had been provided protection. The rights of the common people had no place in it. Henry Marsh says:

> And if Magna Carta had done no more it would have been a charter for the great land owners' and nothing else.

In 1355 the British Parliament while approving and accrediting the Magna Carta passed the bill of Due process of law, under which no person could be evicted from his land or imprisoned without proper legal action against him in a court of law, nor could he be sentenced to death without trial.

***Machiavellian Theories :*** From the fourteenth to the sixteenth century Europe was swayed by the Machiavellian theories which encouraged and strengthened dictatorship and the hand of monarchs and made the acquisition of authority the sole objective of life. In the seventeenth century the theory of natural rights came up once again with full force. In 1679 the British Parliament passed the bill of Habeas Corpus and it became a law, and served as a protection against unjustifiable arrests and detentions. In 1684 the revolutionary army denned the limits of the powers of the British parliament. In 1689 the Parliament passed the most important document, the Bill of Rights. In words of Lord Action. This is the greatest achievement of the English people. This bill is regarded as the completion of the freedom movement in Britain since through it the fundamental rights were clearly defined. In 1690 John Locke wrote out a book *Treatises on Civil Government*, justifying the revolution of 1688-89, in which he presented the Social Contract theory and discussed the rights of the individual with strong arguments. In 1762, the well known French thinker, Rousseau

(Jean Jacques 1712-78) wrote a book under the title *Social Contract* in which he reviewed the Social Contract theory presented by Hobbes and Locke from a new angle. He made an attempt to create a sort of harmony between the Sovereign of Hobbes and the Democracy of Locke. His theories not only paved the way for the French Revolution but had a profound influence on the political thought of Europe, and played an important role in getting the rights of the individual against the state recognized.

On 12th June, 1776, "The Charter of Rights" drafted by George Mason of the American state of Virginia was issued in which the freedom of Press, freedom of creed, and the right of legal proceedings in a court of law were guaranteed. On 12th July 1776 the American Declaration of independence was issued. Its draft was prepared by Thomas Jefferson. Most of his principles were based on the views of the British thinkers and those of John Locke in particular. In the preamble of this declaration, with reference to the natural law, it has been said, "All human beings have been created equal and their creator has conferred on them inalienable rights which include protection of life, freedom and pursuit of happiness. In 1789, three years after the enforcement of the constitution, the American Congress passed those ten amendments known as the Law of Rights. In the same year the National Assembly of France passed the Declaration of the Rights of Man.

In 1792 Thomas Paine published his famous booklet, *The Rights* of *Man*, which made a profound impact on the thought of the western people and further promoted the cause of the protector of human rights. During the nineteenth and the twentieth centuries inclusion of fundamental rights in the constitution of governments became a common tradition. In 1868 the fourteenth amendment of the American constitution was passed in which it was said that no state of America shall deprive any body of his life, freedom and property without due legal proceedings against him, nor shall it refuse to provide him with equal legal protection.

After the First World War, Germany and numerous other new European countries incorporated fundamental rights in their constitutions. In 1940, the famous man of letters, H.G. Wells in his book, *New World Order* suggested the issuance of a charter of Human Rights. In January 1941, President Roosevelt appealed to the Congress to offer their support to Four Freedoms. In August, 1941 the Atlantic Charter was signed whose objective, according to Churchil, was the end of war along with the upholding of Human Rights.

After the Second World War, the inclusion of Human Rights in the written constitutions became more prominent. France included in its constitution of 1946, its charter of Human Rights of 1789. In this year, Japan made Human Rights a part of its constitution. In 1947, Italy guaranteed Human Rights in its constitution.

As a result of efforts for the Human rights, at the national and international levels, at last on 10th December 1948, the U N Charter of Human Rights was issued in which all those rights had been incorporated that already existed in the constitutions of various European countries, or could possibly occur to the human mind. At the time of voting in the General Assembly 48 countries voted in favour of the charter and eight abstained, Russia being among the abstainers. To keep a watch over the enforcement of the charter, and safeguarding the rights guaranteed therein and to offer suggestion for the determination of other rights, a permanent commission of Human Rights was set up.

After narrating this brief history of Fundamental Rights, we shall take stock of its theoretical aspects and find out the sources of the western thinker's concept of Rights, and also whether inclusion of these rights in constitution or just preparing and passing a universal charter of Human Rights has really guaranteed the protection of these rights satisfactorily, and whether the man living in the twentieth century is leading a life of greater safety, peace and is free from fears of impending dangers, as compared with the enslaved and oppressed man of the twelfth or the sixteenth century.

## Various Issues

Concepts analogous to human rights have certain precursors in the Islamic heritage of philosophy and theology, but human rights lack precise equivalents in medieval fiqh (jurisprudence). In fiqh, the category haqq al-ad, the right of the individual Muslim, was used to distinguish cases in which legal actions against a wrongdoer were left to the discretion of the injured party or parties from other cases belonging to the category of the right of Allah, haqq u-Allah, in which prosecution was mandatory and was to be undertaken by the government.

One settled fiqh principle corresponding to a modern right was the right of the owners of property to seek legal right against interference with their property. Rather than constructing doctrines or proposing institutions designed to curb the powers of the ruler or to protect the individual from the ruler's oppression, Islamic legal thought long concentrated on defining the theoretical duties of believers, including rulers, vis-a-vis Allah.

According to the prevailing perspective, rulers had the obligation to rule according to Shariah law; their subjects were to obey them unless ordered to do something constituting a sin. The development of institutions that could place real curbs on rulers' despotism or make them accountable to those whose rule was neglected. Rebellion was commonly proposed as the remedy for tyranny.

To deal with the practical problems of protecting rights and freedoms, Muslim intellectuals and statesmen began to adopt the principles of European constitutionalism in the nineteenth century. In the latter half of the twentieth century, after the common acceptance of the principles of constitutionalism, the related question of the compatibility of international human rights principles with Islamic doctrine was raised.

The strongest influence on Muslim's ideas came from French concepts and legal principles developed during the Enlightenment and the French Revolution. These included the first great statement of modern human rights, the 1789 Declaration des Droits de l'Homme et du Citoyen, and the 1791 French Constitution, as well as concepts of public liberties.

In the areas of the Muslim world ruled by Britain, which lacked a written constitution expressly guaranteeing specified rights, the models were democratic freedom as developed in the common law tradition and Britain's system of parliamentary government.

Many nineteenth-century officials, diplomats, and writers from Muslim countries played roles in disseminating European ideas of constitutionalism and public liberties. They included the Egyptian

Sheikh Rifa an Raff-al-Tatawi (1801-1891), an al-Azhar scholar who studied at French legal and political institutions in Paris from 1826 to 1831. He prepared a report on concepts of political rights, the rule of law, liberty, equality, and the ideas of the Enlightenment, and translated the French Constitution into Arabic; in 1839 his report was translated into Turkish.

Persian diplomat Mirza Malkom Khan (1833-1908), who educated in Paris and had lived in Turkey, later becoming Persian ambassador to Great Britain, wrote extensively on European concepts of government, the rule of law, and liberty, claiming that these could be reconciled with Islam. In the Ottoman realm, the literary figure Namik Keman (1840-1888) was prominent in disseminating ideas of rights and freedom and the notion of their compatibility with Islam.

***Doctrines vs Modernity :*** In the nineteenth century clashes between inherited Islamic doctrines and modern norms regarding rights came on the question of the equality of Muslims and non-Muslims before the law. The issue was joined as European powers pressed for the elimination of the disabilities traditionally placed on non-Muslims.

A fundamental pact announced in Tunisia in 1857 under European pressure guaranteed equality for all before the law and in taxation as well as complete security for all inhabitants irrespective of religion, nationality, or race. Tunisia was the first Muslim country to promulgate a constitution, doing so in 1861 and affirming the rights established in the pact; however, the constitution was suspended by the French Protectorate (1881-1956).

In Tunisia as in many other Muslim countries, the independence struggle against European domination accentuated people's consciousness of the importance of rights and democratic freedom. After independence, the 1956 Tunisian Constitution stated that the republican form of government was the best guarantee of "human rights."

The most important early reforms in the direction of realizing rights were undertaken in the Ottoman Empire, which had many non-Muslim subjects and which, owing to its military and economic vulnerability, was also exposed to pressures from European powers.

The hatt-i-serif of 1839, reinforced by the hatt-i-humayun of 1856, was part of a series of modernizing reforms in the Tanzimat period that aimed to establish the security of life, honour, and property, fair and public trials, and equality before the law for all Ottoman subjects irrespective of religion. The principle of nondiscrimination based on language and race was added by the hatt-i-humayun. In 1840, the new penal code affirmed the equality of all Ottoman subjects before the law.

By mid-century, reformist pressures prompted the adoption of the 1876 Ottoman Constitution, which contained a section on hukuk-i-umumiye, or public liberties, of Ottoman subjects, providing for equality regardless of religion, free exercise of religions other than Islam and freedom of worship, inviolability of personal freedom of worship, and guarantees against arbitrary intrusions, extortion, arrest, or other unlawful violations of person, residence, or property.

There were also provisions for freedom of the press, association, and education. This constitution was suspended in practice and not revived until after the Young Turk Revolution in 1908, a central goal of which was reviving the constitution and establishing the equality of all Ottoman citizens. The Young Turk's reforms expanded constitutional rights protection, prohibited arrests and searches except by established legal procedures, abolished special or extraordinary courts, and guaranteed press freedom. Turkey's second republic saw in 1861 the promulgation of a constitution that undertook in its preamble to ensure and guarantee "human rights and liberties" and made men and women equal. (Article 12)

In the area of free exercise of religion, conditions were imposed to safeguard the policy of secularism adopted by Mustafa Kamal Ataturk (1881-1938), the first President of the Turkish Republic. Article 2 of the 1982 Turkish Constitution proclaimed Turkey to be a law-state that respects human rights.

In Republican Turkey the energetic pursuit of Kemalist secularism, beginning in 1925, led to the repression of various Islamic groups, especially dervish orders. In Soviet Central Asia, the atheistic policies of the Soviet Union curbed the religious freedoms of the Muslim populace until the collapse of the Soviet state in 1991.

Suppression of Islam and denial of religious freedom also occurred under the Marxist regimes that ruled Albania from 1945 to 1991 and Afghanistan from 1978 to 1982. Elsewhere in the twentieth century regimes with secular orientations often indulged in harsh persecutions of Islamic fundamentalists.

Popular agitation against the despotism of the Qajar Shah culminated in Persia's first constitution in 1906-1907. Persia's Shih clerics were divided about the religious legitimacy of constitutionalism and its attendant rights provisions. The Supplementary Constitutional Law of 1907 included Islamic qualifications of two rights provisions; publications were said to be free except where heretical or harmful to Islam (Article 21) and the study and teaching of science, education, and art were to be free except as prohibited by religious law (Article 18). Moreover, ministers in the government were required to be Persian Muslims (Article 58). However, the country's inhabitants were to enjoy equal rights before the law (Article 8).

After the 1978-1979 Islamic Revolution in Iran, official spokesmen invoked Islam as the reason for the clerical regime's hostility to international human rights, which they often dismissed as products of an alien, western cultural tradition; however, Iran did not repudiate its ratification of the International Covenant on Civil and Political Rights.

The 1979 Iranian Constitution in Article 20 expressly provided that all citizens enjoyed human, political, economic, social and cultural rights according to Islamic standards; Article 4 provided that Islamic principles prevailed over those in the constitution. Notwithstanding the reference in Article 20 to economic, social, and cultural rights, the concern seemed to be with using Islamic criteria to curb civil and political rights-many of the latter being expressly limited by Islamic criteria. The principle of equality and equal protection for women and religious minorities were breached in many ways.

In the name of implementing Islamic criminal justice, the regime ignored principles of criminal procedure designed to protect the rights of the accused both before and during trial, as well as prohibition of cruel and inhuman punishment. Religious minorities and individuals and groups opposed to clerical rule or the regime's religious ideology were excluded from the political process and were often subject to harsh persecution.

Islamic and Western concepts were combined in the Afghan Constitution produced between 1921 and 1924. For example, all inhabitants were to be equal before the government without distinction of religion and sect, and it was provided that all Afghans would be equal before the Shariah and the laws of the State. Nonetheless, Hindus and Jews (the only recognized non-Muslim communities) were required to pay the Zizya, the poll-tax traditionally imposed on dhimmis (protected non-Muslims), and to wear distinctive emblems.

By the end of the twentieth century all Muslim countries had adopted constitutions containing some or all of the rights principles set forth in international human rights law. The 1989 Algerian Constitution was noteworthy for its guarantee of equality before the law regardless of gender (Article 28), fundamental liberties and human rights (Article 31), and human rights advocacy (Article 32). Like most Muslim countries, however, Algeria retained Islamic personal status rules and constitutional provisions according Islam a privileged status, perpetuating the ambiguous relationship between religious and constitutional norms.

Fiqh survived longest as the official law of the land in Saudi Arabia. However, changes inaugurated in 1922 suggested that the country might be moving gradually towards a governmental system that would accord at least limited recognition to rights and constitutionalism, albeit subject to Islamic criteria. The principle that Islam entails on human rights was adopted in the Basic Law of Government promulgated by the Saudi Arabian regime in 1922; Article 26 provided that "the State protects human rights in accordance with the Islamic Shariah."

What the Shariah limits on rights would entail was not defined. The basic law provided for many citizen entitlements in the area of social welfare, but only a few rights in the political or civil area were recognized. These included the provision that no one should be arrested, imprisoned, or have his action restricted except as provided by law (Article 36); chat homes should not be entered or searched save in cases specified by statutes (Article 37); that communications should not be confiscated, delayed, read or listen to except in cases defined by statutes (Article 40); and that private property must be protected and could only be taken for the public interest and with fair compensation (Article 17).

***Women's Rights :*** One of the areas where the clash between inherited Islamic principles and international human rights norms was most acute was that of women's rights. Although conservatives propounded the nation that full equality for women violated Islamic precepts, feminists argued that it was patriarchal attitudes and inadequate study of the Islamic sources that led to the notion that Islam required keeping women in a subordinate position.

Already in the late nineteenth century liberal writers like the Egyptian Qasim Amin (1865-1908) had propounded the thesis that certain problems facing Middle Eastern societies—despotism, moral degeneration, and the degraded status of women—were not intrinsic to Islam but were the products of corrupting influences and social customs. While not advocating full equality for women, Amin demanded that women's rights should be enhanced. He also linked the cause of women's freedom to the realization of freedom and rights for citizens in general. Feminists such as the Egyptian Huda Sharawi (1882-1947) became prominent advocates of women's rights and emancipation.

One of the boldest attempts to reconcile Islam with full equality for women was offered by al-Rahir-al-Haddad, a Tunisian graduate of al-Zaytunah, who in 1930 published Imra 'atunafi al Shariah wa-al-mujtama (Our Women in the Shariah and Society), which propounded the idea that Islam had envisaged a progressive emancipation of women; he advocated the reform of Islamic laws to eliminate obstacles to male-female equality in the domestic as well as the public sphere. For the boldness of its thesis, the book was condemned with particular vehemence by conservatives and its author denounced as a heretic.

Unequivocal support for full equality for women came from Kamal Ataturk, who in the wake of the Turkish war of independence proclaimed that women had the right to be equal; he subsequently took measures to remove the disabilities imposed by Turkish custom and Islamic law—without attempting to reconcile his reforms with Islamic precepts.

In the Arab world, the most dramatic reforms was embodied in the Tunisian Law of Personal Status of 1956 promulgated by President Habib Bourguiba. Presented as an Islamic law, the code undertook bold reforms improving women's status, such as abolishing polygamy and establishing equal rights for men and women in divorce.

Into the late twentieth century, Muslim countries preserved laws that discriminated against women and denied them full civil and political rights, often in the face of constitutional provisions mandating the equality of all citizens. In general, laws afforded women considerable equality outside the family; it was in the area of personal status that discriminatory features taken from fiqh were retained. Saudi Arabia was notable for its reliance on Islam to justify its refusal to grant women rights and freedoms widely enjoyed elsewhere in the Muslim world.

Few Muslim countries ratified the 1979 Convention on the elimination of all forms of discrimination against women, and those that chose to rectify did so subject to reservations regarding various central provisions. The reservations made by Bangladesh, Egypt, Libya, and Russia were specifically justified by their need to adhere to Islamic law.

***Human Rights Movements :*** Independent, non-governmental organizations founded for the defence of human rights have spearheaded campaigns to improve respect for human rights in Muslim countries. One of the earliest Muslim human rights organizations was established by Moroccans in December, 1933 in the Spanish-controlled enclave of Tetouan as an affiliate of a Spanish human rights organization.

A human rights group with Islamic affiliations, the Iranian Committee for the Defence of Freedom and Human Rights, was formed with the participation of several religious figures; it aimed primarily at achieving democratization and the elimination of torture and in camera political trials. A central participant was Mehdi Bazaragan (b. 1907), a proponent of Islamic liberalism who went on to become Iran's first prime minister immediately after the

Islamic Revolution. He and his associates later suffered persecution when their stance on human rights put them at odds with the central regime.

Human rights organizations in which educated professionals were prominent proliferated throughout the Muslim world in the 1980s in the face of daunting obstacles and dangers. One of the most important was the Arab Organization for Human Rights, which, like the overwhelming majority of independent human rights organizations, espoused the human rights programmes.

***Muslim States and International Human Rights Law :*** It was in the aftermath of World War II that the modern international formulations of human rights were produced, setting standards that became incorporated in public international law. Muslim countries were among the founding members of the United Nations, whose 1945 Charter called for respect for human rights and fundamental freedoms; all Muslim countries eventually joined the UN.

Aspects of the Universal Declaration of Human Rights passed by the General Assembly in 1948 provoked criticism for representatives of Muslim countries, although in the end only Saudi Arabia failed to support its passage.

Muslim nations different greatly in their willingness to ratify the human rights conventions subsequently drafted under UN auspices. Muslims sometimes charged that international rights norms had a Western or Jude-Christian bias that precluded their acceptance in the Muslim milieu.

In terms of the compatibility of international rights norms and Islamic law, the alleged conflicts centered around civil and political rights; problems of the compatibility of Islam with economic, social, and cultural rights were rarely raised. The principles of freedom of religion—notably the right to convert from Islam to another faith—and the full equality of persons regardless of sex or religion seemed to pose particular problems.

The Charter of the Organization of the Islamic Conference (OIC), an international organization founded 1973 to which all Muslim countries belong, indicated in its preamble that the members were "reaffirming their commitment to the UN Charter and fundamental human rights." In 1980, however, the OIC issued the Cairo Declaration on Human Rights in Islam, which diverged significantly from international human rights standards; it was not made clear how this declaration was to be reconciled with the conflicting obligations undertaken by OIC members in ratifying international human rights covenant or in their individual constitutional rights provisions, which in many cases corresponded to the international norms.

Like the many other self-proclaimed "Islamic" human rights schemes that proliferated from the 1960s onward, the OIC declaration extensively borrowed terms and concepts from the International Bill of Human Rights, presenting a hybrid mixture of elements taken from Islamic and international law. The OIC declaration asserted that "fundamental rights and universal freedom in Islam are an integral part of the Islamic religion," but proceeded to insert 'Islamic' qualification and conditions on the rights and freedom guaranteed under international law—in conflict with international human rights theory, which does not permit religious criteria to override rights. Representative provisions included the rule in Article 24 that all the rights and freedoms stipulated in the declaration were subject to the Shariah, without defining what limits this would entail.

There was no provision for equal rights for all persons regardless of sex or religion. Instead, Article I stated that "all human beings are equal in terms of basic human dignity and basic obligations and responsibilities (not 'right'), without any discrimination on the grounds of race, colour, language, sex, religious belief, political affiliation, social status or other considerations." Article 6 further provided that "woman is equal to man in human dignity" ['not rights'], but it imposed on the husband the responsibility for the support and welfare of the family. In contrast, Article 13 provided that men and women were entitled to fair wages "without discrimination." Article 5 provided that on the right to marry there should be "no restrictions stemming from race, colour or nationality," but did not prohibit restrictions based on religion.

The provisions regarding religion did not aim at neutrality : Article 2 stated that Islam was the religion of unspoiled nature and prohibited "any form of compulsion on man or to exploit his poverty or ignorance in order to convert him to another religion or to atheism." Article 9 called for the State to ensure the means to acquire education "so as to enable man to be acquainted with the religion of Islam."

The favoured treatment of Islam carried over to freedom of speech, with Article 22 (a) stating that expressing opinion freely was allowed "in such manner as would not be contrary to the principles of the Shariah. Article 22 (c) barred the exploitation or misuse of information "in such a way as may violate sanctities and the dignity of Prophets, undermine moral and ethical values or disintegrate, corrupt or harm society or weaken its faith." Article 18 stipulated a right to privacy in the conduct of private affairs, in the home, in the family, and regarding property and relationships. Article 15 set forth "rights of ownership to property acquired in a legitimate way, barring expropriation except for the public interest and upon payment of immediate and fair compensation."

Noteworthy by their absence were provisions calling for the observance of democratic principles in political systems and guarantees of freedom of religion, freedom of association, freedom of the press, and equality and equal protection of the law. Although torture was prohibited in Article 20, there were no provisions explicitly endorsing international rights norms in the area of criminal procedure—only the vague assurance in Article 19 that the defendant would be entitled to "a fair trial in which he shall be given all the guarantees of defence." Since Article 25 stated that the Shariah "is the only source of reference of the explanation or clarification of any of the articles of this Declaration."

"The possibility was left open that a trial would be deemed 'fair' as long which were historically underdeveloped in the area of criminal procedure. There was no principle of legality per se. The provision in Article 19 that there should be no crime or punishment except as provided for in the Shariah seemed to open the door to the application afta'zir (discretionary) penalties, as well as rules regarding hadd crimes. Article 2 prohibited taking away life except for a reason prescribed by the Shariah. Reflecting the third world setting in which Muslim nations elaborate their position on rights, Article II prohibited colonialism and stated that "people's suffering from colonialism have the full right to freedom and self-determination."

In sum, the OIC Declaration suggested that the official approach of Muslim countries to civil and political rights was distinguishable from that of non-Muslim countries by reason of their reliance on Shariah rules.

Governments and individuals throughout the Muslim world continue to take many positions on human rights that are by self-designation 'Islamic.' Given the variety of approaches and principles involved, it is evident that Muslim opinion remains divided on the relationship between international human rights principles and the Islamic legal heritage, and on the compatibility of the two.

In conclusion, one cannot but view the future with some apprehension. If Muslims persist in their acceptance of the absence of social justice among them, if they continue to separate worship in the mosque from the social justice to be observed in lands where the spirit of Islam is to be sown, and to separate the places of prayer from business and industry; if they uphold the hypocrisy of a worship without soul, showing themselves "mean towards those who needs help," then woe betide them in this world, and woe betide them in the Hereafter, even if they are not among those whom the Quran says "neglect their prayers."

Having seen the failure of the constitution in safeguarding the fundamental rights on the national level, let us now have a look at the measures undertaken to ensure their protection at the international level and find out how far they have succeeded in their objective.

The world charter of Human Rights declared by the General Assembly of the United Nations on December 10, 1948, is so to say, the zenith of human efforts in this context. This charter comprises 30 sections which are as follows:

1. All men are born free and are equal in status in the matter of dignity and rights.
2. Every individual without any discrimination on the basis of race, colour, sex, language, religion, political or other views, national and social status, properties, birth or any other aspect or distinction of any sort whatsoever shall be

intervention and with any means and without consideration of the frontiers.

20. (1) Every individual has the right of peaceful assembly and organization.

    (2) Nobody can be compelled to be associated with any particular organisation.

21. (1) Every individual has the right to participate, in the government of his country directly or through the elected representatives.

    (2) Every one has equal right of getting a government service in his own country.

    (3) The real basis of the authority of the 'government shall be the will and desire of the people which shall be manifested through elections in the form of free voting and secret ballot.

22. Every individual shall have the right of social protection for life with dignity and building up his personality and, through national effort and international cooperation and according to the resources of the state concerned shall be entitled to economic, social and cultural rights.

23. (1) Every individual shall have the right to work, to take to a profession of his own choice, to secure better and fair conditions of work, and security against unemployment.

    (2) Every individual without any discrimination, shall be entitled to equal wages for equal amount of work.

    (3) Every individual has the right of getting better and fair remuneration for his family ensuring a dignified living and if necessary, some other means may also be provided for his social security.

    (4) Every individual shall have the right of forming trade unions and participating in them for safeguarding his interests.

24 Every individual shall have the right to rest, entertainment, reasonable fixation of working hours, and leave with pay.

25. (1) Every individual has the light to maintain a reasonable standard of life for his own health and prosperity and that of his family, which includes security of food, clothes, residential space, medical aid, essential service, unemployment, sickness, disability, widowhood, old age and such other conditions.

(2) Maternity and suckling period shall be deemed deserving of special attention and help. And all babies, whether born in or out of wedlock, shall receive equal social security.

26. (1) Every one has the right to receive education.

(2) The goal of education shall be the perfect building up of man's personality and inculcating deep respect for human rights and freedoms.

(3) The parent shall have the option of selecting the type of education their children should have.

27. (1) Every individual has the right to freely participate in the cultural life of the society, to receive his share of the entertainment provided by the sciences and arts, and to be benefited by the fruits of the scientific progress.

(2) Every individual has the right of the protection to the material or moral fruits of his scientific, literary or technical creative work.

28. Every individual has the right to pass his life in a social and international atmosphere ensuring the benefits given form of the rights and freedoms conferred by this charter.

29. (1) Every individual has certain obligations too, imposed by the society, observing which makes possible the free and perfect freedoms of other people.

(2) In connection with the rights and freedoms every person shall confine himself to those limits as ensure the rights and freedoms of other people.

(3) These rights and freedoms cannot be used against the aims and objects and principles of the United Nations Organisation.

30. No part of this charter shall be so interpreted as to acquire for any state, group or individual the right of engaging in an activity through which these definite rights and freedoms may be sabotaged.

The rights and freedoms declared in this Charter have been later divided into two portions. Under one list, economic social and cultural rights have been brought together and in the second list are included the civic rights and those of the State. The General Assembly approved these two covenants and left it to the discretion of the member states to sign them in case they voluntarily recognized these rights.

The UN Commission for Human Rights has done some further work in this connection. In 1959 it issued a declaration relating to the rights of children and in 1963 for the prevention of racial discrimination. The General Assembly adopted various covenants and resolutions in 1948 for the prevention of genocide, in 1951 for the security of migrants and exiled persons, in 1952 for the rights of women, in 1957 for the determination of the nationality of married women, in 1951 for the total prohibition of slavery and putting an end to it and in 1965 for the condemnation of racial discrimination in South Africa.

The special institutions of UN such as the International Labour Organization (ILO), United Nations Educational Scientific and Cultural Organization (UNESCO), International Rehabilitation Organization (IRO) and the High Commissioner for the displaced persons, have also done considerable work for the determination and protection of human rights.

But what is the outcome of these splendid efforts of the world charter of Human Rights and United Nations' Organization and its subsidiary institutions? Has this charter really redeemed man from the clutches of oppression, tyranny and dictatorship and Fascism so that he can now breathe in a free atmosphere and is in a position to be benefited by his rights? The true position of this Charter and the helplessness of the United Nations' Organization is very well brought out by the Western thinkers and international legal experts themselves.

In 1947 the Commission adopted a report on the subject of

implementation which reversed its previous attitude on the matter. It laid it down as a general rule that the Commission recognises that it has no power to take any action in regard to complaints concerning human rights.

It means that even a year prior to the declaration of the charter it was decided that it would have no legal status. If any country wishes to do so, it may go ahead with its enforcement voluntarily, otherwise it may consign it to that waste paper basket. Hans Kelson comments on it thus:

> Judged strictly from a purely legalistic perspective, the provisions of the Charter do not impose upon the members any binding obligation to recognise and protect these human rights and freedoms to which reference is made in preamble or in the text of the Charter. The language used by the Charter does not allow for the interpretation that the members are under any legal obligation to grant human rights and freedom to their subjects.

What the charter has conferred on an individual to remove the high handedness of the states, Kerl Mannhein writes:

> The Charter does not confer upon the individuals the legal possibility to appeal to International Court and specially to the Principal Judicial organ of the United Nations, the International Court of Justice, in case one of the rights or freedoms proclaimed in the preamble or referred to in the text of Charter is violated. The statute of the court stipulates expressly in Article 34 that only states may be parties in cases before the court.

Exposing the real position of the economic and social rights, mentioned in the charter. Dr. Raphael says:

> The so-called economic and social rights, in so far as they are intelligible at all, impose no such universal duty. They are rights to be given things, such as a decent income, schools, and social services. But who is called upon to do the giving? Whose duty is it? When the authors of the United Nations' Declaration

> of Human Rights assert that 'everyone has the right to social security', are they saying that everyone ought to subscribe to some form of world-wide social security system from which each in turn may benefit in case of need? If something of this kind is meant, why do the draft United Nations covenants, which are supposed to implement the Universal Declaration, make no provision for instituting such a system? And if no such system exists, where is the obligation, and where the right? To impose on men a 'duty' which they cannot possibly perform is as absurd in its way, though perhaps not as cruel, as bestowing on them a Right' which they cannot possibly enjoy.

A.K. Brohi says about these rights:

> But the rights in the current on economic and social rights are not rights in the accepted sense of the term in the reality, they are merely principles of social and economic policy. That incidentally explains the reason why two separate covenants had to be drawn up by the commission instead of one.

He has hinted at the two different ideological camps of the world, which do not only follow diametrically opposite policies but have totally different concepts of rights.

Having had an idea of the UN charter of Human Rights and the helplessness of the UNO, let us now see what a western thinker has to say about it in his frustrating analysis of the future possibilities:

> It cannot therefore be asserted that the legal protection of human rights has a bright future under the United Nations. The Organisation is made up of groups of states each with different conceptions of democracy and of the relationship between the state and the individual. Certain rights and freedoms are considered by the Western countries as fundamental to civilized society. These rights, they claim, constitute foundations for real democracy. The communist states, on the other hand, hold that no rights and freedoms are

> fundamental. According to them, the state is the creator of all rights and is entitled to make regular their enjoyment in the interest of society as a whole. Finally, many of the underdeveloped countries whose ambition is to achieve very quick economic and social developments, see in guarantees of the traditional civil and political rights and freedoms an obstacle to the attainment of desirable economic and social objectives. Having regard to all these differences, it is not surprising that the United Nations has been unable to achieve substantial results in the field of human rights, nor is it realistic to expect it to do so in the very immediate future.

A study of the Charter of Human Rights and the comments on it amply reveal the fact even man's collective efforts at the international level could not secure full guarantees of a dignified and respectable life for him. He is just as helpless before the excesses of the government today as he was in the days gone by. Rather, the ever-increasing sphere of the activities and the powers of the state have rendered the fundamental rights and civil liberties meaningless. The value of the Charter of Human Rights is no more than a beautiful document. A list of rights has certainly been made out very carefully but not one of these rights has any sanction and enforcing power at its back. It neither imposes any legal restraint on the states to prevent them from denying the fundamental rights to their citizens, nor provides for any forum to seek legal remedy for the restoration of the usurped rights of an individual. Thus, the charter is a totally useless and undependable document in protecting human rights.

The maximum good that it has done to humanity is to establish a norm of human rights and has conferred on the world brotherhood of mankind a progressive consciousness of the protection of fundamental rights, has stressed the importance of the individual, and with its help and guidance the newly emancipated countries, when formulating their constitutions, find it easier to decorate the formal chapter of the fundamental rights. The status of this charter is only moralistic having no weight and no value from the legal point of view. As the protector of fundamental rights the strength and importance of this charter can be gauged from the fact that the international organisation concerned with the affairs of political prisoners, the Amnesty International, alone has brought on record in its published report for the year 1975-76, that 113 countries out of the 142 member states were found guilty of serious violation of the fundamental rights, and there has been a disturbing increase on the universal plane in the improper use of power, unjustified arrests, political incarcerations, coercion and violence and incidences of death penalty, muzzling of the press, curtailment of the powers of the judiciary, enforcement of the dictatorial ordinances and even laws, and measures adopted for the annulment and suspension of fundamental rights.

# 2

# Social Justice

## Basic Issues

No man is sufficient unto himself and if he tries to be so, he succeeds only in destroying himself. Islam regards the self-adequacy in human conduct as a source of all evil. This means that his social existence is necessary. It makes him aware of the competition, his own claims on persons and the properties of others and the perpetual necessity of adjustment between them. However, when per necessity men get together, the problem of adjustment of rights and liabilities immediately arises. The men swell into tribes, states and nations and their problems multiply. They become ever more pressing and complex because of the violence men use in the love of wealth *(Surah Adiyat* 100/8) and their contentiousness. *(Surah Israel* 17/100). There are very few men possessed of balanced good sense who restrain themselves and prohibit others from mischief on the earth. The wrong-doers, however, pursue the enjoyment of good things of life which were given to them and persist in sin too. *(Surah Hood* 11/116). Such nations are then destroyed as stated in *Surah Israel* (17/16).

- The philosophers tell us that man is the only true subject and object of justice. That apparently deprives the animals of their due. The mere fact, that the wronged animal is incapable of asserting its own claim to right, should not be taken for granted that it has no right to be treated justly.

Even they react when treated unfairly. It is also known by experience that there is not a mere predatory violence and certainly not unrestricted warfare of one against the other. Some where, within it, is a process of allocation and some rules of the game for the coexistence of even brutes and savages. There is some decree determining as to what is lion's share and what is the jackal's.

- We find thus inbuilt, in all living beings, a mechanism which compels them to revolt against injustice. The revolt may result in physically stopping the perpetrator, if he is weak, or in mere resenting or disapproving of it, otherwise. History bears testimony that no wrong is resented more than injustice, though it may be suffered sometimes willingly, for the sake of higher good. Justice, thus is part of every living being's consciousness, by intuition. It ripens in man by experience and anxious cultivation. It has been rightly said that justice is a reflection of the Divine. God Almighty, says in *Surah Al-Tariq* (86/4) that He is the Protector of all living beings and He taught some rules to the animals as well. The difference is that all that is in the universe, follows faithfully His laws except man who is given volition and power to think and decide. He is also given a code of guidance and made answerable here and in the Hereafter. He can thus be just and loyal or disobedient and transgressor as he wills. In *Surah-Al-Momin* (40/40) is stated that:

  "He that works evil will not be requited but by the like thereof: and he that works a righteous deed, whether man or woman—and is a believer-such will enter the Garden (of Bliss): therein will they have abundance without measure."

- But what is that which restrains the mighty from doing injustice? It could either be the same virtue as mentioned above or because of fear. A French Philosopher La Rochefoucauld says that 'love of justice is, in most men, merely the fear of suffering it'. Thrasymachus says in the *'Republic'* that 'those who denounce injustice, do so, not because they are afraid of doing it, but of suffering it'. It has also been happening generally that some people may evolve concepts, as they suit them, in the name of something good and high, to sound it attractive and acceptable to all, though they themselves may know that the same is just a misrepresentation or farce.

- It has been remarked by C. K. Allen that Abominable injustices have been done in the name of justice, even as terrible oppressions have been done in the name of liberty, because, when men sink to the lowest, they clutch for excuse at the highest'. Quran, however, abhors such a treacherous conduct or a misinterpretation as it says in *Surah Al-Imran* (3/78) :

  "There is among them a section who distort the Book with their tongues, (As they read) you would think it is a part of the Book, but it is no part of the Book: and they say, 'That is from Allah', but it is not from Allah; It is they who tell a lie against Allah, and (well) they know it!"

And in *Surah Baqara* it is quoted that (2/79) :

> "Then woe to those who write the Book with their own hands and then say: This is from Allah, to traffic with it for a miserable price! Woe to them for what their hands do write, and the gain they make thereby."

- It is said that the tones of the society are many and it is the function of justice to blend them. In the situation, the need of justice and that too in its pure, true and effective form is necessary. The term 'justice' as we know and understand, may be equated to the concept of *'Adl'*, *'Qist'*, or *'Mizan'* as used in Quran. These terms are antonyms of *'Zulm'* or 'injustice'. According to Imam Raghib Isphahani, *'Adl'* means. In the view of Syed Sharif, it is the mean of excess and less Abul Baqa Hanafi says it is the antonym of *'Zulm'*. It means that the grievance of a person be redressed and his rights restored to him. Allama Aini says that *'Adl'* is the duty to obey such commands which are entitled to obedience and the injustice be totally eliminated. The justice, as a common man understands, means 'getting a square and fair deal', 'equality before the law and 'sticking to the rules'.

- Justice may be analysed and classified into many different forms, like judicial, constitutional, administrative, social, economic, distributive, natural, positive, universal, political, cumulative, recognitive, national, international and parental, etc. This wealth of terminology and this spectrum of so many hues, does at least suggest that there is scarcely any relationship of life into which the question of justice does not enter. In our dealings, with our fellow-men, our superiors and subordinates, our families and relations, our friends and neighbours, in our conduct under the laws which govern us, in our commitments to others and perpetually in our inmost consciences, we can never escape this mentor. The difference between Islam and other systems is that while Islam enjoins on man to do all sorts of justice and the government or the society may compel its performance, the other systems draw a line in between and the government or the society cannot go beyond some of those, to require performance.
- It is our belief and history bears testimony to it, that Islam offers and dispenses the very required concept of justice. Islam is a religion made up in essentials of a revelation and represents the actual expression of the Divine Will. It embodies eternal truths and is, therefore, good and valid for all times to come. Its doctrines are given in Quran and *Hadith.* Some of the matters are expressly provided for. As regards others we have to rely on the principles or concept as can be gathered from Quran and *Hadith* and chart our course on the basis of *Ijtihad, Ijma, Qiyas,* etc. at every given time or age, to suit the needs of a given society. The norms and precepts which are expressly provided are rigid and immutable possessing absolute and eternal validity. They are not susceptible to change or modification. As regards the norms and concepts which are expressed in terms of general principles, they can admit of varying interpretations and varying applications according to the circumstances of the time. We do also

follow the interpretations made by our predecessors, if the circumstances have not changed.

- Islam means unreserved and unconditional obedience of, and compliance with, the directives of God Almighty, their propagation, establishment of an organization for the purpose, and for securing peace and prosperity for the people. Quran says in *Surah Baqara* (2/177) :

  "It is not righteousness that ye turn your faces towards East or West; but it is righteousness—to believe in Allah and the Last Day, and the Angles, and the Book, and the Messengers; to spend of your substance, out of love for Him, for your kin, for orphans, for the needy, for the wayfarer, for those who ask, and for the ransom of slaves; to be steadfast in prayer, and practise regular charity; to fulfil the contracts which ye have made; and to be firm and patient, in pain (or suffering) and adversity, and throughout all periods of panic. Such are the people of truth, the God-fearing."

As also in *Surah Nisa* (4/1 25) :

> "Who can be better in religion than one who submits his whole self to Allah, does good, and follows the way of Ibrahim the true in faith? For Allah did take Ibrahim for a friend."

- Islam also combines temporal and spiritual affairs into one indivisible whole and does not permit a division as done in Christianity or other religions. The *Din* of Islam is a way of life and Quran is the Code to follow. This has been given to man only, as he only, out of the Universe, is likely to go astray. It is stated in *Surah Nisa* (4/27) that:

  "Allah doth wish to turn to you, but the wish of those who follow their lusts is that ye should turn away (from Him),—far, far away."

In *Surah Nahl* (16/4, 49) the Quran says :

> He has created man from a sperm-drop; and behold this same (man) becomes an open disputer!

And to Allah doth obeisance all that is in the heavens and on earth, whether moving (living) creatures or the angels; for none are arrogant (before their Lord)."

In *Surah Hajj* (22/18) :

> "Seest thou not that to Allah bow down in worship all things that are in the heavens and on earth,—the trees, the animals, and a great number among mankind? But a great number are (also) such as are fit for punishment:"

and in *Surah Yasin* (36/77) it is said :

> "Doth not man see that it is We who created him from sperm? Yet behold he (stands forth) as an open adversary".

- The concept of justice in Islam is thus all pervading and has to be manifested in every sphere of human life. God Almighty warns mankind in *Surah Asr* (103/2, 3) that he is in loss except those who have faith, live clean and pure lives and know how to wait in patience and constancy. It is also in the scheme of things that he is not to be left without guidance as provided in *Surah Qiyamah* (75/36) :

  "Does man think that he will be left uncontrolled?"

- God created heavens and earth, sent down rain from the skies for growing fruit and crops for food and other necessities, made sun and moon, night and day and all that is on the earth subject to him *(Surah Ibrahim* 14/32—34, *Surah Nahl* 16/10—16, *Surah Hajj* 22/65 and *Surah Luqman* 31 /20) so as to provide for every need of man. He created man to do homage to God, to obey and adore his Creator, to praise Him and to serve Him and His servants. He then placed him in the centre of the universe so that he may have authority over it and administer it. It is an obligation of man as an administrator on the earth that in case the mankind be to coexist peacefully, he must preserve a measure of balance by enforcing some regulative principles. According to Kant such a regulation should be 'the idea which proceeds from the condition under which each man's power of action can exist in harmony with the power of action of others, in accordance with a universal law of freedom. The man has thus been told that the universe has been designed and balanced in such a way that a little deviation or imbalance may cause the whole system to crash and so he is required likewise to create a balance in his affairs and dealings with others in order to succeed.

- The Quran in verses 1 to 9 of Chapter *Al-Rahman* says:

> "Allah is most Gracious. It is He Who taught the Quran. He has created man. He has taught him speech. The sun and the moon follow exactly computed courses. Both herbs and trees bow in adoration to Him. He has raised high the vault of Heaven with its clouds and stars and He has set up the balance of justice in order that you may not transgress it. So establish right with justice and fall not short of the balance."

We may also refer to *Surah Al-Hijr* (15/19) which is as under:

> "And the earth We have spread out (like a carpet); set thereon mountains firm and immovable; and produced therein all kinds of things in due balance."

In *Surah Baqara* (2/188) it is ordained :

> "And do not eat up your property among yourselves for vanities, nor use it as bait for the judges, with intent that ye may eat up wrongfully and knowingly a little of (other) people's property." 14.The most important scheme of things in Islam unlike other legal system is that one who acts is burdened with a duty and an obligation to honour and convey to others their rights. It imposes a duty on every man, including the head of the State and its functionaries, not to violate the rights of others and to convey to them their due. Further, it is the bounden duty of the State to protect and preserve the life, liberty and property of its citizens in the light of Quranic injunctions and principles, provide them with their essential basic needs and an equal opportunity in life with others. The Holy Prophet even

directed a son to provide maintenance to his father in the light of *Surah Israel* (17/23) in two different cases. Dower of wife is recoverable through Courts under *Surah Nisa* (4/24). The Western philosophy speaks of rights and powers more than the duties and the obligations. The state functionaries in that system enjoy powers and wield authority but have no responsibility to see and ensure that the rights of the citizens are duly protected or honoured. In Islam, on the other hand, we are reminded again and again to maintain balance as that is the very basis of stability and durability of a social order.

- God Almighty also assures mankind that if it obeys His dictates, it shall have no fear, grief or worry *(Surrah Baqara* 2/21, 38, 11 2 and 262) :

  O ye people! Adore your Guardian - Lord, who created you and those who came before you, that ye may have the chance to learn righteousness;

  We said: 'Get ye down all from here; and if, as is sure, there comes to you Guidance from Me', whosoever follows My guidance, on them shall be no fear, nor shall they grieve.

  Nay,—Whoever submits his whole self to Allah and is a doer of good, —he will get his reward with his Lord; on such shall be no fear, nor shall they grieve.

  Those who spend their substance in the cause of Allah, and follow not up their gifts with reminders of their generosity or with injury,—for them their reward is with their Lord; on them shall be no fear, nor shall be no fear, nor shall they grieve."

  This Book is complete in all respects with regard to all matters and furnishes all the required details as stated in *Surah Nahl* (16/89), *Surah Bani Israil* (17/9), *Surah Rum* (30/58) and *Surah Sumar* (39/27).

- As said above, the command of God to do justice, is directed to the individuals as well as to the functionaries of the State and if everyone follows it faithfully there will be no disputes and insignificant litigation in Courts. It will be appreciated that Courts are the institutions where an aggrieved person complains against an injustice done to him either by a fellow man or a functionary of the State. Thus if justice is done in all directions and at all levels, we do not need Courts. There will be no waste of time and money and no worries on this account at all, inasmuch as that it will give rise to an ideal social order. It is for this reason that the command in Quran, to do justice, is addressed to all human beings. I may refer here to a few verses in :

*Surah Shura* (42/15) :

"I am commanded to judge justly between you in accordance with the Book which Allah has sent down and in which I believe."

*Surah Al-Aaraf* (7/'29) : Say, My Lord has commanded justice.

*Surah Maida* 5/9 :

"O ye who believe! stand out firmly for Allah, as witnesses to fair dealing, and let not the hatred of others to you make you swerve to wrong and depart from justice. Be just: that is next to piety: and fear Allah, for Allah is well-acquainted with all that ye do."

*Surah Nahl* 16/90 :

"Allah commands justice, the doing of good, and liberality to kith and kin, and He forbids all shameful deeds, and injustice and rebellion: He instructs you that ye may receive admonition."

*Surah Nisa* 4/58 :

"Allah doth command you to render back your Trusts to those to whom they are due; and when ye judge between man and man, that ye judge with justice: Verily how excellent is the teaching which He giveth you! For Allah is He Who heareth and a seeth all things."

In *Surah Sad* (38/26) Hadrat Daud was directed :

> "O David! We did indeed make thee a vicegerent on earth: so judge thou between men in truth (and justice): nor follow thou the lusts (of thy heart), for they will mislead thee from the Path of Allah: for those who wander astray from the Path of Allah, is a Penalty Grievous, for that they forget the Day of Account."

In *Surah Nisa* (4/105) it is said :

> "We have sent down to thee the Book in truth, that thou mightiest judge between men, as guided by Allah: so be not (used) as an advocate by those who betray their trust;"

God Almighty directed the Holy Prophet in *Surah Al-Anam* (6/114) :

> "Says shall I seek for judge other than Allah when it is he who sent unto you the Book explained in detail."

In *Surah Maida* (5/45) it is ordained :

> "If thou judge, judge in equity between them, for Allah loves those who judge in equity."
>
> It is ordained that the judge must give full weight to the facts and circumstances of the case in accordance with his capacity, capability and lights and does justice even if a near relative is concerned. (6/152).

It is said in *Surah Maida* (5/47) as under :

> "Therefore, fear not men but fear Me and sell not My signs for miserable pittance. If any do fail to judge by the light Allah has revealed they are unbelievers.

5/48: And if fail to judge by the light of what Allah has revealed, they are wrong-doers.

5/50: Let the people of the Gospel judge by what Allah hath revealed therein. If any do fail to judge by (the light) of what Allah hath revealed, they are (no better than) those who rebel."

- Thus God Almighty ordains expressly at the pain of penalty and the society finds it necessary to maintain equilibrium in human affairs so that justice must be done to all. It is, however, not optional. It is the duty of the State that man honours the rights of his fellow-man and the State functionaries discharge the trust reposed in them. In case of an omission or negligence to do, it is provided to compel obedience and performance. Reference be made to *Surah Hadid (57/25)* :

It is important to note that despite the fact, that the *Sunnah* of the Guardian-Angels (82/11) are beyond suspicion and God Almighty also knows the truth of the matter *(see* 2/77, 4/42, *Hajj* 22/1 7, *Al-Imran* 3/119), the person who was killed (81/8-9), the earth on which offence was committed, (99/4) the tongue, hands, feet (24/24) and even the Prophets and other witnesses (39/69) shall be called to depose if any objection is raised on doubt expressed. Such is the right of defence in Islam. Can anyone quote a better procedure anywhere? Such being the right of defence no-one can offer anything less in scope in an Islamic system, for no-one can amend or change the Quran. *See* 5/89, *Yunus* 10/59. It will be appreciated that even the Prophet has not been allowed to bring about change in the express provisions as laid down in *Surah Yunus* (10/15) and *Al tahrim* (56/1). Also refer to the case of Shahid Afzal (PLD 1977, Lahore. 117).

Here it is worth to mention that 'bias in a judge which makes even an order correct, on facts and in law, as void, has no place in the Islamic Concept of Justice. In Islam, a judge is expected to do justice in all circumstances and if he severs from that path for any reason whatever, he is not a fit person to act as a judge. It is, therefore, the correctness of the order which is to be looked into and not the interest of the Judge. This is the view of the Federal Court also.

This may be compared with the Western concept where even decision of a Lord Chancellor was set aside on the ground that he held some shares in a company which was one of the parties before him in a case. *See* Dimes *v.* Grand Junction Canal Company Proprietors (1852) 3 HLC 759). The poor judge died of that shock later. This concept is based on a principle that justice should not only be done but should manifestly be seen to have been done. If this be the justification for striking down an order then perhaps in all those cases where government or other powerful and influential persons are pitched against weak, poor and uninfluential persons there will be no possibility of any justice, whatever. If the reason be of frailty of human-beings then why cannot a judge fall for greater temptations such as bribe, offer of higher position, etc. Even fear may prevent him from doing justice. Again there are hundreds of laws in force in many countries where one is a judge in his own cause. Can the courts strike down those decisions or have they done it on that score? Thus Islam looks for a better man as a judge. His attributes and qualifications are also given in the letter of Hadrat Ali.

The Quran aims at building a better social order and teaches individuals to develop very high integrity so that no person can conceive even for a moment that a judge who undertakes to decide a matter will go astray for any reason whatever. I refer here to a case which came up before Hadrat Umar. Hadrat Umar issued an order against acceptance of gift by anyone holding office since it is a type of bribe. Hadrat Umar prohibited taking or acceptance of gifts by office holders. The Quran thus ordains judges to decide against themselves, their parents, relations, friends, etc.; *(Nisa* 4/135) if the situation so requires, and not to decide against an enemy just only for that reason *(Maidah* 5/8).

Here, we can also mention that some of the legal principles that we generally follow in deciding cases are given in the Quran. Their origin is not to be credited to the modern system of law and justice :

(i) Judge with justice (4/58).

(ii) Apply your mind anxiously (1 7/35).

(iii) One is innocent unless proved guilty (24/12-13).

(iv) No offence without men's rea (33/5 and 6/54).

(v) No offence can be created retrospectively (44/22, 8/38, 5/96 and 2/275).

(vi) There is no offence if an act is done under compulsion (16/106).

(vii) The punishment should be commensurate with the offence and not more (2/194, 10/27, 22/60, 40/40, 42/40 and 16/126).

(viii) Self defence is no offence (42/41).

(ix) An abetter is also guilty (16/25).

(x) No-one can be held responsible for offences of others (42/15 and 39/7).

(xi) Writing is necessary for contracts except if it is unavoidable (2/282).

(xii) Agreement is binding but not so if the other side has broken it (8/56 and 9/4).

(xiii) The aggrieved is entitled to compensation (17/33).

(xiv) No more burden will be placed on one than he can bear (2/286).

(xv) Decide according to the evidence produced (4/105).

You will find 100 such principles, as embodied in *Mejellah,* in PLD 1966, Journal 50.

No-one is considered above law in Islam and so no-one can claim legal immunity. It is in direct conflict with the British notion that the "king can do no wrong" or the Western concept that the head of State or certain other functionaries are neither answerable to anyone nor can they be sued or prose cited. A legacy of this concept has been finding a place in our Constitutions. Article 248 of the 1973 Constitution may be quoted for reference. It is as under:

> Formerly, all witnesses appeared together. Qadi Shuraih made an important change that they should appear separately. Evidence could be oral, documentary, direct or circumstantial. Oral evidence could be direct or hearsay. The latter was permissible to prove paternity, death and reliable character. It had to come from competent witnesses. An adulterer, a person noted for dishonesty, bad character, drunk and a known liar were not considered reliable witnesses. Evidence of a slave in favour of his master was not admissible. Arbitration was allowed but either party could retract before award was given. Award when made became conclusive and could be referred to Qadi for execution.

The emphasis was on reformation and not imposition of sentences for crimes. Forgiveness was preferred to penalty. The Quran, Traditions of the Holy Prophet and, in their absence, personal judgement, were to be resorted to. *Ijma* and *Qias* were added to later by *Khulfa-i-Rashidin.* Hadrat Umar created a new precedent by accepting the evidence of an expert in a defamatory suit filed by Zibriqan bin Badr against a poet Hutaya. The verse which was the cause of dispute was vague and therefore it was decided on the opinion of another poet Hassan bin Sabit. No court fee had to be paid for seeking justice.

It seems appropriate in this respect to reproduce a letter written by Hadrat Umar to Abu Musa Ashari about Qadi's functions:

> "After the praise to God the Administration of Justice is a duty. The Court must observe equality between the parties so that the weaker party may expect justice and the stronger may not expect concession. The burden of proof is on the plaintiff and the defendant may be put on oath, but let this not defeat the ends of justice and law. If you have decided a case, then after due care and thinking you may revise your decision. If you are doubtful in a point which is mentioned in the Quran and *Hadith* then think over it again and again and then apply *'Qiyas'* (a process of deduction). When a party wants to tender evidence then fix a time limit and if he proves his case then decide accordingly. All Muslims are fit to be witnesses except those who have received the prescribed punishment (flogging) for *Hadd* (fornication, adultery) and those who have tendered false evidence."

The system of judicial administration remained more or less the same even under the Umayyads. It is, however, unfortunate that special care was taken in appointing to office only persons who owned loyalty to the executive head and belonged either to the same family or shared in status as clients. The Qadis were appointed and dismissed publicly. During this period the judges were given executive powers like appointment of guardians of infants, administration of *waqf* properties, execution of punishments and looking after testamentary dispositions.

There were no regular Courts of Appeals but usually the Khalifah himself performed the duties of a High Court of Appeal. During the rule of Khalifah Al-Mamoon, a *Nazir-fil-Mazalim* or Board for Inspection of Grievances was established. It was presided over by Khalifah himself. It included the Chief Qadi, the Chief Wazir and one or two Secretaries of state and jurists or *Muftis* as members to correct miscarriage of justice. There was no set procedure as we know it today. The Board could apply the principles of equity to secure the ends of justice. Its powers were similar to the constitutional jurisdiction of the High Court.

During the rule of Abbasides science of jurisprudence flourished, traditions of Holy Prophet were collected and commentaries on the Quran were written. The four great schools of *Sunni* Law were established in this period. Administration of justice commenced on definite lines which had close resemblance to the modern systems. If the case was settled or terminated by a decision, a written judgement had to follow. The Qadi also had the right to pass an *ex-parte* decree. He could review his own judgement. The Abbasides developed a procedure for consulting specialists in the *Shariah* Law through *'Muftis'* and jurists who also assisted the litigants with written opinions or *'Fatwas'*.

*Muhtasibs* or Ombudsmen were also appointed during the Abbasid period. They were responsible for the enforcement of moral duties and obligations in accordance with the Quranic injunctions. The *Muhtasib* had the power to act *suo-moto* and enforce obedience by striking fear of the Hereafter. He was concerned with observance of prayers, fastings and other religious acts, non payments of debts without excuse, failure to fulfil official obligations, nuisances, right of way, easements, etc. The *Muhtasib* exercised control over attorneys and *vakils* so that they did not tamper with the administration of justice.

I propose now to wind up my address by pointed reference to the difficult task which lies ahead of all of us, to achieve the avowed objective of shaping ourselves as true Muslims, as best as one can, and adopt and practice the Islamic System of doing justice. The enormity of the task is indisputable but it is not impossible to achieve. It entails care and caution so that we reduce to the minimum the chances of trial and error.

Let me quote in the end a Latin—American saying :

> "It is better to know where to go, but know not how to go, then know how to go but know not where to go."

Thus what is important is the destination. In so far as we Muslims are concerned God Almighty has given us our destination precisely and also the way to reach it. So my friends you are the lucky ones, the chosen ones and the blessed ones. If we stick to the faith and righteousness and obey the commands of *Rabb-e-Zuljalal,* of the Holy Prophet, and of those provided by a body of resolute men of faith and firmness, we are, *'Insha-Allah',* bound to succeed.

## Judicial Perception

Islam presents a well articulated and coherent model of justice. The Islamic view of justice includes an understanding of how society can maintain a balance in its network of social relationships and how it can prepare individuals to accept and adopt the Quranic mandate reflecting the Will of Almighty Allah. This view of justice can be completely vindicated by empirical methods.

The Concept of Justice in Islam is contained in the principle: "to each his due". The just state of affairs in Islam is that in which each individual has exactly those benefits and liabilities which are due to him by virtue of his personal characteristics and circumstances. Common examples are the claim that justice means giving each man what he deserves and it also means equality.

The definition of justice in Islam has two important corollaries. First, it implies that where two men are equal in the relevant respects (so that their dues are the same) they should be treated the same way. Islam endorses the principle "Treat Equals Equally' . It is also supported by another fundamental principle "Render To Each His Due". An inference can be drawn from these two statements that the amount of benefit a person enjoys or the amount of burden he suffers should be proportional to the quantity of the relevant attribute which he possesses.

A possible distributive principle of Islam is that everyone should retain what he currently possesses. Resources have to be distributed in such a way that the greatest total amount of happiness is produced. The distribution of resources is recommended as a means to an aggregate goal, not as an end in itself.

***Justice as Virtue :*** Justice is regarded as a virtue in an Islamic social setting. There is usually a natural urge to perform acts of justice, as there is for acts of benevolence, such as helping a man who is in pain. Justice is vital to Muslim society. It is founded partly on the concept of *Ummah's* interest. Justice and the interests of *Ummah* are interdependent.

Justice in Islam serves the general happiness, conforms to the laws of life and gives each individual what he deserves. An adherence to distribution according to capability is guaranteed to produce maximum happiness. Islam endorsed the view that men should have rights in proportion to their merit.

The domain of justice in Islam can be sub-divided into two spheres of legal justice and social justice. Legal justice includes *"Tazeer"* which concerns the punishment of wrong-doing and the compensation of injury. It stipulates the conditions under which punishment may be inflicted and adjusts the scale of punishment to fit the nature of different crimes. In the sphere of civil law, the legal justice regulates the amount of restitution which must be made for injuries. Both the sections of legal justice lay down procedures of a fair trial and also rights of appeal. Social justice concerns the distribution of benefits, material and otherwise, and liabilities throughout the Muslim society as it results from social, economic, religious and political institutions. It deals with such matters as regulation of wages, administration of profits, protection of individual rights, allocation of food, clothing and shelter, and provision of education, health and welfare benefits.

The concept of justice in Islam tends to preserve the existing order of rights and possessions and restores it when any breach has been made. It consists in the recognition and protection of legal rights and also comprises principles for maintaining these rights according to the Quranic standard. The concept emphasises, in all segments of political life of Islamic society, the notion contained in the maxim "To each according to his or her rights".

Rights generally derive from publicly acknowledged rules, established practices, past transactions, current behaviour and individual qualities. Rights are also concerned with the citizens' expectations from the state and with ensuring that they are not disappointed. Men ought to be rewarded according to their deserts. A man's deserts may be measured by the accomplishments, his productive efforts, his capacities and capabilities. Thus Islam presents a healthy amalgam of three principles "To each according to his rights; To each according to his deserts; To each according to his needs". Each of the three principles embodies an important reason why Islam works out their synthesis.

The three principles whose synthesis is produced by Islam demand that a person's share of goods to which he is entitled by virtue of someone rule and by virtue of its affiliation to the other two principles should be made available to him. This availability should be a factor contributing to the maximum possible happiness. Given certain empirical assumptions, maximum possible happiness can be produced by recognising the claims of rights, deserts and needs.

Granted that it would be useful for Muslims to adhere to this synthesis; more happiness will be produced if desert is generally rewarded. The expectation of reward in the case of private citizens and of promotion in the case of public servants encourages people to acquire useful skills and perform deserving actions.

A more specific conception of justice within the Islamic framework expresses itself in the requirement that each person is to have an equal right to the most extensive basic liberty compatible with a similar liberty for others. Social and economic inequalities are to be minimised. They must provide great benefit to the least privileged. All public officers and positions have to be laid open to all under conditions of fair equality of opportunity. The principle of fair equality of opportunity demands that positions and offices should be assigned on the basis of ability and skill rather than on the basis of birth and influence. It covers such issues as freedom of conscience and the rights of citizens to participate in the affairs of Government.

It can safely be maintained that justice in Islam is not mostly procedural as it is in Roman Law. Islam provides reasonable criteria for judging whether a given allocation of financial resources to persons or institutions is just or unjust. Such an allocation can, however, be just if it has arisen through the operation of fair procedures. Islam visualises an institutional framework within which these criteria can be applied.

There is to be a competitive market economy, a "transfer branch" of government to guarantee a basic social minimum, another branch to prevent the formation of monopolies, and so on. The Quranic law will then provide a guideline as to how wealth and other goods should be distributed to persons. Once institutions are established on the Islamic model, individuals participating in these institutions will form certain expectations about how they are to be treated, and these in turn will give rise to entitlements.

Islam does not endorse the socialistic conception that the position of the under-privileged should be materially improved by expropriating wealthy landowners without just compensation. The expectations of the landless and of the land-owners have to be kept in proper balance. The objective of land reforms in Islam is not to deprive the land-owners of their landed property and to make them the under-privileged members of society.

Islam accepts in full the common-sense precepts of justice, such as the precept "to each according to his contribution" or the precept "to each according to his effort". Someone who makes a larger than average contribution is creating more value for the Muslim society, and it is, therefore, worth paying him a larger wage. Rewards and incentives are essential to encourage the Muslims to acquire skills, work harder, and take on unpleasant work. Islam provided justifications for the payment of exceptionally high rewards to people with scarce but useful talents. Surely all of those currently receiving high rewards must deserve them.

Islamic social system does not discard the belief that every man must have the opportunity to climb the social ladder and to achieve the highest rewards that the society has to offer. Islam does not impose barriers of a legal, social or economic type that could prevent a citizen from gaining rewards. Anything that a man may justly claim he must earn by exercising his capacities in a socially useful way, in which case the institutions of property, contract and exchange will ensure that he gets a fair return.

The Islamic society makes service to the community the dominant motive in work. The social well-being is eventually broken down into individual benefits and the chief constituent of individuals' well-being is the satisfaction of needs. Thus the better-off can show their own rewards to be just by meeting the just claims to their services made by those in need.

The cardinal feature of Islamic society is that the Muslims characteristically evaluate the social distribution of benefits by reference to Quranic standards of distribution. The general criteria of social justice can only be implemented by establishing Quranic doctrines and principles, and thus by conferring certain positive rights upon individuals. Once a right has been established, it gains its own intrinsic value because individuals come to govern their actions by reference to Quranic standards.

In an Islamic social setting, the traditional network of social relationships produces a commitment to values such as generosity. The society is concerned with the protection of human rights as well as with the relief of the needy.

The Islamic view of justice incorporates a number of distinguished characteristics. For example, each man can choose the kind of occupation he will adopt, instead of being assigned to it by birth or authoritative command. He works for the rewards which he can gain, not under compulsion or for fear of sanctions. He competes freely with other individuals for these rewards. He is free to make contracts with others as he wishes. There is no inherited social status: a man's place is determined by his actions, by the agreements he makes, and the rewards they bring him.

There are no rigid institutions which constrain people to act in ways they would not otherwise do, whether by compulsion or by the sanctity of custom; every institution is created and sustained by the free agreement of the individuals who wish to use it to gain certain specific ends. Efforts of the people are combined, in an Islamic society, for mutual advantage. Occupations are determined by the principle of efficiency. The social institutions are erected on the basis of free contract. Contracts are not simply expressions of mutual self-interest. They are subject to the moral control of society which determines the forms of contracts that are permissible.

The economic system is composed of independent producers who group themselves into associations for mutual advantage. Within the association, independence is preserved and competition of a nondestructive type is continued and rewards are proportional to merit. There are no status barriers between men. Thus justice is not a constraint on individuals seeking their private ends. It becomes instead an expression of their independence, of their individuality and of the religious milieu.

In an Islamic society any expenditure of talent and energy which is socially useful must be recompensed at the appropriate rate, which is agreed on in advance. Rewards gained in the open society are just, because to gain them a man must have contributed sufficiently to the welfare of society. Every individual should receive a fair recompense for his labour, and this is given quantitative expression in the principle that he shall be rewarded according to his competence and capabilities. Justice is satisfied when each gets out of the undertaking an equivalent of what he has put in.

The Islamic Concept of Justice can be rationally defended. The defence consists partly in showing that the conception corresponds to Allah's Will, partly in showing that it represents the rational choice of individuals placed in a real situation in which they are cognisant of their personal qualities and of their place in society. The whole enterprise of delineating a conception of justice on the basis of rational choices abstracted from Holy Quran is well taken, because these abstracts have the prerequisites for making a sound conception of justice. It follows from this thesis that Muslims hold conception of justice as part of specific Islamic views of society, and that they acquire these views through their experience of knowing, assimilating and following the Quran.

## No Discrimination

Justice, as an abstract quality, is difficult to define. To say that it enables distinction to be made between right and wrong does not simplify the matter because opinion on rights and wrongs vary widely. To say that every human being is equipped with a sense of justice is of little help, since the thought of each individual is limited by the conscious knowledge he possesses. It is clearly a quality attaching to actions, and therefore to living things that are capable of action. The effect of an action could be particular in a certain aspect, such as the Courts deal with, on a large scale, as between human beings. Despite the scope of the judicial function, within a community, being ever on the increase, it yet does not, in my opinion, represent the widest stretch of the meaning of the word 'justice'. That, perhaps, is to be found in the relationships of all living things to everything in their natural environment. With the exception of man, all other things have limitations upon the extent of their activity, which are designed to operate for promotion of a balanced life for all, so that the Will of the Almighty should be fulfilled by the continual betterment of His Creation.

The agency of man, to whom has been entrusted control of everything else in nature, is an element of the greatest importance in that fulfilment. If, in exercising that control, he is to carry out the Divine purpose, he must have appreciation of the exactness of the adjustments that nature, in its justice, has provided for the governance of relations between living beings and inanimate things in creation. Lately, evidence has been gathered which shows the enormous damage done to the environment by the naked pursuit of advantage and profit to themselves, by groups of human beings, notably in Western countries. They had interfered with the economy of nature, without understanding of the linkages between and the justice operating through all its creatures, animate and inanimate, until the detriment to themselves started them in the face. They had done injustice to their environment and punishment had followed.

A definition of the quality of justice has been attempted in the great work of Shah Waliullah, entitled *Hujjatullah al-Baligha. Adalat* is there specified as one of four faculties, by the fostering and development of which, perfection in human happiness may be attained. *Adalat* is that quality in a member of a society which enables him, without effort and with perfect naturalness to act always so as to strengthen the bonds of union in the society. The ideal is that of a healthy body, made of perfectly co-related parts operating in unison, free from internal obstruction. The just man has the special capacity, by his actions in everyday life, of assisting towards the end that all the members of the society live together, in their separate walks, as limit of a single corporate, integrated body. Such a person furthers the intention of Allah, in respect of all human communities, that their affairs should be conducted in the best possible way, to ensure continuous improvement. Being imbued with a feeling of total involvement in the activities of the people, in the manner of a head of a family, being sensitive to their innermost feelings and thoughts, cognizant as their settled technique in the implementation of their desires, he is competent to guide their energies into beneficial channels. Possessing the basic virtue of gentleness in thought and action, and free from harshness and hatred, his adaptation to the human environment is such that all his action's are in just proportion to the occasions. Such a person, with this special quality, is, in Shah Waliullah's opinion, well suited to control the affairs of a State. Among those affairs, not the least in importance is the function of the judiciary, for the dispensation of justice in the wide area of conflict of interest between citizens and the ruling authorities.

Among the many distinctions to which the religion of Islam can lay claim, one that in the context of human affairs can claim the highest importance is that its acceptance and establishment proceeded concurrently with the establishment of the Islamic State, under the inspired leadership of the Apostle of Allah, the Holy Prophet Muhammad (peace be upon him). In the first thirteen years after he received the call to Prophethood, he received the bulk of the revelations vouchsafed to him by the Almighty, while being tested and tempered through a fierce fire of determined and seemingly invincible opposition by his own people in the holy city of Mecca. Under Divine guidance, he then moved to the city of Medina, and immediately the number of his followers multiplied to the extent that it fell to him to lay down the Constitution of his State, and to provide it with the full apparatus of a Government.

That he did so in the light bestowed upon him by Allah is apparent from the fact that a great proportion of the Divine injunctions relating to human affairs is to be found in the four *Surahs,* Nos. 2 to 5, which were revealed at Medina. Under direct guidance from the Almighty, the Holy Prophet conducted all the central affairs of the new State, laid down principles of government and organization, established institutions, directed foreign affairs, conducted negotiations and concluded treaties, sent out embassis carried the war with his Meccan opponents to a successful conclusion. He at the same time, in direct touch with all his followers, accessible at all times to each of them, and he judged every case himself. The record of the revelations he received is contained in the Holy Quran; the record of his actions as reported by his personal Companions or other reliable persons who had received it from the Companions is in the *Sunnah*. It is from these two Scriptures that the governing principles of justice in Islam are derived. Over and above the detailed and particular principles, there is to be read the direction of Allah, contained in *Surah* IV, verse 106 :

> "We have revealed the Book comprising the Truth, so that you would judge men in the light of Allah."

And it is made plain that the dispensation of justice is to proceed on regulated lines in the injunction to King David, in *Surah* 38, verse 27 :

> "And judge between men on right principle, and do not follow your own inclinations, for they will cause you to stray from the path of Allah."

Decisions were not to be based on whim or caprice, but on proper canon and justice and equity. A model was thus set up for the Holy Prophet, and his successors, to follow, and indeed they followed it. Equity, which may be described as mitigation of the harsher aspects of justice according to the circumstances, is a basic rule of Islamic Justice.

The Holy Quran is replete with injunctions that are relevant to justice. In *Surah* IV, verse 136 it is said 'Believers! bear aloft the standard of justice', and verse 9 of the *Surah* V proclaims that justice has quality that brings it near to piety and the fear of Allah. Verse 9 of *Surah* V and verse 153 *of Surah* VI warn against allowing ill-will or affection to colour a judgement. In the matter of private retributive justice, there are several directions for the observation of equality and proportion, and each is supplemented by a recommendation to mitigation or forgiveness. For instance, verse 178 of *Surah* II, says that for murder, the retaliation must be equal, freeman for freeman, slave for slave, woman for woman, but immediately thereafter comes the mitigation in His Mercy, Allah ordains that the next-of-kin has the option to refrain from retaliation on receiving material compensation, which should be agreed in proper manner, and received graciously, that is retaining no rancour. Verse 127 of *Surah* says — 'Believers! if you must take revenge, do it in proportion to the injury suffered and immediately after 'but if you suffer patiently, that is better for the sufferers'. Self-defence is approved in verse 39 of *Surah* 42, where it is said 'the return for an evil deed is a similar deed—but he who forgives has his reward with Allah verse 47 of *Surah* XXIII takes the matter even further, when it says-'Meet evil by repaying it with good and this is repeated in verse 35 of *Surah* XLI, which reads — 'Good and evil are not alike; repay evil with good, and your enemy will become a sincere friend.

The jurisprudence of a particular system of justice is founded on maxims, rules, principles and precedents. These are not to be expected, in precise form, in such a Scripture as the Quran, but there is a great deal to be found which is of directory effect to the spread of justice within the community of Islam, as well as to the dispensation of justice. The entire field is placed under the religious obligation, surrender to the Will of Allah, and answerability on the Last Day. But there are rules of conduct laid down in many matters out of which resort to law most frequently arises, which may be recounted briefly.

Thus, provocation which is a common cause of conflict, is frowned upon in verse 12 of *Surah* XLIV, where the faithful are enjoined against mocking, calling names, fault-finding, spying and the nursing of suspicions. Verse 149 of *Surah* IV says—'Do not use foul language, even if wronged', and in verse 54 of *Surah* XVII, it is said—'Use gracious words to each other, for Satan is alert to create discord among you. Aggressiveness in behaviour is condemned in verse 34 of *Surah* VI and verse 92 of *Surah* XVI, in the words — 'Allah forbids unlawful aggression'. 'Oppression is blameworthy' says verse 42 of *Surah* XXXVII and verse 10 of *Surah* XLIX requires that the aggressor should be humbled. Oath-taking in order to deceive is expressly forbidden in verse 95 of *Surah* XVI which says—'You will thereby abandon firm ground and incur punishment'. Scandal-mongering receives special treatment at many places. Thus, *Surah* 104 declares 'Woe to all backbiters and slanderers', and a biting condemnation is contained in verse 13 of *Surah* XLIX, in the words — 'Avoid backbiting: would you wish to eat the flesh of a dead brother?

The spreading of rumours not based on knowledge is declared 'a grave fault' in verse 15 of *Surah* XXIV, of which verse 27 says that calumniators cannot injure any people. Indecency in behaviour, both open and hidden, is forbidden by Allah in verse 34 of *Surah* VI, and a painful punishment in both the lives is declared for those who spread immorality. Privacy of homes is safeguarded by injunctions in verses 28 to 30 of *Surah* XXIV, where entry only with permission and after greeting the inmates is enjoined. Careless behaviour in this regard could be a source of grave trouble. Correct and respectful behaviour between the sexes is particularly prescribed in verses 31 and 32 of the same *Surah:* men are to lower their gaze on meeting women, and women must do likewise when meeting men, and at the same time, should cover themselves up.

Extravagance being contrary to just behaviour, a bad example to others, and a way towards sinful acts, is specially mentioned in verse 188 of *Surah* II, where it is said — 'Eat not up your property in vanity' and in verse 27 of *Surah* XVII, squanderers are characterised as 'brothers of the devils'. Drinking and gambling are condemned in verses 90 and 91 of *Surah* V, as 'Satan's handiwork out of which enmity and hatred grow' and as such make you 'forget prayer'. In both, says verse 21 9 of *Surah* II, is great sin.

For the dispensation of justice, an indispensable requirement is evidence, oral as well as documentary. It is important that evidence should be forthcoming, and verse 283 of *Surah* II gives the direction 'Do not conceal testimony: to do so in sinful', and verse 136 of *Surah* IV says 'Let no low motives keep you from the path of justice'. 'Bear true witness' says verse 9 of *Surah* V, and in verse 64 of *Surah* XXV it is said 'The servants of Allah the Gracious One, do not give false evidence'. Those who stand by their testimony are said, in verse 33 of *Surah* LXX to be 'saved from hell'. To give evidence 'for the sake of Allah' without fear or favour, is enjoined in verse 136 of *Surah* IV, where it is said 'Bear testimony even against yourself, your parents and your kinsfolk'.

Documents have value for avoidance of falsity and fraud, and the Holy Quran prescribes the writing of deeds in, at least, five cases, viz. loans, sales, wills, divorces and the freeing of slaves. A debt should be put into writing; the scribe should not refuse to record it; the contents should be dictated by the debtor, and there should be at least two witnesses; persons asked to witness should not refuse. *(Surah* II, verse 282).

The same verse requires that sales should also be put into writing and witnessed in the same way, and the scribe and the witnesses should be held free of harm. By verse 2 of *Surah* LXV, it is directed that when a woman is given release from her marriage, a deed should be inscribed, attested by two witnesses. Special provision is made for wills to be in writing, attested by two witnesses from among the relations, by verse 107 of *Surah* V, and the testator may put these witnesses to the oath that they will, when the occasion arises, support the will, and not back out for money or for fear of offending other heirs. It is even laid down that if the attesting witnesses back out, others may be produced, who should be put to the oath that their testimony is true. One sees the great care taken to ensure that truth and justice should prevail. By verse 33 of *Surah* XXIV, it is required that a slave should be given a written release if he asks for it. In certain cases, e.g. the attesting of wills, a standard of competency for being a witness is laid down: they must be 'just men.' Certain persons, e.g. those found guilty of preferring a false charge of unchastity against honourable women are debarred for life from giving evidence *(Surah* XXIV, verse 5). To keep the judiciary free from corruption, the faithful are warned by verse 188 of *Surah* II not to use their money to gain the favour of judges, and so to devour the property of others.

To ensure the orderly devolution of estates, bequests are recommended, in verse 180 of *Surah* II, to be made to parents and near relatives, as a 'safeguard against sin', and those are commended who advise the testator on making a fair distribution. Blood relations are to be preferred above other believers and the refugees, but even to a friend, a bequest may be made *(Surah* XXXIII verse 7). A person approaching death should make special provision for his wife, leaving enough for a year's maintenance, while living in his house *(Surah* II, verse 240). These precautionary admonitions are clearly designed to secure the doing of justice to all entitled persons in the distribution of the estate of a deceased relative, out of which commonly great and lengthy disputes are apt to arise.

To the same purpose, there have been provided clear rules of succession to such estates in *Surah* IV, verses 7, 12, 13 and 177. These are too well-known to require mention by me. They are still in force throughout the Muslim world. The scheme is elaborate and, what is more, unique among known systems of succession. It is so close to the ideal both from the viewpoint of the beneficiaries as well as the health and well-being of the economy that, in India, Hindu Judges of High Courts have applied it to the distribution of estates in regard to which the personal law of the parties was not clear, at the same time observing that the system was both just and beneficial.

Similar comprehensive rules are laid down in the Holy Quran in regard to the regulation of matrimonial affairs, out of which troubles are apt to arise in all societies. These too are very well-known, and there is need to only touch upon them briefly. Women were not to be forced into marriage against their will. The practice of widows being forced to marry a kinsman of the deceased husband, as a matter of inheritance, was forbidden in verse 19 of *Surah* IV. The consent of the relatives of a slave-girl was made requisite, by verse 34 of *Surah* XXIV, for her marriage to her owner. By the same verse, the man was required to give a portion at marriage to the wife, even if she were a slave, and taking back of what was so given was forbidden by verse 20 of *Surah* IV, unless the women were guilty of flagrant lewdness. In case of disagreements between the spouses, recourse was first to be had to reconciliation (verse 129 of *Surah* IV) but when a total breach was feared, their case was to be referred to two *hukma* (judges or Arbitrators) one from each side. (Verse 34 *of Surah* IV).

The care of the Almighty for the good of the parties was indicated by the words in the same verse—'if they are inclined to peace, Allah will bring them to agreement, but if they are bent on separation, verse 131 of *Surah* IV gives the assurance that 'Allah will fulfil the needs of both'. Elaborate rules to govern divorce are contained in *Surah* II. Two golden threads run through the entire code of divorce, namely :

(1) kindness and consideration for the woman, and

(2) avoidance of haste in divorcing. A period of waiting was imposed upon the divorced wife before she could marry again, for the obvious purpose of keeping the lines of pedigree pure. Such women were not to be prevented from marrying again.

Rules are also laid down in the Holy Quran in regard to such matters as trusts, and business relationships. By verse 283 of *Surah* II and verse 58 of *Surah* IV, fulfilment of trusts is enjoined, and *Surah* 70 imports the religious obligation when it says that paradise is assured to those who are faithful to their trusts and convenants. Honesty in trade is enjoined by the injunction 'Weigh and measure full and fair' contained in verse 153 of *Surah* VI and verse 36 of *Surah* XVII, and *Surah* 83 condemns traders who demand full measure from others but give less themselves. Observance of contracts is made obligatory in verse *2, Surah* V and verse 35 of *Surah* XVII, and again the religious sanction is brought in by the words 'you must account for them'. There are severe injunctions against usury, by which money is doubled and quadrupled; some practice it under the cover of trade; it is a thing of the Devil and Allah puts a blight on it. (verse 275 of *Surah* II and verse 130 of *Surah* III).

Orphans being easy victims for their guardians, the Holy Quran makes special provision in many places to ensure proper treatment for them, and proper care of their property during their minority. *Surah* 93 condemns ill-treatment and contemptuous behaviour and *Surah* 89 forbids harshness, towards orphans. The best course, says *Surah* II, verse 220, is to improve their lot, and bring them up as brothers. Deal fairly with orphans' property, says verse 153 of *Surah* VI, and verse 35 of *Surah* says. Do not touch orphans' property, except for a proper purpose. Verse 2 of *Surah* IV gives a comprehensive direction—Look after orphans till they reach marriageable age, then give them their property, and have the transaction witnessed. During their minority, be careful in spending their money, do not mix their property with your own, and charge your expenses reasonably.

There is much more in the Holy Quran that is relevant to law and justice, but for the present purpose, this account of the directions on certain subjects is sufficient to establish that a comprehensive jurisprudence was given to the faithful of Islam thereby. That the injunctions were to be observed as law appears from following verse, among others - 'When they consult you concerning women, say' Allah has given you decrees and the Scripture that has been recited to you" (Verse 127 of *Surah* IV). In verse 59 of *Surah* IV, there is the overall injunction— 'If you are at variance over any matter, refer it to Allah and His Messenger'. This has throughout been interpreted to mean that the line of decision is to be sought in the Holy Quran, and the word of the Holy Prophet (peace be upon him) spoken in his lifetime and as recorded in the *Ahadith* or *Sunnah* after his death.

We have not dealt with the matter of crimes and punishment that are detailed in the Holy Quran, as these are very well-known. The best known matters seem to be the *Hadd,* i.e. the maximum punishment. What is much less known is that the principle of mitigation in relation to the circumstances has been applied from the very first days of Islam. In Verse 178 of *Surah* II, which is mentioned earlier, where blood-money was declared to be an acceptable alternative to equal retaliation, the words were added 'this mitigation is provided through the mercy of your Lord'. Shah Waliullah, in the *(Hujjatullah Al-Baligha)* points out that the *Hadd* punishments were applied to offences of three kind :

(1) those subversive of public order and disturbing to the community,

(2) such as, if not prevented early, could be repeated so as to become habitual, and

(3) such that the victim could not get redress for himself.

For treason and sedition, the most severe punishment was prescribed and mitigation was inadmissible. For theft, the punishment was prescribed in the Holy Quran, namely, hand-cutting, the offence being one easy to commit, and therefore apt to become both habitual and widespread. The Holy Prophet (peace be upon him) as a law giver is reported to have imposed this punishment only where the value of the stolen property was more than a quarter of a *dirham.* He also laid down the principle that for applying this punishment, the taking must be from actual safe-custody, or under protection, besides being of the requisite value. So, for plucking fruit from a tree or taking animals that were straying in the hills, lesser punishments were given, including a fine of double the value of the thing taken. Cases of crimes which cannot be requited by the victim are outraging the modesty of respectable women, highway robbery, false imputation of unchastity, and for these the *Hadd* punishments were appropriate. Mitigation was also laid down for slaves, who did not possess full freedom of will; for them punishments were halved. The Holy Prophet (peace be upon him) said — 'if a female slave commits an offence, beat her; if a male slave commits theft, sell him'. Another tradition is to the effect that when a complaint was made against a slave by his owner, that he had committed theft, the Holy Prophet said 'both belong to you; one is merged in the other'.

There are traditions also with reference to the *Hadd* punishment for adultery that qualified mitigation was applied, according to the facts. With regard to intoxication through drink, the Holy Prophet strengthened the Quranic injunctions by declaring it to be *Haram.* He ordered the punishment of 40 lashes to a drunken person. Here too, the offence is one easily committed, and apt to become habitual so that full severity in punishment was justified. Later, it was increased to 80 lashes. A very impressive instance of the Holy Prophet's inclination towards mercy is to be found in the tradition that when a man brought before him, as an offender who had incurred a punishment of 100 lashes, proved to be sick and a cripple, he said 'take a branch with a hundred twigs and give him one blow with it'.

During the period when the Holy Prophet (peace be upon him) was the sole Judge of his people, he enlarged the jurisprudence of Islam in several directions. The record of his decisions and dicta is contained in the *Ahadith.* It was he who laid down the rule that in the trial of suits, the onus of producing evidence to support his claim is on the plaintiff; the defendant must take an oath that his case is true. The reason given was that if relief were always given to plaintiffs on evidence alone, unjust results could follow. Another rule that he laid down is that in cases of doubt, the antecedents of witnesses should be checked. Supplementing the rule of the Quran that one who is proved to have made a false imputation of unchastity against an honourable woman is for ever disqualified as a witness in judicial proceedings, the Holy Prophet disqualified also persons who have committed breach of trust or adultery, as well as those who were enemies of a party. Rules were laid down as to the taking of oaths—the formula of words, the time and the place.

The words should bring to mind the total power and the total knowledge of Allah; the time should be after the *Asar* prayer; in Mecca the place was within the precincts of the *Kaaba,* and in Medina, at the mosque of Tayyiba. The Holy Prophet greatly disapproved of litigious persons saying that in the view of Allah these were the most troublesome, but those who avoided contention were praised as magnanimous. False evidence and false cases were regarded with a very severe eye; they show disrespect to Allah, they disturb the harmony of society and so attract the wrath of Allah, who loves not the troublemaker and desires that social order should be maintained. The Holy Prophet said—'he who makes a false case to get another's property is not of my people; he should find his place in Hell'. A judgement does not make that lawful which is itself unlawful, and the Holy Prophet added great emphasis by saying :

> 'Remember that I am like one of you. If a clever litigant, by artful words, convinces me so that I decide a case in his favour, such a litigant will go to Hell.'

In his decisions, the Holy Prophet always upheld the principle of public good. Thus in a case of damage to a garden by a stray camel, he laid down that if it happened in the daytime when the garden-owner should have guarded his property, there was no blame to the camel-owner, but if it happened at night, when the camel-owner should have kept his animal secure, the camel-owner was liable. The maxim *'al-khiraj-biz-zaman',* meaning that the profit from a thing belongs to him who is responsible for its existence, from which is derived the corollary *'al-uzm-bil-ghanam'* meaning he who pays for a thing is entitled to the benefit from it, comes from the Holy Prophet himself, and in his time was laid down the salutary principle that all transactions that predated the advent of the Islamic State were to be left as they were, untouched by the new order of things.

The rule favouring the person in possession, where the ownership of property is involved, and the evidence is either doubtful or equal on the two sides was applied by the Holy Prophet in a case he decided. With regard to property of which no owner could be found, he laid down that its disposal should be governed by the element of benefit to all Muslims as well as to the thing itself, and secondly, by the element of prior possession; failing these, by the casting of lots. He held that contracts should be enforced to the letter, unless anything agreed makes that *halal* (lawful) which religion declares to be *haram* (unlawful). Where the parties are not agreed as to the terms of a contract, it should be declared void, and in a particular case, the Holy Prophet said—'When seller and buyer are not agreed, and the word of neither can be accepted, if the thing allegedly sold be there, the word of the seller should be accepted, but if the buyer does not agree, the contract should be declared void." Many cases are recorded in which the Holy Prophet (peace be upon him) laid down canons of justice of general application.

The paternity of the child of a slave-girl being contested, one party claiming that his brother, when dying had said the child was his and should be looked after in his family, and the other declaring it is the child of my father's slave, and was born in my father's house, the Holy Prophet pronounced judgement as follows : 'the child belongs to the owner of the house in which it was born; for the adulterer there is stoning.' He decided that in a built-up area, where trouble had arisen through the paths being encroached upon by builders, the minimum width of the path should be seven cubits; so a public nuisance was removed. In a case where a person had cultivated land belonging to another tribe than his own, without authority, the Holy Prophet decided that the man had no right to the produce, but could ask for payment of his expenses of cultivation. He laid down the principle in a pre-emption case, that the 'right of pre-emption exists only so long as partition has not been effected, so that rights remain joint; when every field has been demarcated, and each owner has his separate way, no right of pre-emption remains'.

These could be found examples in Shah Waliullah's book, to which reference had been made earlier and there is no doubt that many other precedents are recorded in the main books of *Hadith.* What has been said so far is sufficient to show that by the time that it became necessary for the Holy Prophet (peace be upon him) to send Qadis (judges) to the new provinces which had acknowledged Islam and the rule of the Prophet, there was already established, in the Holy Quran and the record of decided cases, a sufficient volume of maxims, rules, principles and precedents to constitute the Islamic Jurisprudence. The procedure of trial of cases through presentation by the parties, supported by evidence in the face of the Court, was well established. A code classifying offences and the *Hadd* punishments therefore, as well as the grounds of mitigation, had already been settled. It is recorded that the Holy Prophet interviewed a person who was to go as Qadi to the new Province of the Yemen; part of the dialogue was as follows:

Q. On what will you base your legal decisions?

A. The Quran.

Q. But if that contains nothing for the purpose?

A. Then upon your tradition and practice.

Q. But if that also fails you?

A. Then I will follow my own opinion.

The Holy Prophet approved these answers. In common with many persons who have read that little dialogue, it seems that the Holy Prophet was only testing the man's faith and allegiance to the Holy Quran, and to himself. Its true significance was brought home to me, in the course of the study that has gone into the present paper. The Holy Prophet (peace be upon him) was making sure that the man realised that he was being sent to operate and propagate the new jurisprudence of Islam, according to right principles and that he knew where those principles were to be found. He was not to dispense justice in the manner of the pre-Islamic period, the *Jahiliyat,* or in the indigenous way of the people who had been recently brought within the authority of Islam.

The fact was recognised also that the code, being new, was not complete so as to provide, in detail, for every kind of case, and so the appointee was permitted to use in such cases, his own judgement. The compilation of the *Ahadith* went on for almost a hundred years, and we may be sure that copies were sent to all the administrators and judges, far and near. Work on the formulation of the *Sham,* the comprehensive code for the guidance of Muslims, continued for the next three hundred years, when it was completed separately, with variations, by the four great *Imams.* It was settled that the laws of the Muslims were to be derived firstly from the Quran, secondly from the *Sunna* of the Holy Prophet, thirdly by assemblies of the learned, known as *Ijma,* and lastly, by *Ijtihad,* meaning ratiocination by individuals. Three of these sources were in operation from the outset, with the approval of the Holy Prophet himself, as we have seen. The fourth, the making of laws by assemblies failed of its purpose, since the assemblies were to be confined to scholars of individual schools, and the results produced lacked universality. But one thing is clear, namely, that from the very inception of Islam, the dispensation of justice has proceeded on regulated lines, on principles formulated in writing, and with the aid of precedents, in the form of judicial decisions that go back to the Holy Prophet himself. The people of Islam can take just pride in the thought that their judicial system was placed from the beginning on lines that in substance are no different from those of the best systems of today. Compared with the other prevalent systems, it was distinguished by a higher degree of humanity towards criminals, even towards prisoners taken in religious wars, and a deeper understanding of the basic needs of human beings living in settled communities. In the common belief, that remains the condition even today.

The progressive elements among the recognised sources of law in Islam are those of *Ijtihad,* the advancement of law through ratiocinative processes, and *Ijma,* which means codification and modernisation of laws through deliberative assemblies. Our poet-philosopher, Iqbal, relates *Ijtihad* to the original thinking of exceptionally gifted persons, a very acceptable view, but it is possible to see that at the level of our superior Courts, the process of *Ijtihad* is applied in every case where under minute examination, the Judges are expected to apply the law to new and unanticipated situations, and even in some cases, to fill gaps in the law. As for *Ijma,* under modern conditions, and in the enlarging fields of human affairs that are outside the strict teaching of the four main schools, it is possible to regard the legislative assemblies of today as being competent to discharge that function in this aspect of modernisation.

The task of codification has been frequently attempted by Muslim rulers of the past. Such an attempt was made by the Mughal Emperor, Aurangzeb Alamgir, and the result was the *Fatawa-e-Alamgiri,* which retains importance even today despite its character of a compilation of judicial dicta, often related to particular facts, whose application to new cases gives rise to difficulty. The collection was made about 275 years ago. Another attempt at codification of Islamic laws was made by the Sultan of Turkey, entitled *'Mejelle-el-Ahkam-i-Adliya'*. It is much more recent, having been completed and promulgated as the law of the vast territories of the Turkish Empire about a hundred years ago. It was replaced by a new Code in 1926.

An English translation of this valuable source book of Islamic law has been published in Pakistan, by the All Pakistan Legal Decisions of Lahore, and is readily available. When published originally, it was described as 'A Complete Code of Islamic Civil Law', though it excludes the important subject of marriage *(munakiahat)* and is confined to 'dealings between people and their relations with and conduct towards each other' that are included within the comprehensive description of *muamlat.* The book is prefaced by a collection of a hundred maxims, followed by 1851 Articles, adapted for application by the *Nizam* Courts, as distinguished from the *Shariah* Courts. Although the propositions of law are not set out or worded in the manner of statutes in the English mode, and the translation is cumbrous through being too literal, yet the book has the merit of being arranged in chapters, subject-wise, from contracts of sale and lease, surety and pledge, to torts, pre-emption, judicial guardianship, partition and partnership, limitation, etc. and so is practically usable for reference. It contains elaborate provisions for implementation of the Holy Prophet's injunction 'proof is for the plaintiff; oath for the defendant' besides rules of evidence. The Holy Prophet's direction to examine the credibility of witnesses is carried out in a set of rules on the subject.

This compilation was the work of a Commission of Jurists appointed by the Sultan for 'the production from the practical part of the *Shar' (Fiqh)* of a beneficial work, so that it shall be sufficient for application to the transactions of people, which happen everyday' in the words of the compilers, who purported to follow 'those opinions of *Hanafi* doctors which are most in harmony with the exigencies of modern life and business' (from the Foreword by Mr. Justice S. A. Rahman of the Supreme Court of Pakistan). The duty of adherence to *Shar'* law in the *Hanafi* school was borne in mind by the compilers, and there is thus assurance of such conformity for those who seek guidance in the paths of Islamic jurisprudence from this book. For that purpose, it can safely be recommended for study by the great number of persons in Muslim countries, who have been encouraged by recent events to hope for the establishment of a genuine *Nizam-e-Mustafa* in Muslim countries.

And it has given me very great pleasure to demonstrate to you that the edifice of justice in Islam was founded and built up to a substantial degree by no other than the Apostle of Allah, Muhammad *Mustafa* (peace be upon him). There can be no greater proof of its excellence and its right to be accepted with total confidence.

## Various Angles

1. The Concept of Justice in Islam is different from the concept of the remedial justice of the Greeks, the natural justice of the Romans or the formal justice of the Anglo-Saxons. Justice in Islam seeks to attain a higher standard of, what I might call, 'absolute justice' or absolute fairness as suggested by the *'Meezan'* for Balance. The Holy Quran proclaims :

   "We sent aforetimes Our Apostles with clear signs and sent down the Book and the Balance, that men may stand forth injustice (25—57)."

2. This verse clearly postulates two essential principles. Firstly, that justice is to be done not only in accordance with law but also in such a way that it results in complete fairness. Secondly, that the doing of justice is not the concern of the judge alone but the collective responsibility of the community as well. Every member of the community is

involved in this process. If an injustice is being committed to a person's knowledge he cannot stand apart as a silent spectator even if he is not personally affected. Allah commands :

> "Oh ye who believe! Stand out firmly for justice, as witnesses to Allah, even as against yourselves, or your parents, or your kin, and whether it be against rich or poor; for Allah can best protect both. Follow not the lusts of your hearts; lest ye swerve, and if ye distort justice or decline to do justice, verily Allah is well acquainted with all that ye do." (4—135).

3. This too indicates the degree of fairness demanded in the Islamic system. The *'Meezan'* not only symbolizes this degree of fairness but also refers to the God given faculty by which a person can judge between right and wrong even as against oneself or one's parents or kin. *'Adl'* according to Islamic concepts thus demands a perfect standard of comparison or estimation which cannot be swayed by any other consideration.

4. The Arabic word *Al-Adl* though used in various senses in the Holy Quran nevertheless always imports a moral duty to act with fairness. Justice is, therefore, also a religious duty which has to be performed "as witnesses to God" and the importance that is attached to it is so great that it has been placed next to *Taqwa,* i.e., piety itself. Allah ordains:

   > "Oh ye who believe stand out firmly for Allah as witnesses to fair dealing, and let not the hatred of others to you make you swerve to wrong and depart from justice. Be just; that is next to Piety." (5—9).

5. It follows from the above that the exercise of *Al-Qada* is a vital principle of religion and the administration of justice is a devotional act—a *Fard-Al-Kifayah*-a collective obligation upon every Muslim. Another consequence which flows from this is that Law and Morality become merged. Whatever is immortal is also illegal, because, no law can sanction that which is prohibited by the Holy Quran or is opposed to the practices and precedents of the Holy Prophet (peace be upon him).

6. Justice being also one of the attributes of Allah has to be done in His name and bearing in mind that He is All-Seeing and All-Knowing from Whom nothing is or can be hidden. The administration of justice is, therefore, not based only upon the overt acts but has to search out the innermost motives of man and then determine what will be just in a given case. The principle that the Devil himself knoweth not the mind of man and as such his (latter's) intention is to be deduced from his words and deeds is not acceptable under the Islamic system. Motive is always relevant and has to be ascertained as far as humanly possible.
7. Islamic justice is not also blind justice. The Holy Quran itself commands:

   "Allah commands justice, the doing of good and liberality to kith and kin" (16-90). Justice in its comprehensive sense, as Abdullah Yusuf Ali puts it in the notes of his translation of the Holy Quran under the above verse, "may include all the virtues of cold philosophy" but Islam asks "for something warmer and more human". This 'something warmer' is called 'Ehsan or goodness proper. *'Adl'* simpliciter, according to the Islamic concept is the doing of good for good but *'Ehsan'* is the doing of good even where *'Adl'* does not strictly demand it and there is no question of receiving any reciprocal benefit. Justice, according to the command of Allah has, therefore, also to be tampered with mercy and it is on this principle that an otherwise legal claim may be withheld or a legal obligation not imposed upon considerations of hardships or the best interests of the community as a whole.
8. The principle that Allah is the Fountain-Head of Justice being the Supreme Law-Giver and that Sovereignty vests in Him firmly establishes the Principle of Equality before the Law and the equal application of the law. There is no room under this system for bringing in any concept of 'equal but different'. Islam permits no distinction on the basis of race, caste, colour, creed or birth. All Muslims are equal and no-one how high so ever is above the law.

15. In the first Islamic State formed in Medina by the Holy Prophet (peace be upon him) himself under the Charter of Medina, the Holy Prophet (peace be upon him) was the paramount judicial authority for all Muslims and non-Muslims—and was the final court of appeal. The administration of justice was, however, a matter of common concern, in so far, as all were collectively responsible to see that no one dared to harm or encroach upon the rights of others. Everyone, according to the teachings of the Holy Quran, had to act with absolute fairness, free from any kind of bias or partiality, fear or favour even though it be against one's own interest or the interest of one's parents, kinsmen or tribesmen. The rule of decision so far as Muslims were concerned was the *Shariah* Law.

16. So far as non-Muslims were concerned they were to be governed by their own laws, customs and traditions except that the custom of revenge and counter revenge was totally banned and no interference on the basis of kinship or tribal affinity was permitted, particularly, in the affairs of administration of justice. They had complete freedom of religion and also administered their common law through their own ecclesiastical courts.

17. In disputes between Muslims the Holy Prophet (peace be upon him) administered justice according to the Holy Book but his decisions also became precedents for the future because his interpretation of the Quranic *Ayats* had of necessity to be most accurate for whenever he was in doubt he received revelations giving him the solution of his doubts. Nevertheless he never hesitated to point out that he decided the disputes brought before him upon the evidence adduced and that he was liable to err like any other human being. Such error, however, on his part was unthinkable and it is for this reason that his decisions treated as *"Ahadith"* which along with the Holy Quran form the main sources of the *Shariah* Law.

18. During this period the judicial power was not delegated in Medina to anybody although the savants of Medina consisting of the senior most companions *(Sahabis)* were

sometimes consulted. However, when the territories of the State expanded and Provinces were set up this power was also delegated to the Governors of the Provinces. When Muaz-bin-Jabal was appointed Governor of Yemen he was asked by the Holy Prophet (peace be upon him) as to how he would decide cases. He is reported to have replied that he would judge by the Quran but if no solution can be formed therein he would seek guidance from the precedents of the Holy Prophet (peace be upon him) but if even that did not provide a solution he would set according to his own *'Qiyas'* or independent judgement. Upon this it is reported by both Abu Daud and Tirmidhi that the Holy Prophet (peace be upon him) praised God and said that he agreed with this procedure. *'Qiyas'* did not, however, mean whim or caprice but had to be based on analogical deductions from Quran and *Hadith.* This was really the basis of what later came to be known as *'Ijtihad'* which was resorted to for meeting new situations not covered by Quran and *Sunnah.*

19. The *"Al-Mazalim"* jurisdiction was introduced by the Holy Prophet (peace be upon him) himself. This was a wide jurisdiction for enforcing both *Huquq-ul-lah* and *Huquq-ul-ibad* i.e., the rights of God and of Man. Under this jurisdiction persons doing each other wrong *(Mutazalimun)* could be compelled to do mutual justice and even litigation could be prevented by deterring the refutation of just claims.

20. During this period the procedure was simple but even in this period the rule had been established that the parties must be present personally during the proceedings, that the burden of proof lay on the party asserting a claim and that the party refuting the claim had to deny it on oath. Only upon such denial the party asserting a claim was called upon to adduce evidence in proof of his claim. If there was no denial on oath this was treated as an admission and a decree was passed on this basis. Possession was treated as *prima facie* proof of title to property. Thus where evidence of both sides claiming a property was equal the decision went in favour of the party in possession.

21. The rules of evidence were also simple but evidence could be either oral or documentary or even circumstantial. The Holy Quran advises that trans actions should be recorded in writing by a scribe in the presence of two witnesses. On the analogy of this normally two male witnesses were considered necessary for proof of any fact unless the Quran required a larger number of witnesses as in the case of *Zina* where at least four witnesses were required. Where there were only female witnesses the number had to be doubled for two females were equal to one male witness. Adulterers or persons who had once given false evidence or had the reputation of being dishonest were incompetent to give evidence. Similarly, the evidence of a close relation or slave was not admissible in favour of the relation or the master as the case may be.

22. The Holy Prophet (peace be upon him) also laid down two important constitutional principles. The first was that everyone was equal before the law and the second was that no-one enjoyed any immunity. Even the Head of the State could be sued both as a private individual also in respect of his public acts. He established this by his own acts and precepts. Thus he once declared that even if his daughter (Fatima) committed theft he would cut off her hand. Again during the course of his last sermon *(Khutba)* at the *Hajjat-ul-Wida* he publicly offered to the community that if he owed anything to anyone or had done any harm to anyone's life, reputation or property he was present there to answer for it. The audience was amazed but one person came forward to demand a few *'dirhams'* which were immediately paid.

23. After the Holy Prophet the *Khulafa-e-Rashidin* followed the same pattern of administration of justice but to meet new situations *'Ijtihad'* had often to be resorted to even though disputes were few and the people by and large acted with utmost fairness. Under the first Khalifah, Hadrat Umar was appointed the Qadi of Medina but it is reported that not a single case was brought before him for adjudication. Hadrat Umar, however, on assumption of

office as Khalifah brought in certain reforms. The reforms were as follows:

(i) Separation of judicial office from other offices of the State;

(ii) Setting up of a department of police called the *'Ahdas'* under a *'Sahib-ul-Ahdas;'*

(iii) Setting up of jails and the introduction of the punishments of imprisonment and transportation;

(iv) Introduction of the *'Ifta'* jurisdiction under which the judiciary could also consult *'Muftis'* on complicated questions of *'Fiqh';* and

(v) Constitution of a *'Majlis-e-Shura'* which apart from advising the Khalifah on matters of State also served as a forum for evolving a consensus on questions of law. This became the *'Ijma'* of the *Ummat* and the *'Shura'* a legislative body to that limited extent.

24. As regards the procedures to be followed they can best be gathered from two *'Firmans'* issued by Hadrat Umar himself. One to Qadi Shuraiah the Qadi appointed at Basra and another to Qadi Abu Musa Al-Ashari appointed at Kufa. The first reads as follows:

> "If a case is presented which is treated in the Quran then decide accordingly and do not go against the Quranic injunctions and if such a case is presented which is not treated in the Quran, then follow it in the *Hadith* and decide accordingly, but if a case is presented about which there is no provision in the Quran and *Hadith,* then look for its solution in the *'Ijma-ul-Umma,* and follow that decision. However, if such a case is presented about which there is no precedent in the Quran and *Hadith,* and not even decided by anyone before you then you may decide according to your own judgement after due care and caution. I approve of such a course."

### *The Next is as follows*

'The Court must observe equality between the parties so that the weaker party may expect justice and the stronger may not expect concession. The burden of proof is on the plaintiff and the defendant may be put on oath, but let this not defeat the ends of justice and law. If you have decided a case, then after due care and thinking you may revise your decision. If you are doubtful in a point which is mentioned in the Quran and *Hadith* then think over it again and again and then apply *'Qiyas'* (a process of deduction). When a party wants to tender evidence then fix a time limit and if he proves his case then decide accordingly. All Muslims are fit to be witnesses except those who have received the prescribed punishment (flogging) for *'Hadd'* (fornication, adultery) and those who have tendered false evidence."

25. To preserve the independence of the Judges, Hadrat Umar prohibited them from doing any trade or business and gave them an allowance which was considered to be sufficient to meet their needs. Hadrat Ali the fourth Khalifah turned this into a salary which was expected to enable them to live in a manner befitting their position and keep them away from temptation.
26. During this period the Khalifah under his supervisory jurisdiction *(Al-Mazalim)* was the final court of appeal and any citizen could complain to him against any authority, executive or judicial. At first these complaints were made on the occasion of the Hajj which was attended by all officials but later they could be made at any time.
27. So far as the law of evidence is concerned Hadrat Umar and Hadrat Ali both clarified that cases were to be decided not merely on the basis of the number of witnesses, but on the basis of truth as the essential principle of Quranic teaching that justice could only be done on the basis of unimpeachable evidence. It is the quality of the evidence and not its quantity that matters. Hadrat Umar also set a new precedent by admitting evidence of an expert in a defamation suit filed by one Zibriqan-bin-Badr against a poet Hutaya. Since the defamatory verse was not clear another poet Hassan bin Sabit was examined as an expert and the case decided according to his opinion.
28. During this period there were no separate criminal courts. The same Courts had jurisdiction over both civil and criminal

matters but in criminal matters proceedings were initiated by the *Sahib-ul-Ahdas,* the Officer-in-charge of the Department of Police *(Ahdas).* The procedure followed was also the same. The rules of evidence were also same for both civil and criminal matters but the principle that the benefit of doubt should go to the accused was strictly adhered to from the earliest stages. The presence of *mens rea* or criminal intent was a necessary condition for the infliction of punishment This is deductible from a *Hadith* which is to the effect that "my community is excused for what it commits under duress, in error or as a result of forget fullness". The principle of self-defence was also duly recognized on the basis of verses 42 and 43 *of Surah 'Al-Shura'*

"42. There is no blame on those who defend themselves after they have been wronged;" and

"43. The blame is only on those who wrong men and transgress in the Earth without justification."

29. In the process of administration of criminal justice the judge was in fact bound to take into account all such circumstances as were likely to affect his criminality, such as his capacity to do the act (infancy or insanity), the nature of the offence, the circumstances in which committed (duress, mistake, defence or even necessity) the previous history of the offender, the character of the offender, his personal details and other relevant circumstances (Al-Mawardi—*Ahkam-at-Sultaniyah,* pp. 344-350). Indeed the rule followed was that "it is better to discharge an accused by mistake rather than to punish by mistake" (A. A. Qadri-Islamic Jurisprudence, p. 290).

30. With the assassination of Hadrat Ali and Imam Hassan, the republican period of Islam came to an end and a hereditary dynasty was set up by Muawiyyah yet the system of administration of justice set up by the *Khulafa-e-Rashidin* survived in more or less the same form even under the Umayyads with minor organizational changes necessitated by the exigencies of a far-flung empire extending from Persia to Egypt. There was a Chief Qadi at Damascus and

Qadis for each of the provinces and under them were subordinate Qadis with limited jurisdictions. Those with such limited jurisdiction were restricted either to the duties or to the territories specified in their *Firmans* of appointment but the others had jurisdiction overall things authorized by law.

31. An important change was, however, made in the reign of Khalifah Al- Mamoon. He set up a *Nazir-ul-Muzalim* or Board for the Inspection of Grievances consisting of the Khalifah, the Chief Qadi, the Chief Wazir, one or two Secretaries of State and Muftis or Jurisconsults. This Board had control over the judiciary and could correct all miscarriages of justice. It was thus the final court of Appeal but the Khalifah still remained the court of ultimate appeal if he had not participated in the proceedings of the Board in that particular matter.

32. In this period the judiciary also came to be burdened with certain other executive duties such as the appointment of guardians of infants, administration of *waqf* properties, looking after testamentary dispositions, supervision of law officers like public notaries and some secretaries. The execution of punishments prescribed by law *(hadd)* was also made their responsibility.

33. The Umayyads did not also have separate criminal courts but the Qadis were vested with the *Mazalim* jurisdiction which extended to correcting all wrongs. It is through this jurisdiction that the judges also came to exercise jurisdiction to review executive acts in somewhat the same manner as is now done under the writ jurisdiction. Since the Khalifah invariably presided over the Board of *Mazalim* it could also check cases of injustice committed by members of the royal family and thereby also acquired some influence over the sovereign himself.

34. This was, however, still the formative period of the Islamic system of administration of justice in a vast empire spread over the best part of then known civilized world but the system flowered into perfection in the Abbaside period (749—1258 A.D.). It is during this period that the science

of Islamic jurisprudence attained its golden age. It is in this age that traditions *(Hadith)* were methodically collected and verified, commentaries on the Quran were written, the science of the sources of law developed and the four great schools of *Sunni* Law, *Hanafi, Shafii, Maliki* and *Hanabali* came to be established. The administration of justice also came to be conducted upon a definite system.

A department of Justice known as the *"Dar-ul-Adl,* was set-up with *"Qadi-ul-Qazzat"* as its head. Though appointed by the Khalifah he was independent of executive control. The entire judiciary was under his supervision and control. Each city had its own Qadi. Some big cities had also Naib-Qadis or Deputy Qadis. The *ifta* system for consulting specialists in the *Shariah* through *Muftis* or jurisconsults was further developed. Litigants could also obtain their advice free of charge but later *Muftis* were also permitted to charge a fee and still later to appear before Qadis as *Vakils* under the Islamic Law of agency or mandate by submitting a *Tawakkil Nama* or power-of-attorney. The origin of this practice lay in the fact that Muslim States treated it as their responsibility to provide citizens with legal aid so that no-one should suffer due to ignorance of law. As against this the common law principle is that ignorance of law is no excuse.

35. The Board for the Inspection of Grievances now called the *Dewan- ul-Mazalim* was continued but a modification was introduced by providing that in the absence of the Khalifah it would be presided over by a *Rais* or *Sadar* whose position was higher than that of the *Qadi-ul-Qazzat.* The latter as a Member of the *Dewan* came under the *Rais* and thus the judiciary also came under the *Rais.* Apart from the *Rais* and the Chief Qadi the Principal Secretaries of State *(Wazirs),* some nominated *Muftis* and the *Hajib* or Chief Door-Keeper were also made Members of this *Dewan.* The last named came in as the person responsible for the protection of the Khalifah against the free access of petitioners. Nevertheless the Khalifah under the Persian influence retained the right to receive complaints and hear

appeals as an ultimate court for setting right cases of grave miscarriage of justice.

36. The powers of the *Rais* of the *Dewan-ul-Mazalim* were very wide. He was authorized to apply the Principles of Equity *(Isthasan)* to secure the ends of justice. He supervised and corrected not only miscarriages of justice by Qadis but also corrected cases of injustice and tyranny committed against the people by Governors of Provinces and other executive officers, e.g., injustices in the levy of taxes, claims of illegal reduction or withholding of pay of government servants. Claims for the restoration of property taken by force, the government of *Auqaf* and the suppre-ssion of open civil cases which had not been suppressed due to the weakness of *Muhtasibs* also came within the jurisdiction of this *Dewan*. This is wider than the writ jurisdiction as we now know it and the *Dewan-ul-Mazalim* may well be compared with the Star Chamber of the English Court or the Council of State or the Privy Council.

37. The *Muhtasib* or Public Censor was an officer responsible for the enforcement of moral duties and obligations. His duties were concerned with matters relating not only to *Huquq-ul-lah* but also the *Huquq-ul-ibad* and to both. He could act *suo moto* and his jurisdiction was very wide. He enforced not only the observance of religious duties but also all obligations of the public, individual or collective; such as non-payment of debts without any excuse, rights of way, easements, nuisances and even irrigation rights. He exercised disciplinary control over attorneys and *vakils* and saw to it that they were not encouraged tamper to with the administration of justice in any way.

38. It is in this period that separate criminal courts Were also set up under magistrates—at first called *Sahib-ul-Mazalim* but later *Qadi-us-Shurtah.* The *Shurtah* was a department set up for the investigation of crimes and other breaches of law as also their disposition. Such magistrates supplemented the authority of the Qadis and were responsible for securing compliance with the orders and decrees of Qadis more or less like executing courts.

39. The system of court officials developed in this period was that each court had a *'Katib'* who kept the record of the cases and was thus the Registrar and Court Clerk rolled into one. Under him were *"Awans"* or auxiliaries who maintained order within the court and a Door-Keeper called *"Abwab"* who was the Security Officer responsible for the protection of the Qadi. There was also an official translator or interpreter called the *"Muslim"*. In addition there was a *"Khazin-Diwanul-Hakam"*, who maintained the archives of the court, and can be compared with the modern Record-keeper, and an *"Ammat-ul-Hakam"* who looked after the properties of orphans. He can be said to be the official Trustee of the present times. An another important official whose equivalent does not exist now was *'Muzakki'* who investigated the character of the witnesses and kept a record of the persons who were not competent to give evidence such as those who had been convicted with the *'Hadd'* punishment or were persons who had the reputation of having bad moral character.

40. In the *Nazir-ul-Muzalim* or the *Dewan-ul-Mazalim* there used to be attached in addition to the above officials a panel of judges to carry out research and find solutions of difficult questions of law like the law clerks attached to judges of the Supreme Court in USA or research officers in our own Supreme Court. The judges of this ultimate Court had also secretaries to keep the minutes of their proceedings.

41. This system was perfected by 1176 A.D. when Nuruddin Mahmud, a President of the *Nazir-ul-Mazalim* set up a *'Dar-ul-Adl'* a High Court of Judicature and settled the hierarchy of Courts with the High Court and *Nazir-ul-Mazalim* at the apex as courts of final appeal from the Courts of *Qadi-ul-Qazzats* in the Provinces. The latter heard appeals from other Qadis under their jurisdiction.

42. Such was the final pattern of Courts under the Islamic system of administration of justice which remained more or less unchanged under the Ottomans and also the Mughals in India apart from changes in the nomenclature

of officials and in the organizational pattern. The Umayyads in Spain also followed this pattern with the addition of a system of *ad hoc* Courts of *Mazalim* to try very high officials. This was the origin of the system of State-Trials.

43. The Ottomans improved the *'Ifta'* jurisdiction and made it a department of State under the *Sheikh-ul-Islam* with *Mufti-e-Azams* in the Provinces. These alone had the power of advising the Khalifah and the Qadis and of issuing *'fatwahs'*. This had become necessary with the change in the concept of sovereignty. The Turkish Sultans claimed the power of supplementing the *Shariah* by royal '*Firmans'* and, therefore, there had to be an institution for advising the Sultan on the legality of the *Firman,* because, even the Sultan could not make a *Firman* which was repugnant to the Quran and *Sunnah.* Under the Ottoman system the *Sheikh-ul-Islam* became a very important person as he had the power to veto legislation and he often exercised this power very effectively.

44. The Muslim rulers of India up to Sher Shah Suri followed the same pattern and we have records of many instances in which the Qadis or the *Muftis* came into clash with the executive. It is on this principle that Qadi Mughisuddin of Jaunpur incurred the wrath of Sultan Allauddin who did not like ecclesiastical interference in matters of law. He (the Qadi) had told the Sultan that he had no right over the *Bait-ul-Mal.* He could only take what was given as pay to a chief officer and in addition such sum as was needed for meeting legitimate State expenses.

45. The procedure followed in these Courts were as follows. In civil matters all litigants, no matter how high or how low were treated in an impartial and strictly equal manner. The case was started by a *Dawa* (plaint). If this made out a *prima facie* case then both sides were summoned on a particular day and the judge listened to the pleadings of the parties. The plaintiff *(Muddai)* addressed the Court first. Then if the defendant *(Muddah Alaih)* denied the claim on oath the plaintiff was called upon to prove his claim. He was considered to be a person who has no right

without proof *(Hujjah)*. The trial was conducted in open court and in the presence of the parties. Where defendant was not available a representative had to be appointed for watching his interest according to the *Hanafi* School. The *Shafii* School, however, permits the passing of an *ex-parte* order without the representative. Witnesses are then examined, the evidence is taken down verbatim by the *Katib*. Cross-examination is made both by the opposite party or his *Vakil* and even by the Court. After conclusion of trial a written judgement *(Ilam)* is delivered giving its reasons and a formal decree *(Hukum)* is drawn up so that the same cause is not again litigated upon. Thus the rule of *Res judicata* was also observed. Copy was supplied to the successful party and also to the losing party, if requested. After judgement the losing party could commence a claim in rebuttal (enter a *caveat)*. If this failed or no such claim was filed then the decree was put into execution.

46. The Court was not permitted to reconsider its judgement except by way of a review on the ground that it was not in conformity with the principles of the *Shariah*. The Court could, however, correct accidental or clerical errors. Judgements could also be revised in appeal by superior Courts right up to the Khalifah upon the principle that complete justice should be done.

47. The law also made it compulsory that for the protection of minors, insane persons or those suffering from any other legal incompetence a legal representative or *guardian-ad-litem* should be appointed if the person did not have a competent natural guardian. Joinder of parties was also permissible for doing complete justice. The Courts had also the jurisdiction to pass interim orders if considered necessary for protecting the interests of the parties *ad-interim*.

48. Arbitration was encouraged. Indeed every judge was required to attempt to bring about an amicable settlement without taking sides. The arbitrator had to possess the same qualifications as a Qadi and was bound by the same

code of conduct *(Adab-al-Qadi)* drawn up for judges. An award when made had to be referred to a Qadi. He confirmed it if he agreed with it and put it into execution in the same way as a decree. This is what we now call making the award a rule of the Court.

49. The *Adab-al-Qadi* was an elaborate document laying down in detail the rules of conduct the judges were required to observe so as to abstain from doing anything which might destroy "the majesty of the Court" as the *Mejelle* puts it. He could not be a judge in his own cause or in the cause of his near relatives. He could not accept presents or invitations from litigants or meet only one of the parties or even speak to one of the parties either by sign or language unknown to the others. He had to avoid doing anything which might even cause suspicion of bias or partisanship. *(Mejelle*-318 and *Minhaj-et-Talibin* — 504).

50. On the criminal side the complaint was required to give a precise account of the offence *(Istighasa)* mentioning whether it was premeditated or voluntary or whether there was any accomplice or not. If the complaint did not make out a *prima facie* case it was dismissed in *limine.* If such a case was made out then the accused was summoned and the trial was continued after administration of oath to accused. The rest of the procedure was the same as in a civil case. The accused was thus a competent witness.

51. Crimes were divided according to punishments into three categories, namely, (1) those involving *'hadd'* punishment, (2) those involving *'Qisas',* and (3) those involving *'Tazir'.* The Penal Law of Islam had been worked out most comprehensively. It had a dual function. It provided both for the punishment *(Uqubat)* of the wrong-doer as also for remedying the wrong caused by such violation *(Masiyah).* It thus combined with it the law of torts. It is applied and enforced on all criminals irrespective of their being Muslims or non-Muslims. Muslims committing offences outside the limits of an Islamic State are indictable on their return to the Muslim territory on the basis of the extraterritoriality of the *Shariah* Law.

*(Minhaj-e-Talibin* —Books : 47 to 56).

52. We don't have not the time at our disposal to go into the details of the *Usul-e-Fiqah* (jurisprudence) regarding the administration of criminal law but since this branch of Islamic Law has been made the target of attack by Western critics, it is necessary to mention here that most of this criticism is based on ignorance of the concepts of Islamic jurisprudence and what is worse ignorance of their own concepts which prevailed even up to the 18th Century. These critics seem to forget that in their own countries thieves were hanged, robbers were hung from a tree on a highway crossing, perjurers were pilloried, witches were burnt alive and adulterers were branded. Even civil trials were conducted on the basis of oracular predictions, omens, ordeals, compurgation or battle while the Muslims had long before perfected an adversary system of trial on the basis of evidence by fully observing the principles of natural justice in a humane and civilized manner with such perfection that law, morality, equity and mercy all came into play at one and the same time.

53. Thus even in a case involving the imposition of *'hadd'* which are punishments provided by the Quran and *Sunnah,* the principle based on a *Hadith* was that every effort should be made to avoid the imposition of such punishment. The benefit of every doubt went to the accused. So much so that even if a person had confessed his guilt and sentence had been passed yet he retracted from his confession before the execution of the sentence the *'hadd'* punishment could not be imposed upon him. It could only be imposed upon a mentally capable, careful, strong and legally fitted offender. Thus it cannot be imposed on a pregnant woman, a minor or an instance person or when the act is committed under a mistake of law or fact. Hadrat Umar actually suspended the *'hadd'* punishment for *Sarqa* (theft) during a period of scarcity. Emperor Aurangzeb by a Firman of 1672 directed :

"If a man has committed theft only once either less than or only up to the amount of *Hisab* then chastise *(Tazir)* him. But if he repeats the offence then after

defendant in a civil case and an accused in a criminal case should also be required to take the oath.

59. The office of *Muzakki* should be re-introduced for keeping a record of the witnesses called before Courts and to make local enquiries as to their character and reputation. This will enable judges to make proper appreciation of their evidence.

60. The accused should be made a competent witness and should be allowed to be cross-examined as is the practice even in the United Kingdom. The law of evidence will also be required to be brought in line with the Islamic rules of evidence. With these changes our existing court system will be able to satisfactorily administer *Shariat* Law if the judges make themselves familiar with the *Fiqh* and the *Usul-ul-Fiqh* or Islamic Jurisprudence.

# 3

# Basic Freedom

## Freedom of being Safe

Out of the fundamental rights conferred by Islam on its citizens, we shall take up, to begin with, those rights which are equally enjoyed by all the citizens as human beings without distinction of creed. Later on we shall take stock of the exclusive rights of Muslims and non-Muslims.

***Security of Life :*** Islam regards human life extremely sacred, and maintaining murder of one man as the murder of entire humanity, has stressed the security of human life. A parallel is not to be found any where in the world in the religious, moral or legal literature. God says:

> If any one slew a person... unless it be for murder or for spreading mischief in the land ...it would be as if he slew the whole people. And if any one saved a life, it would be as if he saved the life of the whole people.
>
> (Al Quran V 32.)

At another place it has been said:

> Nor take life...which God has made sacred...except for just cause. (Al Quran XVIL33)

Islam has limited taking of life for just cause to the following situations:

(a) Qisas (or life for life) for a deliberate murder.

(b) In Jihad against those resisting the advancement of the True Faith.

(c) As a punishment to those trying to overthrow the Islamic order.

(d) As a punishment to a married man or woman for adultery or fornication.

(e) As a punishment for apostasy.

(f) As a punishment for highway robbery.

Barring these six exemptions the violation of the sanctity of human life can never be allowed.

Such instructions have been repeated in the Quran so often—VI: 152, 11:178-179 and XXV: 68. Taking of human life is such a serious and heinous crime in the sight of God that its perpetrator even after being executed under the Islamic Law is to be consigned to Hell-fire after death, and is the target of Divine wrath and eternal damnation (except those who repent sincerely before execution are forgiven. Tr.):

> If a man kills a believer intentionally, his recompense is Hell, to abide (there in) (for ever): and the wrath and curse of God are upon him, and a dreadful penalty is prepared for him. (Quran IV: 93)

The Quran also forbids talking the life of one's own offspring for fear of hunger and poverty:

> Kill not your children on a plea of want;
>
> We provide sustenance for you and for them;
>
> (Al Quran VI: 151)

And the same instruction has been repeated in Surah XVII: 31 and VI: 140 also. The Arabs during the days of Jahiliyah so often buried their daughters alive—(this heinous practice was partly due to poverty and partly due to false notions of honour—the daughters were not a source of strength but were taken away by the enemies in case of attack by a rival tribe for mere plunder if not blood-fend. Tr.) Pointing to the severe punishment in the life Hereafter, God says in an extremely wrathful tone (without so much as addressing the culprit directly. Tr.):

When the female (infant), buried alive is questioned for what crime she was killed;

(Al Quran LXXXI 7-8)

God has not only forbidden taking the life of others but not to take one's own life either. And in the way the path of suicide has been barred:

And do not kill or destroy yourselves:

(Al Quran IV 29)

And after these very definite Quranic injunctions relating to the sanctity of human life, now we shall take up some sayings of the Prophet on this theme and some incidents of his period.

In his harangue on the occasion of the last Hajj, the Prophet said:

O ye people; your blood, goods and honour dignity have been declared totally sacred, one's for the other. Their sanctity is eternal as the sanctity of this day and of this month of Zul Hajjah in this town (of Mecca). Beware! Lest you should take to beheading each other after I am gone, and be 'associated with the group of unbelievers.

(Bukhari, Abu Daud, Nasai and Musnad Abroad.)

Later, presenting the first example of putting this instructions into practice he says:

All the blood-fends are being ended herewith. The first vendetta which I end here and now is connected with my own family... the blood of the suckling baby, the son of Rabia bin-al-Harith, who had been murdered by Bani Huzail. I now forgive them for it.

(Bukhari, Abu Daud, Nasai, Musnad-e-Ahmad)

Once the Prophet said:

In comparison to the murder of a believer, the degradation of the whole world has no value in the sight of God. (Muslim)

And it is not the blood of a "Muslim" alone that is sacred but it is true for every servant of God. If an innocent zimmi is killed by a Muslim, the latter's entry to heaven is barred:

> Whoever murdered a zimmi. God closed the doors of heaven upon him. (Nasai)

> One who killed a zimmi, would be denied even the fragrance of heaven. (Bukhari.)

Once it happened that some children of the unbelievers were accidentally killed in a skirmish against the registers of the faith. The Prophet was very much grieved. The companions said, "They were only children of the polytheists." The Prophet said in reply:

> The children though polytheists are better than you. Beware! Never kill the children. Every living thing has been created on the nature conferred on it by God. (Musnad-e-Ahmad)

Ibn-e-Abbas reports that during the period of the Prophet, a dead body was found, but the murderer could not be traced. The Prophet, very much irritated said in his harangue:

> O ye people! How is this that a person is murdered while I am here amongst you, and his murderer is untraced. If the entire creation in the heaven and the earth concurs on the murder of one person, God will not let any one of them go unpunished. (Tabrani)

In a certain skirmish, a woman got killed. The Prophet on seeing her dead body, said:

> Oh! What have you done? She was not among the combatants. Go and tell Khalid not to kill women, children and the disabled, old, infirm and cripples not combat-fit. Tr.

A correct idea of the sanctity of human life and the attitude of the Islamic state in this behalf can be had from the general amnesty granted on the occasion of the conquest of Mecca. So long as the unbelievers were in the position of aggressors and were after wiping out the Islamic state of Medina, they were treated as combatants of an aggressive country. As against the opinion of Abu Bakr that the prisoners of war of Badr be freed against payment of ransom, the suggestion of Umar that they must all be put to sword received Divine approbations and the following verse was revealed:

> It is not fitting for an Apostle that he should have prisoners of war until he had thoroughly subdued the land, Ye look for the temporal goods of this world; but God look to the Hereafter and God is exalted in might, wise. Had it not been for a previous from God, a severe penalty would have reached you for the (ransom) you took. (Al Quran VIII: 67-68)

Now that the situation had changed after the conquest of Mecca, their state had been liquidated and with it its aggressive character and the position of the unbelievers as aggressors, they, as the citizens of the conquered territory came under the authority of the Islamic state, became its citizens. And according to the Divine Will they became "subdued" (brought low):

> Until they pay the Jizya with willing submission and feel themselves subdued. (Al Quran IX:29)

Therefore, the Prophet, who had been given the glad tidings of the conquest of Mecca by God, as head of the Islamic state, before the stage of the conquest could attain completion, while the war had not yet laid down its spoils took extraordinary care to save the lives of the new citizens of his state.

Mecca was the stronghold of the blood-thirsty enemies of the Prophet and deadly antagonists of Islam. Here lived those who had strewn the paths of the Prophet with thorns, brought great afflictions to him and his companions, kept him confined to Shob-e-Abi Talib, (a narrow gorge between the mountains in Mecca), plotted and made attempts on his life. And when he had migrated to Medina, they did not allow him to live in peace either. Made repeated surprise attacks on Medina with murder and pillage. In the battles of Badr, Uhud and the battle of Clans, thrust on Medina, they killed many of his faithful and trustworthy friends and wounded him also. Those of his companions who had migrated from Mecca to Yaman, Syria, and Abyssinia were not left undisturbed there either. At the time of the conquest of Mecca, Wahshi, the murderer of the Prophet's uncle Hamzah, Hindah who had tried to chew the liver of Hamzah, and Ikramah b. Abu Jehal, Safwan b. Umayyah, Kaab b. Zubayr and many such other enemies of Islam were in Mecca. The Prophet was now in a position to settle old scores with them. But he, in spite of the power to avenge himself, issued to his army the following orders to save their (his enemies) lives:

1. He who discards arms should be spared.
2. Whoever enters Kaaba should not be killed.
3. Whoever takes shelter in the house of Abu Sufyan should be left alone.
4. Whoever takes shelter in his own house, should be spared.
5. One who betakes himself to the house of Hakeem-ibn-Hizam should not be killed.
6. One who takes to his heels should not be pursued.
7. No wounded person should be killed

After the conquest of Mecca when people gathered before the Kaaba, the Prophet addressing them said:

> Do you know, What I am going to do with you to day?

There arose a response from the crowd:

> You are a noble brother and the son of a noble brother.

The Prophet said in reply:

> This day let no repreach be cast on you. Go you are all at liberty.

The great example of magnanimity and forgiveness set by the Prophet became an important chapter of the Law pertaining to war. And during the period of the rightly guided caliphs on all the occasions of the conquests of Syria, Iraq, Egypt, Iran and the Roman territories abstention from blood-shed was the rule after the enemy had been subdued. A glance at the orders issued by Abu Bakr, 'Umar, 'Uthman and Ali to their military commanders and the governors shows clearly that they had on them a deep impression of the general amnesty of the conquest of Mecca.

An important question in connection with the security of life is when it becomes applicable. All the laws in the world commonly regard the right of the security of life applicable only after the birth. But the Divine Law makes it applicable from the time of initiation of pregnancy. We find that the Prophet abstained from immediately pronouncing the punishment of stoning to death on Ghamidiyah even after her clear confession of fornication, since she had also stated in her confession that she was pregnant. She was meted out this punishment after the birth of the child and the termination of period of suckling the child. If this punishment had been immediately enforced, an innocent life (of the unborn child) would have been lost.

The legists have determined the applicability of the right of security of life from 120 days after conception, since during this period the embryo starts taking shape from an agglomerate of rapidly multiplying cells, and then the term "human entity" is applicable to it. This opinion of our legists after centuries has now been recognized by the modern medical science. The American Supreme Court in a case Reo versus Wade have pronounced the decision with reference to the findings of modern embryology that the "human entity" in the mother's womb would be recognized three months after conception.

***Security of Property :*** In the Islamic state all such private properties as have been legally acquired and from which all the rights and' obligations such as Zakat, Sadaqah (charities), the expenses of the upkeep of the parents, wife and children, brothers and sisters and those under purchase and sale and other maintenances and obligations have been paid, and the regular and temporary taxes levied for defence, administrative needs, public welfare or to meet the emergency needs like war, famine, flood, earthquake and epidemics have also been paid, and also that they are not being surrendered on illegal and unapproved pursuits (of lusts) or business of this nature, shall be immune against the interference of the state, and the owner shall be entitled to the following rights relating to the properties :

(a) The right of their utilization, management and control (change, sale, gifting, donation etc. Tr.)

(b) The right to invest them in business to earn profits.

(c) The right to transfer them.

(d) The right to protect them. There is a definite Quranic injunction:

> And do not eat up your property among yourselves for vanities. (Al Quran II; 188)

If the government has to acquire some body's private property in public interest, it will do so with the consent of the owner after paying compensation at the market rate.

The piece of land that the Prophet selected as the site for the mosque belonged to two orphans. They offered it as a free gift, but the Prophet had its value estimated, and purchased it at the market rate of that time.

On the occasion of the battle of Ummah the Prophet asked Sufyan bin-e-Umayyah for some armours. And when he said, "O Muhammad, are you taking them from me without payment," the Prophet said in reply, " We are taking them temporarily for use and all those damaged or lost shall be paid for." Qadi Abu Yusuf says in his *Kitab-al-Khiraj*:

> The Imam (government) has no right to take any thing from the (rightful) possession of an individual without a proved legal right (of the government to that item.)

In the harangue of his pilgrimage to Mecca what the Prophet said about the sanctity of property along with that of life, has already been mentioned. The security of proprietary rights can be had from the following tradition:

> Whoever is killed in the protection of his property is a martyr. (Bukhari)

***Security of Honour and Dignity :*** An important right of every citizen of the Islamic state shall be that his dignity and honour be protected. The Prophet in his harangue of the last pilgrimage included the sanctity of the dignity and honour also along with life and property. God says in the Quran:

> O ye who believe! Let not some men among you laugh at others:
>
> It may be that the (latter) are better than the (former): nor let some women laugh at others: it may be that the (latter) are better than the (former): nor call each other by offensive nik-names: (Al Quran XLIX : 11)
>
> And do not speak ill of each other behind their backs. (Al Quran XLIX: 12)

Further, it occurs in the same verse:

> Avoid suspicion as much (as possible): for suspicion in some cases is a sin: (Al Quran XLIX 12)

Use of harsh and abusive language has also been strictly prohibited in mutual conversation:

> God loveth not that the evil should be noised abroad in public speech, except where injustice hath been done: (Al Quran 148)

In this verse where it forbids man to use àbusive language, he has been permitted to raise his voice against the oppressor with full force.

> Say to the believing men that they should lower their gaze and guard their modesty: (Al Quran XXIV: 30)

> And say to the believing women that they should lower their gaze and guard their modesty: (Al Quran XXIV: 31)

In these verses the believers have not been addressed directly but these instructions have been conveyed through the Prophet means that while the Muslims are to practise them individually in their lives, the Islamic state has also to keep an eye on that they are being practised. And where their violation is noticed it should be effectively stopped. In other words, it is the obligation of the state that it should make efficient arrangements for the protection of the honour and dignity of the people and stop spread of immodest practices.

The Prophet, in many of his sayings, has forbidden beating people and insulting and bringing them to disgrace. Once he said:

> The back of a Muslim is sacred (he cannot be beaten), except when he comes to deserve it through guilt. Whoever beats a Muslim will have to face Divine wrath. (Tabrani)

> If a person does not help a Muslim where he is being disgraced and his honour is at stake God will not help such a person where he is most in need of His Help and implores Him for it. And if a person helps a Muslim

> in a situation where he is being disgraced and his honour is at stake, God helps him in situation where he needs God's help most and prays to Him for it.
> (Abu Daud)

In another tradition the Prophet has said:

> Whoever has insulted another person or disgraced him or has wronged him in any other way should have it forgiven today (in this life), before the Day when there will neither be money nor other goods of this world, save his own good deeds which will be taken away from him and given to those wronged by him in this world according to the measure of his crimes. And if all his good deeds fail to compensate for his wrongs, the evil deeds of the wronged victims will be cast upon him. (Bukhari)

The Prophet has termed disgrace of a person the worst oppression.

> The worst oppression is unjustified attack on some body's honour. (Abu Daud)

Umar, when giving a send-off to his executive officials, used to give them the following instructions:

> I am not sending you out as tyrants and oppressors, but as leaders and guides. Take heed! Do not disgrace and debase Muslims by beating them.

In cases of defamation the Islamic principle is that every member of the society is honourable no matter what his position, rank and financial status, which is the same as to say when some body is filing a suit of defamation against any one he need not prove that he is honourable, and by the action of the defendant he has really been disgraced. It was on the basis of this principle of equality that 'Umar, the second caliph, got Muhammad b. Umar the son of Umar b 'As, the governor of Egypt, beaten by an Egyptian since he had beaten him (the Egyptian) for his only fault that his horse had beaten all others in a race and (Muhammad) had said. "Take these stripes of the lash, I am the son of the noble." Umar called both the father and the son to Medina and handing over the lash to the Egyptian, said, "Beat the son of the noble." And after he had been thrashed, 'Umar said to the Egyptian, "Now a few stripes for Umar bin-al-'As too, for, by God, the son dared beat thee on the strength of the father's authority and power.

It was in connection with protection of honour that two murders were committed during the caliphate of Umar but he dropped Qisas against both murderers. In one of the incidents a member of Bani Hazail tribe criminally assaulted his host's daughter, who threw a stone at him fatally damaging his liver. Umar pronounced his decision, "He has been murdered by Divine arrangement, no blood money can be allowed in this case."

The other incident is this that two young men fraternised with each other. One of them went out for Jihad and deputed the other to look after his family. One night he saw a Jew in a compromising position with his brother's wife and slew him. He threw his naked dead body out on the road. In the morning the Jews brought up a complaint to the court of Caliph 'Umar, who, on hearing the statement of the young man, said to him, "God bless thy hands," and the murder of the Jew was declared unworthy of any legal action.

'Umar, the second caliph, sentenced the three persons, who had brought accusation of fornication (for adultery) against Mughira-bin-Shabah, the governor of Basra, to eighty stripes each of the lash for false accusation in support of which they could not produce requisite evidence.

Abu Musa Ashari had a person flogged (twenty stripes of lash), for demanding greater share from the spoils of war, and got his head shaved. He went straight to Medina and complained to 'Umar about the insults heaped on him. Umar sent Abu Musa a written order. "If you have disgraced him publicly, in herewith bind you by an avowal to God to allow him to avenge himself on you publicly. And in case it was in privacy let the revenge be taken in privacy." People tried to make him to forgive the offender but he did not agree. At last Abu Musa offered himself in public to receive chastisement at the hands of the wronged person, who at this stage, raised his eyes towards the heavens and said, "O God! Be Thou witness to it, I forgive him."

An idea of temperament of Islam in the matter of security of honour and dignity can be had from the Quranic verses (XXIV: 11-19), in which censuring those accusing 'Aishah, God testified to her chastity and modesty and severely warned Muslims against inventing lies and bringing false accusations against innocent people:

> Those who brought forward the lie are a body among yourselves: Think it not to be an evil to you; on the contrary it is good for you; to every man among them (will come the punishment) of the sin that he earned, and to him who took on himself the lead among them, will be a penalty grievous. Why did not the Believers—men and women, when ye heard of the affair,—put the best construction on it in their own minds and say, "This (charge) is an obvious lie?" Why did they not bring four witnesses. to prove it? When they have not brought the witnesses, such men, in the sight of God, (stand forth) themselves as liars! Were it not for the grace and mercy of God on you in this world and the Hereafter, a grievous penalty would have seized you in that ye rushed glibly into this affair. Behold, 'ye received it on your tongues, and said out of your mouths things of which ye had no knowledge; and ye thought it to be a light matter, while it was most serious in the sight of God. And why did ye not, when ye heard it, say —It is not right of us to speak of this: Glory to God! this is a most serious slander! God doth admonish you, that ye may never repeat such (conduct), if you are (true) believers. And God makes the Signs plain to you: for God is full of knowledge and wisdom. Those who love (to see) scandal published broadcast among the Believers, will have a grievous Penalty in this life and in the Hereafter: God knows and ye know not.
>
> (Al Quran XXIV: 1-19)

The Quran stresses, in general, the security of honour and dignity of every individual, but special emphasis has been laid where security of women's honour is concerned, and God has seriously admonished those violating it:

> Those who slander chaste woman, indiscreet but believing, are cursed in this life and in the Hereafter:

> for them is a grievous Penalty ...on the Day when their tongues, their hands, and their feet will bear witness against them as to their actions. On that Day God will pay them back (all) their just dues, and they will realize that God is the (very) Truth that makes all things manifest. (Al Quran XXIV:23-25)

It was due to these instructions that in the numerous stories of oppression and tyranny and coercion and violence during the history of the Muslims, there is not a single instance where a ruler to bring down their enemies to their knees might have violated the chastity of their women folk.

***Security of the Private Life :*** Perfect security of the private life has been provided to the citizens of the Islamic state, and the enclosure of a private residence has been given the position of a citadel, where nobody has a right to pry. The Quran says:

> O ye who believe! Enter not houses other than your own, until ye have asked permission and saluted those in them: That is best for you, in order that ye may heed (what is seemly). If ye find no one in the house, enter not until permission is given to you: if you are asked to go back, go back: that makes for greater purity.
> (Al Quran XXIV : 27-28)

The Prophet has instructed the believers not to enter even their own houses unannounced, so that there may be no chance for them to look at their own women folk in an embarrassing position which is deemed immoral.

Only those buildings are exempted from these restrictions which are not residential:

> It is no fault on your part to enter houses not used for living in, which serve some (other) use for you.
> (Al Quran XXIV : 29)

Under this category fall offices, public buildings, hotels, inns, guest houses, shops, schools and other places like them. Along with instructions not to enter houses without permission, the Muslims have also been told not to meddle into the private lives of other people. The permission granted by the owner to enter his house, does not mean that the visitor should stay there longer than necessary and not allow the owner of the house to pass his time even in his own house according to his will and programme:

> O ye who believe! Enter not the Prophet's houses,— until leave is given you, for a meal, (and then) not (so early as) to wait for ita preparation: but when ye are invited, enter; and when ye have taken your meal, disperse, without seeking familiar talk....
>
> (Al Quran XXXII: 53)

In connection for entry to a house and to stay there only as long as barely necessary, it was also said that if one has to take some thing at the door, he must ask for it from before the door screen:

> And when ye ask (his ladies) for any thing ye want, ask them from before a screen.
>
> (Al Quran XXXIII; 53)

Similarly, peeping into other people's houses has been strictly forbidden. The Prophet said that if somebody catches any one peeping into his house and blinds him by sticking it. He has also forbidden to look into somebody else's letter or even cast a side glance at the letter somebody is reading.

Along with provision of security to a citizen's house from outside interference, the Quran has also impressed it on Muslims that they should strictly abstain from prying into each other's secrets, and spying on each other:

> And spy not on each other, nor speak ill of each other behind their backs: Would any of you like to eat the flesh of his dead brother? Nay, ye would abhor it.
>
> (Al Quran XLIX 12.)

Man through spying on others comes to learn some of their secret faults and infirmities and then takes a morbid pleasure in disclosing them to others, and thus becomes the means of their defamation and disrepute. The Quran strictly forbids both spying and back-biting.

The Prophet once said:

> If you are bent upon learning the secrets of other peoples,, you will corrupt them or at least make their approach to corruption certain. (Abu Daud)

In another tradition he says:

> Whoever noticed somebody's fault and kept it to himself (abstained from exposure,), he, as it were, quickened a living corpse. (Abu Daud, Nasai)

The Prophet has specifically prohibited the rulers from spying on their people:

> When a ruler comes to search for reasons behind mere suspicions, he is sure to corrupt them.
> (Abu Daud)

In this connection an incident of the period of 'Umar gives us an idea of the limits to which the Amir of the Islamic state can go in the matter of interference in the life of a citizen, and how strong a defence he has been provided against such meddling. Once he ('Umar) heard (on one of his nightly vigilance rounds) somebody singing in his house. Suspecting dirty game, he scaled the wall and entered the house, to find that there was not only wine there but a woman also. 'Umar called out to him saying.

O enemy of God! Art thou under the (erroneous) impression that thou will be allowed to go on with thy transgression against God and He will not expose thee. In reply he said, O Amir-al-Muminin Don't be hasty. If I am guilty of one sin you have committed three. Allah forbade you to spy on people and you have spied on me. Allah commands you to enter houses through their gates and you have scaled the wall to my house. Allah has ordained that permission is necessary for entry to the houses of other people, and here you are without my permission. Hearing this Umar confessed his fault and took no action against him, but made him promise that he would take to the path of righteousness.

Tafheem-al-Quran, Vol. V, p 89, with reference to Makarim-ul-Akhlaq.

Another incident of the period of 'Umar in which a girl to escape the limit set by God, tried to commit suicide with the help of a knife but could not succeed in her attempt. And then she repented for her sin. A certain person who was ignorant of her former guilt proposed to her. The guardian of the girl asked 'Umar, "Shall I enlighten the would be groom the tragic event in her life? 'Umar said in reply, "Will you reveal what God has kept concealed? By God, if you let a breath of it pass to any body I will make you an admonitory example for people. Marry her off as chaste virgins are married."

This is how Islam protects private life and maintains its sanctity. How can the government, that is committed to these commandments and instructions of the Shariah, justify it, conduct in weaving a network of espionage, set a spy or informer in pursuit of every citizen, dug people's private apartments and offices, tap their telephones, censor their letters and keep their photostat copies for record, photographing people's private apartments, and resort to other measures of black-mailing their (political) opponents?

***Security of Personal Freedom :*** In the Islamic state no citizen can be imprisoned without proving his guilt in an open court. Arresting people on mere suspicion and incarcerating them without proper trial in a court of law is not permissible under the Islamic order. Whatever is being done under the name of "Preventive Detention" in the "interest of the state", there is no room for it in the Islamic Law. There is a definite injunction of the Quran that the freedom conferred by God on his servants, not to speak of a common ruler, even the Prophet of God cannot take away:

It is not (possible) that a man, to whom is given the Book, and wisdom, and the Prophetic office, should say to people: "Be ye my worshippers rather than God": On the contrary (He would say):

> Be ye worshippers of Him who is truly the cherisher of all: for ye have taught the book and ye have studied it earnestly." (Al Quran III; 79 )
>
> Say: "Shall I seek for judge other than God? When He it is who hath sent unto you the Book, explained in details." (Al Quran VI: 114)
>
> What! Have they partners (in goodhead), who have established for them some religion without the permission of God? (Al Quran XLII:21)

The Islamic attitude in this behalf is that as far as possible punishment should be avoided, and reasons and evidence should be sought, not for punishment, but for acquittal the Prophet says:

> As far as possible spare Muslims (citizens) from punishment. If you can find any excuse for that, acquit them. It is better for the Imam (ruler) to err on the side of acquittal than in the matter of punishment.
> (Tirmidhi)

> So long as you can find a way for it, spare people from punishment. (Ibn-e-Majah)

A remarkable instance of this attitude of the Prophet is reflected by the incident connected with Maiz bin-e-Malik. He became involved in fornication. He came to the Prophet and said, "O Prophet of God! I am guilty of fornication be so good as to cleanse me of this filth." Now it is remarkable the way the Prophet sought ways to avoid meting out punishment to him. To begin with he turned his face away from him, and said to him, "Go and repent and ask forgiveness of God." But he (Maiz) came before the Prophet and repeated his request. The Prophet once again turned his face. He came before him for the third time and made the same request, and the Prophet once again turned his face away from him. Abu Bakr warned Maiz that if he confessed his guilt for the fourth time, the Prophet would have him stoned to death. But he was adamant, and repeated his request for the fourth time. Now the Prophet became attentive and asked him, "Perhaps you indulged in kissing and hugging, or indulged in preliminaries or looked at her with lust." He replied," "No". The Prophet asked him, "Were you in the same bed with her?" He said, "Yes". The Prophet again asked him, "Did you cohabit with her?" And he said. "Yes". He was again asked. "Did you copulate with her?" And he said, "Yes". Similarly to the further three (very definite) question of the Prophet he replied in the

> affirmative. Finally, he asked him, "Do you know what is fornication?" He said, "Yes, I did to her illegally what a husband does with his wife lawfully." Prophet asked him, "Are you married?" And he said "Yes" The Prophet asked him, "You are not drunk, I hope?" He said, "No". Then the Prophet asked his neighbours about his sanity, and they testified that they had never witnessed any thing in his wits to the contrary. The Prophet said to Hazzali-bin-Naim, who bad brought up Maiz, and had advised him to request the Prophet to seek forgiveness of God on his behalf: "It would have been better for you to keep his guilt concealed". And then he gave the decision to have Maiz stoned to death. He was taken out of the town and stoned to death. When he was being stoned, he tried to run away and said, "O people take me to the Prophet. My tribesmen have brought me to this end. They deceived me that the Prophet would not have me executed". But those entrusted with stoning him, did their job and killed him. When the Prophet was told of it, he said, "Why did you people not let him go? If you had brought him to me, it was possible he would have repented and God would have forgiven him"
>
> (Tafheem-al-Quran, Vol.111, p.335-336.)

In this incident every question of the Prophet put to Maiz makes it evident that he was doing all that was possible to save Maiz, and was trying to find a flaw in his own statement or the evidence of the neighbour that could provide cause for doubt, and through benefit of that doubt his life can be saved. He also sought for the doubts arising from drunkenness and witnesses. But when there was no plea left for his defence he gave the decision. And then he was sorry for the sentence being executed. This incident also reveals to what extent thorough investigations are necessary to get to the true facts of the case before pronouncing a decision, especially when passing a sentence.

Numerous incidents of the period of the Prophet and those of the rightly guided caliphs that in the Islamic state no citizen be incarcerated without trial and proving his guilt:

> Once the Prophet was delivering a haraugue in the mosque. A certain person stood up and said, "O Prophet of Allah! For what crime have my neighbours been arrested". The Prophet made no reply and he again put the same question to him. The Prophet continued his harangue and made no reply even then. When he rose for the third time and repeated his question, the Prophet ordered the release of his neighbours. (Abu Daud, Kitab-al Quzat)

Why the Prophet kept quiet twice was due to the fact that the Police Officer was present in the gathering in the mosque, and if there had been any justifiable excuse for their arrest he would have spoken out. But when he kept mum the Prophet concluded that then arrests were unjustified and therefore he ordered the release.

During the period of 'Umar's caliphate a certain person came from Iraq and approaching the caliph said, 'Amir-al-Muminin, I have come to you in connection, with a certain affair which is very complicated, revealing neither head nor tail." 'Umar asked him, "What is that?" He said, "The nefarious practice of false evidence has started in our country", 'Umar said. "Has it"? He said, "Yes". 'Umar said, "Don't you worry on that score. By God, no body can be incarcerated without justice being against him."

Moatta, Chapter on the conditions for Witness :

> The Incident of 'Umar's period in which he called Umro-bin-al-'Aas, the Governor of Egypt and his son Muhammad bin-e-'Umro, heard the case of the Egyptian against them and had Muhammad bin-e-Umro flogged by the wronged Egyptian has been mentioned earlier. 'Umar allowed him to give some stripes of the lash to' Umro-bin-al-'As also, whose gubernatorial authority and powers had most probably encouraged his son to disgrace a citizen. But plaintiff said, "O Amir-al-Muminin, I have avenged myself. I am satisfied that I have beaten the person who had beaten me." At this juncture 'Umar addressing Umro-bin-al-'As, made the historic remark, "O 'Umro! Since when you have made men your slaves; their mothers had delivered them as free individuals."

From these precedents it is evident that under the Islamic order, the Islamic state can neither inflict any punishment on a citizen nor depriving him of his freedom, can imprison him. The Quran announces in clear terms:

> And when ye judge between man and man, then ye judge with justice: (Al Quran IV: 58)

Along with this general order for the believers, the first ever head of the Islamic state of Medina, the Prophet, had been particularly ordered to do justice:

> And I am commanded to judge justly between you.

The words of the first verse clearly indicate that justice is not an arbitrary decision. It has a norm of its own, a well known concept, a firm regulation and as such the decision must of necessity be according to due process of Law, meeting all its conditions. In this matter, the course of the judicial process of the Islamic state is made evident by a decision pronounced by the Prophet himself:

> It happened a little before the conquest of Mecca, while the Prophet had been making preparations for his march towards Mecca, and the success of his plan of action depended on strict secrecy so that the Meccans may not be forewarned. A certain companion of the Prophet, Hatib-bin-e-Abi Baltaah, for consideration of the safety of his family, sent a letter of warning to the Quraish through an old woman going that way. The Prophet learnt of it in time and sent Ali and Zubayr in hot pursuit of the woman bearing that (dangerous Tr.) letter. They obtained that letter and came back with it. When it was opened and read out, it was found to contain the information that the Quraish were to be shortly attacked. When Hatib was called to explain his conduct in an open court he remorsefully said,' 'O Prophet of God, I am neither an apostate nor an unbeliever. I didn't do it as' a traitor to the cause of the Islamic state. My family is in Mecca. There is no tribe there on whose support I could count. I had written this letter with a view to oblige the Quraish so that they may not harm my wife and children.

> Apparently, it was a case of high treason. If this letter had found its way to the Quraish, the entire plan of war prepared by the Muslims would have gone topsy-turvy. In face of the gravity of the crime, 'Umar got up and said, "O Prophet of God, permit me to behead this traitor." But the Prophet who had been commissioned by God as a Mercy to the peoples, said very gently, "Hatib is one of Badr-fame, and the plea he has put forward in his defence is according to the fact." 'Umar was so overwhelmed with passion (righteous anger Tr.) that he began to weep, and sat down saying, "Allah and His Apostle know best."

This acquittal of Hatib is an unparalleled example of the sanctity of human life, hearing of the most serious case in open court and giving the accused the chance of defence. No other government in the world would have brought the perpetrator of a crime of this nature to an open court for trial. Nor any court would have sentenced the culprit, with solid documentary evidence against him, and his own confession, to anything less than capital punishment. But the Prophet in view of the past life of Hatib, his services in the battle of Badr and his most honest and sincere statement, not to speak of death penalty, acquitted him honourably, considering the lowering of his prestige for the time being among the believers enough punishment for him. This incident has come for mention in the Quran (LX:1). (For greater detail of the incident see *Tafheem-al-Quran* Vol.V, P. 422).

The behaviour of the Kharijites during the period of Ali has come for mention earlier. He never put any member of this group behind the bars for their antigonism to him. He was all patience upto the last, adhering to the principle that so long as they do not rise in an armed rebellion against the state, the caliph cannot take any step against them.

'Adi bin-e-Artat, an executive of the government headed by 'Umar bin-e-Abdul Aziz, wrote to him (the caliph) that the people of the territory under his charge were such as did not pay the revenues due from them unless they were tormented in some degree, and solicited permission to adopt that measure. In reply 'Umar bin-e-Abdul Aziz wrote back:

> I am amazed to find that you seek permission to torment people which amounts to saying that I shall be able to save you from the Divine wrath and His torment, or my approval of your actions will stand between you and the Divine torment. On receiving my letter make it a rule to realize the dues only from those who willingly pay them to you; and those who do not pay, take an oath from them and let them go. By God! I would much rather have people going before God (on the Day of Reckoning) with the burden of their own crimes, than that I should be brought before Him with the crime of tormenting them.

Qadi Abu Yusuf, the Chief Justice of the Abbasid period, has written about Detention:

> It is neither allowed nor is there any room for such allowance that a person should be detained in the custody of police or jail just because some body has accused him of some crime. If such a situation arises, both the plaintiff and defendant should be summoned. If the plaintiff has proof of the crime, decision in his favour should be given, failing which the defendant should be released against security. If later the plaintiff brings forward proof of the crime, suitable action will be taken against the defendant strictly according to law, otherwise he will be let alone.

These Islamic laws are not dependent on the existing conditions at any particular time or place. They cannot be held in abeyance by proclaiming a state of emergency. They will remain enforceable under any circumstances whatsoever. Therefore, in the Islamic state, the citizens shall enjoy perfect protection against unjustifiable detention.

## The Protection

A citizen in an Islamic state shall also have the right not be held responsible for other people's actions. The Quran has determined the following rule in this behalf:

> Every soul draws the need of its acts on none but itself: no bearer of burdens can bear the burdens of another. (Al Quran VI: 164)

The same thing has been repeated in Surah Fatir (XXXV:18). In such Baqarah (11:193) it has been clearly stated:

> Let there be no hostility except against wrong doers. (Al Quran II: 193.)

In the presence of these commandments his father, sons, mother, sisters or other relatives cannot be arrested in place of the accused. Such examples are to be met with in the highly developed so-called democracies of the twentieth century. The entire Muslim history before the period of western colonization is free from such incidents. Hajjaj bin Yusuf is notorious for his tyranny and murders. But with all his ferociousness, he was not found guilty of beheading the relatives of his opponents. A well known incident of his period is that he got arrested a person named Qatari bin-e-Faqaat and told him that he would have him murdered. Qatari asked him the reason for this drastic action, and Hajjaj said in reply, "Because your brother has brought an attack against us." Qatari said, "I have a letter from the Amir-al Mominin to the effect that should not be implicated for my brother's crime." Hajjaj asked him to produce that letter and show it to him. Qatari said in reply:

> I have a letter more worthy of compliance. God says:
>
> No bearer of burdens can bear the burden of another. (Al Quran VI: 164)

Hajjaj was pleased with the answer, smiled and released him.

## Different Free Acts

***Right of Protest :*** Islam has conferred on the citizens of the Islamic state the right that in case of tyranny they can raise their voice against it, are not to be cowed down by the tyranny and not to take his tyranny lying down. Allah says:

> God loveth not that evil should be noised abroad in public speech, except where injustice has been done. (Al Quran IV: 148)

What is meant here is that speaking ill of others, however disagreeable, when, tyranny has crossed all limits and patience is tried, and the oppressed speaks ill of the tyrant in a passion over which he has no control, in spite of the highest moral teachings, such ill speech on the part of the oppressed is forgivable in the sight of God. The oppressed has a right to complain and in so doing if his passion forces him to lose sight of regard for a civil tongue, he is not blame-worthy. A well known tradition runs like this:

> The most superior type of Jihad is to openly declare the Truth (or justice) before a tyrant (a despot).
>
> (Abu Daud, Tirmidhi, Ibn-e-Majah, Nasai, Musnad-e-Ahmad)
>
> When people see a tyrant (oppressing people) and do not hold his hand, it is not unlikely that a general visitation from God may overtake them.
>
> (Abu Daud, Tirmidhi)
>
> Help your brother whether he is an oppressor or oppressed. The companions (wonderingly) asked him, "We shall certainly help our oppressed brother, but how to help him in case he is the oppressor?" The Prophet replied, "Hold his hand to stop his tyranny."
>
> (Bukhari)

The Prophet was an embodiment of mercy, and never oppressed any one in the least. But if any one had any complaint against him, he gave him a chance to put his grievance before him, and presented himself for his revenge.

Once he was getting the spoils of war distributed. A certain person in the crowd came forward in haste and fell on him face forward. The Prophet had a thin stick in his hand and tried to stop him with that stick. By chance the end of the stick came against his face and bruised it. The Prophet said to him:

> You may avenge yourself on me for it. He said, O Prophet of God, I have forgiven you. (Abu Daud)

On the occasion of the Battle of Badr, the Prophet was straightening the rows of the Mujahidin (the fighter in the way of Allah). Sawad bin-e-Ghazyah was standing a little ahead of others in the row. The Prophet with a gentle poke of the arrow said to him, "Fall in line." Sawad said, "O Prophet of God! You have caused me injury, when God has commissioned you to do justice and restoring (usurped) rights to the people. So kindly allow me to avenge myself on you." The Prophet exposed his abdomen and said, "Sawad, avenge yourself." Sawad kissed the exposed abdomen.

A certain person came to the Prophet and demanded repayment of the loan taken by him. He used harsh language in that company. The companions were annoyed by his aggressive style of address and some of them got up to give him a good thrashing. The Prophet said:

> Let him say, let him say what he likes. He who has a claim on somebody can say things like that.
>
> (Bukhari)

The harangues of Abu Bakr and 'Umar have been quoted earlier in which they had asked people to take notice and action wherever they witnessed tyranny and oppression. The incident of complaint against Abu Musa has earlier come for mention under the heading security of honour, in which he had a person gagged and his head shaved. He collected the shaven hair and went to Medina with them. As soon as he approached 'Umar he threw his locks of hair at his chest and said in a very rude manner, "Here, by God, it is Fire." 'Umar said, "Yes, by God, it is Fire." He said, "O Amir-al-Mominin, I am a person with a high pitched voice and exert heavy pressure on the enemy. I have received twenty stripes of the lash and my head has been shaved. Umar instead of getting into a rage at this rude behaviour of his, paid tribute lo him thus:

> By God! If all men were high-minded and resolute like him, I would have liked it more than all the spoils of war God has given us so far.

Islam has not only conferred on men the right of protest against tyranny, but also that of refusing to obey the tyrant and removing him from his office, if their voice raised in protest against tyranny falls on deaf ears, since the first and foremost responsibility of the high position of emirate is crushing tyranny and the establishment of justice. Justice is an essential condition for the emirate. The Quran says:

> (And when God said Ibrahim). I will make thee an Imam to the Nations. He pleaded: And also (Imams) from my offspring! He answered: But my promise is not within the reach of evil-doers.(Al Quran II: 124)

The Muslims have been commanded:

> And follow not the bidding of those who are extravagant (not respecting the limits set by God).
>
> (Al Quran XXVI: 151)

Several Quranic verses and traditions on this theme have been quoted under 'The Limits of Obedience', which clearly bring out the fact that tyrants cannot be tolerated in the Islamic state, and raising one's voice against their tyranny is not only a right but an obligation for any shortcomings in it shall be liable to accountability before the Sovereign.

***Freedom of Self-expression :*** The citizens of the Islamic state do not only enjoy the right to open their mouths when oppressed but also to freely express their opinion about the affairs of the state and problems confronting the country. These traits of the believers have been mentioned in the Quran:

> They enjoin what is right and forbid what is wrong.
>
> (Al Quran III: 110)

This quality can never develop without freedom of self expre-ssion. This verse does not only ensure this freedom but determines the direction of its use also. A Muslim can use it only for promoting what is right but not for spreading an evil, since it is the trait of the character of a hypocrite about whom the Quran says:

> They enjoin evil and forbid what is just.
>
> (Al Quran IX: 67)

The Quran points it out as one of the reasons behind the degeneration of the Israelites:

> Nor did they (usually) forbid one another the iniquities which they committed. (Al Quran V: 79)

Warning the Muslims against this negligence it was said:

> And if ye distort (justice) or decline to do justice, verily God is well acquainted with all that ye do.
>
> (Al Quran IV: 13 5)

What the Quranic verse is intended to convey is this that if you lapse in proclaiming the truth, or under any pressure, threat or avarice, adopt the hypocritic attitude by mincing matters and speaking ambiguously, you may save your skin in this world, but can never escape the punishment of this crime (of concealing the truth) in Hereafter. The Prophet says:

> There are going to be some rulers after me. One who supports them in their falsehood and helps them in their tyranny, he is not from me and I am not from him (God and His faith, Islam, and His Prophet have nothing to do with those who aid and abet tyranny and falsehood. Tr.) (Nasai, Kitab-al-Bai)

It was customary with the Prophet to consult his companions in various matters and encourage them in the expression of their opinions. Several examples of it have been given in this book earlier. On the occasion of the battle of Uhud, the Prophet and his high-ranking companions with seniority in age and advantage of experience were of the opinion that they should meet the enemy in the town of Medina; but Hamzah and the young men among his companions were in favour of confronting the enemy in the open, outside Medina. Seeing that the majority was in favour of facing the foe out of the town, he decided in favour of the young men and went into his room to get in battle array. During this period (in the absence of the Prophet) the elderly men raised an accusing finger at the young men that they did not respect the opinion of the Prophet and put him to some trouble in taking decision. This moved the young men to revise there opinion and they gathered outside the Prophet's room to apologise. The Prophet came out and hearing apologetic revision of their opinion said to them, "It does hot become a Prophet of God to disarm himself before achieving the objective. We shall now engage the enemy in the open outside Medina.

Once, while the Prophet was distributing the spoils of war, somebody remarked "The booty has been distributed against the Divine Will (or Justice)." It was a serious matter, but he forgave the offender. Another voice was heard, "You have not done justice." He said in reply, "If I do not do justice, who will." But he did not take him to task. A certain case of dispute between Zubayr and an

Ansari came up before the Prophet and he decided it in favour of Zubayr. The Ansari in a rage taunted. "You have favoured your cousin!" The Prophet took no notice of his rude remark and did not say a word.

In a certain skirmish against the unbelievers, the Prophet instructed the Muslims to put up tents for sojourn at a certain place. A certain companion asked him, "Is that through revelation from God or your own opinion?" The Prophet said, "It is my personal opinion." The companion then said to him, "This place is not suitable for sojourn; such and such place will be suitable for it." So the place suggested by him was approved for sojourn.

Abu Bakr in his managerial harangue actually invited people to express their opinions. When 'Umar came to occupy the seat of authority vacated through Abu Bakr's death, Abu Ubaidah and Maaz bin-e-Jabal jointly addressed a letter to him, in which they had invited his attention to the responsibilities of the caliphate and accountability of the Hereafter. They had written in their letter.

We seek refuge in Allah that this letter of ours may not be given by you the importance it really deserves. We have written it in a spirit of well-wishing and sincerity.

'Umar thanking both of them in a long letter wrote to them:

> Your joint letter is full of truth. I need such letters (of advice) so remember me in this behalf from time to time.

Sad bin-e-Ubadah Ansari neither took an oath of fealty at the hand of Abu Bakr nor at 'Umars. He neither attended congregations led by them in the mosque, nor the weekly Friday congregation, nor performed Hajj pilgrimage led by them. Ibn-e-Qutaibah has written about him:

> If he had found some supporters he would have attacked the persons in authority. And in case some people had sworn loyalty to him, He would have risen in revolt against them. He was adamant in his attitude. When Abu Bakr died and 'Umar succeeded him, he went to Syria and died there.

In spite of this attitude of Sad bin-e-'Ubadah, neither Abu Bakr, nor 'Umar ever had any thing to do with him, since, in spite of his abstention from taking an oath of fealty and adopting an 'attitude of rebellion against them he never indulged in any mischievous activity.

During the period of 'Umar freedom of self-expression had reached a stage that any person could stop him on the way or interrupt him during a largely attended harangue and question him or put up a complaint before him, or take him to task. And to keep this spirit of self-expression alive he paid full attention to the complaint, and if any one else tried to interfere or stop him he was annoyed and allowed him ( complainant) full freedom to say what he had to say, encouraged him and took immediate action in connection with his complaint. He heard complaints against governors like 'Umar-bin-al-As, Mughira bin-e-Shabah and Abu Musa 'Ashari, publicly, and took action against them. Explained how he came to have two sheets while all ethers had one, in a big gathering, withdrew his suggestion of limiting the dower of women also in public, and thanked the woman who had brought well sustained objection against such limiting, for showing him the right path. And when a person got up in a public gathering and told him that they would bring bin', to the right path with the sword if he deviated from it, he thanked God that there were such individuals among his people who could stop him from going astray. The entire period of his caliphate is replete with incidents of encouragement of self expression. The most important aspect of these incidents is that never any questioner, reckoner or complainant was silenced. Neither he ever took exception to the tone and language which were very often uncivil, even rude and insulting. Here are some instances of this attitude of his:

> A certain person addressed him on the public road and said to him, "O 'Umar fear God." He repeated this sentence several times. At this stage some body tried to stop him saying, "Keep quiet! You have said enough to the Amir-al-Muminin." Umar immediately intervened and said, "Do not stop him. What use are they if they stop saying such things to us. And if we do not accept these things from them we should be shorn of all good, and it would be no wonder if this remark

bin-e-Yusuf?" He replied "Yes, why not?" Hajjaj said to him, "Tell me something about his character." He said in reply, "He is very bad person, unparalleled in transgression against God and his commandments." Hajjaj became red in face with rage and said in a harsh tone, "You rascal, don't you know that he is my brother." He replied very coolly, "Yes I know it well enough, but dost thou not know that Allah is my Lord and Cherisher, and my God, He is much dearer to me and sought after than thy brother is to thee."

Once Haroon Rasheed went on Hajj pilgrimage. While circumambulating the Kaaba, Abdullah 'Umri happened to look at him, and called out to him, "O Haroon!" Haroon came forward and said in reply, 'Respected uncle! this servant of yours is here before you." Abdullah 'Umri asked him, "Can you tell me the number of people who have come here for Hajj pilgrimage?" Haroon said, "A very large number, and God alone knows the real count." Abdullah 'Umri said, "Man! do not forget the fact that every one in this huge crowd is responsible to God for his own deeds, alone, while you are answerable for all of them. Just think what will happen to you at the time of reckoning." Haroon on hearing this much from him began to weep but said nothing to Abdullah 'Umri.

The advice tendered by Qadi Abu Yusuf in the preface of his *Kitab-al-Khiraj* to this same Haroon Rasheed, is a masterpiece of courage in the matter of freedom of the expression of opinion.

Haroon was once delivering a harangue to his audience when somebody stood up and said, "By God, you neither maintained equality nor justice and equity in the distribution of the spoils of war. Instead you were guilty of such and such inequities. "Haroon ordered his arrest. After the prayer was over, Qadi Abu Yusuf was called to his presence. Haroon told him that the person in question had said things never said by any one before that. He was in a rage at the moment and the (outspoken) person was standing guarded on both sides by the executioners. The Qadi putting forth the beautiful pattern of the Prophet's conduct and the precedents of the rightly guided caliphate, said to him taking courage in both hands. "You cannot punish him." Reference to the pattern of the Prophet cooled down Haroon's anger and he ordered immediate release of the (outspoken) person.

Sultan Sanjar, son of Malik Shah Seljuqi, was the ruler of Khorasan. Imam Ghazzali saw him, and said to him "It is a pity that the neck of the Muslims are being broken by adversity and misery, and the neck, of your horses with heavy collars of gold."

Sheikh-al-Islam 'Izzuddin bin-e-Abdus Salam was advised by some body to kiss the hand of the king to end his differences with him, after which he would be reinstated with promotion. The Sheikh said in reply:

> "You simpleton! I cannot allow the king to kiss my hand, not to speak of my kissing his hand. O ye people! You are living in a world different from mine. And I cannot thank God enough that I am free from what holds you in its grip."

It was the same Sheikh Izzuddin who, when celebrations were in full swing and people were presenting their offerings on their knees to the king, called him out in the crowded durbar (court) and said, "O Ayyub! What will be your plea to God's query whether you had been given the rule of Egypt that you may let the people alone to drink freely." The king asked him "Is this a fact?" The Sheikh said, loudly "Yes, at such and such bar liquor is being sold, and other acts too heinous to be named, are going on freely. And here you are enjoying yourself." The king immediately ordered the closure of that public house.

Islamic history abounds in such incidents where Truth was proclaimed with great courage, in a very strange tone and in crowded gatherings and durbars. Even the despots heard them with patience and did not punish those who admonished them.

How many rulers elected by the popular vote are there in this age of democracy, who would allow people to adopt this style of address and present themselves for such impartial reckoning of themselves?

Determining the limits of the freedom of expressing one's opinion in Islam, Allama Shaukani writes:

> The Islamic Shariah does not allow killing of those who believe in revolting against the Imam (ruler), so long as they do not rise in sums to give a practical

> shape to their convidious, or at least make preparations for an upsurge, since the Prophet has said that they should be put to sword only when they rise in revolt.

If a group of people show signs of nursing ideas of a rebellious nature the way the kharijites did, it would not justify their execution. Their murder would be justified only in the event of their number multiplying and arming themselves menacing the lives and properties of people.

These limits clearly indicate that on the basis of mere suspicion even the openly expressed most serious differences of opinion or even opposition, no punishment can be meted out to the opponents so long there is no practical demonstration of rebellious activities. In the Islamic state no government can put a ban or even restrictions on the free expression of opinion, since it will be tantamount to usurp a right given to people by God and as such a rebellion against the Sovereign on the part of the rulers.

***Freedom of Conscience and Belief :*** The Islamic state confers freedom of conscience and belief on every body. The Quran proclaims decisively:

> Let there be no compulsion in religion: Truth stands out clear from error. (Al Quran 11.256)

What the verse is intended to convey is that the right course is the one to which Islam calls, and it has also sorted out the wrong and misleading ideas from the Truth, so that there is a clear line of demarcation between them. Now the will and pleasure of God, and the striving of the Muslims is that the mankind should accept the Islamic message of Truth. But there should be no compulsion in this business. Whoever wants may accept it on the basis of sound reasoning. But those who are not prepared to do so shall not be compelled to accept it. The Quran addresses the Prophet thus:

> If it had been thy Lords Will, they would all have believed, all who are on earth! With thou then compel mankind, against their will to believe.
>
> (Al Quran X 99)

At another place detailing the responsibilities of the Prophet in connection with the call to the Truth, it has been said:

> Thou art not one to admonish. Thou art one to manage (Men's) affairs (a warder over them).
>
> (Al Quran LXXXVIII 21-22)

> The same thing has been repeated over and over again— L:45, X:108, XVII:29, VI: 107, XXIX:46, XXXIX:41.

The only responsibility of all the Prophets commissioned by God, was to convey the Message of Truth without any amendments. They themselves said about their mission:

> And our duty is only to proclaim the clear Message.
>
> (Al Quran XXXVI 17)

Similarly, it has been said to the Prophet:

> But if they turn away, thy duty is only to preach the clear Message. (Al Quran XVI 82)

In Surah Shura (XLII), the Prophet has been instructed to tell the unbelievers and polytheists rejecting and falsifying the faith:

> God is our Lord and your Lord: for us (is the responsibility for) our deeds, and for you for your deeds. There is no contention between us and you.
>
> (Al Quran XLII 15)

The same theme runs in Surah CIX from the first to the last verse:

> Say: O ye that reject Faith! I worship not that which ye worship. Nor will ye worship that which I worship. And I will not worship that which ye have been won't to worship, nor will ye worship that which I worship. To you be your way and to me mine.
>
> (Al Quran CIX: 1-6)

In this matter, the best example of tolerance is the incident of Wasaq Rumi, the slave of 'Umar. He himself relates that "I was slave of 'Umar and he used to say to accept Islam. If you become a believer, I shall give you some responsibility of the affairs of Muslims, since it is not permissible for me to appoint unbelievers to jobs of the trust of the believers." But I did not accept Islam. And he used to say, "There is no compulsion in faith." And when his death was approaching, he freed me and said, "Go where you like."

These incidents relating to Said bin-e-'Ubadah Ansari have been mentioned earlier. He adhered to his opinion regarding caliphate, but neither Abu Bakr nor 'Umar compelled him to take a vow of fealty from him. The freedom of the difference of opinion on minor issues ever continued among the Muslims. During the period of the rightly guided caliphate, many people differed in opinion from the decision of the Amir in advisory council. To the extent of the opinion they adhered to their own but complied with the decisions of the Amir. A good example of it is served by the incident of Uthman not shortening his prayers at Mina. Many people violently disagreed with him, but when it came to prayer led by him, they joined it and finished it according to his manner. This difference continues to this day.

'Umar prayed in a corner of the Christian church of Bait-al-Maqdis. Then it occurred to him that the Muslims might adopt his praying there as a plea for ousting the Christians from this church (and convert it into a mosque Tr.). So he wrote out an edict and entrusted it to the charge of the bishop according to which the church was made an exclusive place of worship for the Christians, and one and only one Muslim could enter the church at any given time.

In the matter of freedom of creed, Islam not only commanded that there should be no compulsion in religion but also forbade injuring the feelings of any one professing a different faith, through disrespect to his deities. God says in the Quran:

> Revile ye not those whom they call upon besides God.
>
> (Al Quran VI: 108)

In religious debates it happens so often that people lose sight of regard for the feelings of others and make the belief of the opponent the target of taunts and revilement, and along with their objects of worship they go on to speak ill of their reverend religious leaders. But the Muslims have been strictly forbidden from indulging in any irreverential behaviour:

> And dispute ye not with the People of the Book, except with means better (than mere disputation).
>
> (Al Quran XXIX, 45)

In this one word Ahsan (better) are included all the fine qualities like gentleness and good manners, patience and tolerance. This commandment is not exclusive to the People of the Book but the followers of all religions.

***Right of Equality :*** The Quran regards all men as human beings, equal in rank:

> O mankind! We created you from a single pair of a male and a female, and made you into nations and tribes, that ye may know each other (not that ye may despise each other). (Al Quran XLIX.-13.)

The same thing was said by the Prophet in his harangue of the last Hajj pilgrimage to Mecca, in these words:

> No Arabian has any superiority over a non-Arabian nor non-Arabian over an Arabian. No person of white complexion has any superiority over a black one, nor a black person over a white one, save for Taqwa or piety.
>
> You are all the offspring of Adam, and Adam was fashioned out of clay. (Bukhari and Muslim)

In the words of the Quran and those of the Prophet all persons living within boundaries of the Islamic state, shall be equal in status in the sight of law. Even in the social sphere of life there shall be no other norm among them for distinction save superiority in Taqwa (Piety). Islam has made the entire human race as a brotherhood on the basis of kinship (blood relationship due to common parentage). And the basis, of belief and Faith has made the Muslims brothers, and as such perfect equality of status exists among them:

> The believers are but a single Brotherhood.
> (Al Quran XL1X: 10)

The Prophet has called not only Muslims but the entire humanity a brotherhood:

> I bear witness that all men are brothers among themselves. (Abu Daud, Kitab-al-Salat)

During the period of the Prophet, that of the rightly guided caliphate and in later periods too, we come across many instances in which master and slave, the rulers and the common citizen, the rich and the poor and Muslim and non-Muslim have been treated with perfect equality in the dispensation of justice. The Prophet kept himself at the same level with others in the matter of rights and dealings. A certain woman of the Quraish, Fatima, committed theft (a young companion and very close to the Prophet Tr.) Usamah pleaded with the Prophet that she should be forgiven. The Prophet replied strictly:

> O Usamah! Dare you interfere in the punishment under the limit set by God, with your intercession? Take heed! Never repeat that mistake again.

Then he ordered Bilal to call the Muslims to the mosque. When they gathered in the mosque, he addressed them thus:

> The Ummahs preceding you met their ruin for the reason that they discriminated among criminals on the basis of their status. They let those lower in status be punished according to the Law, but allowed the high placed ones to go scot free. By God, in whose hand is my life, if Fatima, the daughter of Muhammad had been involved in a case like this, I would have amputated her hand. (Bukhari and Muslim)

The Muslims have been commanded this:

> O ye who believe! Stand out firmly for God, as witness to fair dealing, and let not the hatred of other to you make you swerve to wrong and depart from justice. Be just: that is next to piety: and fear God. For God is well acquainted with all that ye do.(Al Quran V:8)

The Prophet never oppressed any body, yet he was so anxious and careful in the enforcement of the Divine injunctions that he used to invite people to avenge themselves on him if they had even been injured by him. So we find many instances in his life when he offered himself for being avenged upon. Sawad bin-e-Umar says that he once went to see the Prophet with gaudy clothes on. The Prophet on seeing him said, " change them, change them" and gently poked him with the stick (he had in hand at the moment). I said to him:

> O Prophet of God! I shall avenge myself upon you. And he (the Prophet) at once exposed his abdomen before me.

Similarly, he had offered himself to Sawad bin-e-Ghaziyah on the occasion of the battle of Badr, Usaid bin-e-Hazair while talking to him and a certain companion during the distribution of the spoils of war, for their revenge on him because he had gently poked them with his stick.

Referring to these examples established by the Prophet, Dinar, the second caliph had said in reply to the query of Umar-bin-al-'As,the governor of Egypt, whether he would punish the governor of a province for the chastisement of some body (Meaning an ordinary citizen) Tr.)

By God in Whose hand is my life, I shall bring him (the governor) even for revenge, since I have seen the Prophet present himself for revenge.

So we find him strictly adhering to this principle during his ten years term of caliphate. Jabala bin-e-Adham Ghassani to escape revenge for slapping a beduin, had put forth the plea:

> O Amir-al-Muminin! How can you do it? He is a common citizen and I am a king.

To which 'Umar replied:

> Islam has established fraternity and equality between you two. You can excel him in Taqwa, but not in any other way.

Umar by issuing orders of punishment to Abu Musa Ashari, Umar bin-al-'As, his son Abdullah, Abdullah bin-e-Fart, the governor of Hams and Qudam-al-bin-e-Mazoon, the governor of Bahrain, and execution of the limit set by God on his own son Abdullah bin-e-'Umar had established unparalleled precedents.

'Umar's attendance of the court of Zaid-bin-e-Thabit as a defendant, showing displeasure at his paying respect to him ('Umar) saying "It is your initial injustice in this case," sitting by the side of Ubai bin-e-Kab, the plaintiff and consenting to make statement on oath in the absence of a witness that he could produce, and angrily reproving Zaid bin-e-Thabit on his suggestion to Ubai bin-e-Kab for sparing the Amir taking an oath, saying, "Zaid! Unless a common citizen and 'Umar are equal in your sight you are not fit for the responsible post of a judge," is a bright example of equality of men in the sight of law.

Another example of this nature had been furnished by 'Ali in his period of caliphate.In the case of the theft of the armour, he presented himself at the court of Qadi Shuraih when summoned. The defendant was a Zimmi in this case. Qadi Shuraih addressed Ali saying:

"Abu Tureb! Sit by the side of the opponent."

The Qadi realized that Ali had felt his remark, and said, "Abu Tureb! Perhaps you took my remark ill, but it is the demand of equality in the sight of law and judicial process under Islam, that you have to sit by the side of the opposite party."

'Ali replied "I don't feel it that you directed me to sit beside my opponent. What I took to heart was your discrimination of calling me by the title, (Abu Tureb or the father of dust), which was honouring me in comparison to my opponent and as such a manifest injustice."

'Umar had forbidden men to go about with women. He witnessed a certain person praying with women, and flogged him. He said, "By. God, if I was doing a good deed you have been harsh to me. And if I did something evil, you had not informed me of it."

Umar said, "Were you not present when I got it proclaimed?" He replied "No".

Umar threw the lash he had in his hand, before him and said "Take thy revenge on me."

He said, "Not today (some other time)."

Umar said "Well, if you do not avenge yourself on me, forgive me then."

He said, "No, I would not forgive you either." And they parted. Next day when 'Umar met that person, he found, Umar's face a little pale. He said, "Amir-al-Mominin! Perhaps you have taken my words to heart?"

Umar said, "Yes".

He said, "God be my witness, I have forgiven you."

One of the evil traits of character to which Pharroah had degraded himself mentioned in the Quran was that he bad divided his people into high and low and noble and ignoble. And one of these two classes he depressed and degraded. The Quran says:

> Truly Pharoah elated himself in the land and broke up his people into sections, depressing a small group among them. (Al Quran XXVIII 4)

As against this, Islam has it to its credit that bringing the high a little low and elevating the low a little, it created a balance in the society and equality among people. When 'Umar was told by Nafi bin-al-Harith, the governor of Mecca that he had left the freed slave Ibn-al-Bara as his officiating deputy, he ('Umar) inquired about his qualities and was much pleased and said:

> "Why not, our Prophet had said that God would elate some with this Book (Quran) and some he would degrade."

***Right to Seek Justice :*** The very aim and object of the existence of the Islamic State is establishment of justice. God commands the Prophet to proclaim:

> And I am commanded to judge justly between you. (Al Quran XLII:15)

> Say: My Lord hath commanded justice; (Al Quran VI 1: 29)

God says the purpose of commissioning the prophets in the world, revelation of the Scriptures or inspired Books, and the political and fighting force of the Muslims is the establishment of justice in human society:

> We sent afore time our apostles with Clear signs and sent down with them the Book and the Balance (of Right and Wrong), that may stand forth in justice; and we sent down Iron, in which is (material for) mighty war, as well as many benefits for mankind, that God may test who is that will help unseen. Him and His apostle: for God is Full of Strength, Exalted in Might (and able to enforce His will). (Al Quran LVII: 25)

The justice for which the Prophet and after him, the Muslim Ummah as a whole, were commissioned, its norm was also given in great detail so that it may be easy to determine the meaning of this' "Justice" and there may be no ambiguity in the proper understanding of God's will and pleasure:

> O ye who believe! Be ye staunch in justice, witnesses for Allah, even though it may be against yourselves or (your) parents-or (your) kindered, whether (the case be of) a rich man or a poor man, for Allah is nearer unto both (than ye are). So follow not passion lest ye lapse (from truth) and if ye lapse or fall away, then Lo! Allah is ever informed what ye do.
>
> (Al Quran IV: 135)

In this verse not only the meaning of justice has been explained, but all the conditions of the establishment of justice have been put forth. If even one of them is dropped and neglected, justice shall no more be justice but shall become injustice. These conditions are:

1. Do not only establish justice but hold its banner aloft. And where you find it suppressed, do all in your power for its uplift.
2. Bearing of witness should not be for the success or failure of either party but to seek the countenance of Allah, since justice cannot be established without true evidence. Never for a moment be anxious whose interests it affects adversely your own, your parents or your kindred's interests.
3. When testifying in a case not only disregard your relationship with the parties concerned but also be unmindful of their social or economic status, since you can never be a greater well wisher of any body than Allah. Discrimination in evidence is not benevolence but manifest injustice and malevolence.
4. State the facts of the case in your knowledge as they are without any admixture of your own wishes. Wishes pervert the facts, and the person hearing the evidence fails to get to the bottom of the facts, which becomes a hindrance to just decisions.

5. If you state the facts of the evidence vaguely, concealing some and interposing others of your own creation, with a view to save a party, or get one punished, shirking true and impartial evidence, and becoming a means of tyranny and injustice, know it well that your state of mind shall not be hidden from God, and you will not be able to save yourselves from the evil consequences of your doings.

It was in view of this verse of the Quran that 'Umar had written in a letter to Qadi Shuraih:

> In the Majlis-e-Qaza (the court of law) neither try to weigh people, nor wrangle with any body, nor indulge in purchase and sale, nor ever pronounce judgement in a quarrel between two people when you are in a rage.

In short, it is essential for the quality of being just that the person dispensing justice should be free from all such internal and external motivations which can influence a just decision. God says that when you come to sit in judgement, do full justice to it:

> And if ye judge between mankind, that ye judge justly.
> (Al Quran IV: 58)

> Whenever ye speak, speak Justly, even if a near relative is concerned. (Al Quran VI: 152)

In connection with justice, the Quran has also laid down the following principles:

> Life for life, eye for eye, nose for nose, ear for ear, tooth for tooth, and wounds equal for equal.
> (Al Quran V:45.)

And the same rule has been stated at another place in these words:

> The recompense for an injury is an injury equal there to (in degree): but if a person forgives and makes reconciliation, his rewards is due from God: for (God) loveth not those who do wrong. But indeed if any do help and defend themselves after a wrong (done) to them, against such there is no cause to blame. The

> blame is only against those who oppress men with wrong doing and insolently transgress beyond bounds through the land, defying right and justice: for such there will be a penalty grievous. But indeed if any show patience and forgive, that would truly be an exercise of courageous will and resolution in the conduct of affairs. (Quran XLIi: 40-43)

In this verse along with presenting the principle of fit for let in connection with justice, the oppressed person has been directed to restrain himself from oppression in retaliation and persuaded to forgive the oppressor. In other words, he may avenge himself on equal basis if he likes, which will be justice indeed. In case he oversteps in retaliation it will be injustice. And Allah does not love the wrong-doers. But if the oppressed person resorts to forgiveness it will be an act of high mindedness and magnanimity and appreciated by God:

> God commands justice, the doing of good, and liberality to kith and kin, and He forbids all shameful deeds, and injustice and rebellion: (Al Quran XVI: 90)

But "Ehsan" or doing of good, is an individual act. The judiciary of the Islamic state is bound to pronounce judgement according to the dictates of justice when a complaint is made to them. However, the oppressed complainant has all the time the right to withdraw the case against the defendant, and be rewarded for this act of kindness by God. As for the judiciary, it is bound by the commandment:

> If any do fail to judge by (the light of) what God hath revealed, they are (no than) unbelievers.........they are (no better than) wrong.

According to this commandment, it may be an individual, an arbiter, a panchayat, or a regular court of law that judges, must do it by the light of the Book of God and Sunnah of the Prophet. The prophet says:

One day of a just Imam (leader) is better than sixty years of devotional service.

He also said:

> Among the people He has created, God loves most a just Imam. And the one most detestable person in His sight, arousing His wrath, is the Imam who judges unjustly. (Musnad-e-Ahmad)

How the Prophet and the rightly guided caliphs, coming after him, put these commandments into practice, some examples have been mentioned earlier. The Prophet presented himself before people so that they may avenge themselves upon him. 'Umar and 'Ali in their periods of caliphate presented themselves in the courts of law (in the capacity of a common citizen as defendants). 'Umar executed the punishment, prescribed by the limit set by God, in case of his own son, presented himself for being avenged upon by the people who fall offended, chastised his governors in connection with the complaints lodged by common citizens, and removing all the obstacles standing in the way of seeking justice, he made redressal of grievances and deliverance from oppression very easy.

Abu Bakr, appointing 'Umar the Qadi of the Islamic state with its centre at Medina, made judiciary independent of the executive. Umar on coming in authority gave it the shape of an institution, and presenting himself at the court as a defendant, practically demonstrated the superiority of the judiciary over the executive. After him, throughout the Muslim history this system was kept alive. The most important characteristic of this system is that people secured justice free of cost. There were no such things as court fee and the fees of the pleaders. In the Indian subcontinent this system was in practice till the Britishers took over. And the countries that escaped the subjugation of colonialism, this system exists to this day. For example, in Saudi Arabia justice is available for the rich and the poor alike free of cost. Truth to tell, there is no other system of justice in the world that, has not made the high sounding claims of "Equality in the sight of Law" and "Justice for all alike", meaningless by making justice a saleable commodity. How many people are there who can pay the fees that have to be paid to the High Courts and the Supreme Court and the fabulous fees of the advocate pleading their cases at these courts? And if they cannot afford to pay these costs, is it not tantamount to closing the doors of these superior courts of the country upon all such people. And thus deprived of the facilities of getting justice have not all such people been automatically deprived of the protection of law and its support against those who are in possession of the needful resources.

The judicial system of the Islamic state is entirely free from this commercial outlook. Here all the expenses of the establishment of justice are borne by the state. All that is required of distressed person is to knock at the door of the court. And in case he is not satisfied with the judgement of the lower court, he is at liberty to go to the High Court and the Supreme Court. He will not be burdened with any expenses any where. Such a burden on him shall be injustice repeated twice over, that he, coming with the complaint of wrong done to him, may be involved in further financial troubles to get justice.

Moreover, this financial burden in going to the courts discourages poor and indigent people, and establishing the superiority of those in possession of resources further encourages them in their tyranny and oppression.

Islam conferring equality on the rich and the poor, the high and the low, influential and the fundamental, in the sight of the judiciary has made the principle of equality in the sight of law, enforceable in its true spirit, and has brought the fundamental right of seeking justice within easy reach of every citizen.

***Right of Economic Security :*** After 'Fatiha (or the opening surah of the Quran when we start reciting Surah Baqrah (II), in the verses in the very beginning, the following qualities of the Quran and those believing in it, have been mentioned:

> A.L.M. This is the Book; in it is guidance sure, without doubt to those who fear God: who believe in the Unseen, are steadfast in (establish Tr.) prayer, and spend out of what We have provided for them:
>
> (Al Quran II 1-3)

Pondering over these verses it becomes a manifest that belief in the Book of God and the unseen facts stated therein, such as the Entity of God, decrees of God, relating to us men and the rest of the creation, the creation of the universe, creation of Adam, Heaven and Hell, the life Hereafter, and the geni and the angels, two obligations devolve on man. In the sphere of the relationship of God and man, the first and foremost obligation is that he should bow down his forehead before God, and establishing the system of Prayers, he must repeat his covenant with God alleging his own sub-service and God's worshipfulness five times a day.

Immediately after the prayer, the first and foremost obligation devolving on man in the context of relations between man and man, is spending in the way of Allah, or help and support of the needy and the indigent out of that with which God has endowed him. This order of the rights of God and man is not exclusive to this verse, but every where in the Quran we find that Zakat immediately follows Prayer or devotional service to God. Nay, at places the Quran declares the prayers of a person wasted where this worshipping person adopts a miserly attitude in meeting the needs of a needy servant of God. God says in the Quran:

> Seest thou one who denies the judgement (to come)? Then such is the man who repulses the orphan (with harshness), and encourages not the feeding of the indigent. So woe to the worshippers who are neglectful of their Prayers, those who (want but) to be seen (of men), but refuse (to supply even neighbourly needs).
>
> (Al Quran CV1I: 1-7)

The first verse of this Surah now brings before us the fact stated in Surah Baqarah (II) from a different angle. One who does not believe in the unseen or the reward and punishment of the Hereafter, can neither fulfil his obligation to God (Prayers), nor fulfil that of helping his needy brothers through Infaq or spending in the way of Allah. When praying he will manifest lack of earnestness and would like to be seen of men, and the bounty of God he will hoard, neither spending on himself nor on others in need of it. He will kick out the orphan and not only refuse food to the indigent but not persuade others to feed him either. And he will also flatly refuse those asking for loan of very ordinary things of use in daily life. Those adopting this attitude are being warned that such prayers will not at all avail them, but will be thrown back into their faces, and will fail to protect them from the ruination awaiting them for their unfulfilled obligations to the needy and indigent servants, of God.

This is the importance of "the economic problem of men in Islam, and the nature of the injunctions from the Sovereign to the Believers to solve this problem. At more than thirty places in the Quran the payment of Zakat has come up for mention along with the establishment of the system of Prayer, and at more than seventy places Infaq or spending in the way of Allah has been stressed. Unfortunately, the Muslims themselves have assigned Zakat the fifth position in the order of the Pillars of Islam, God only knows for what reason, when the fact is that the Quran has assigned it a position immediately after belief and Prayer, and Fasting and Hajj in order of their importance come after Zakat.

After this preliminary talk on the importance of the economic problem in Islam, let us now see how much stress has been laid on spending in the way of Allah to provide economic protection to man in the Religion of God. What are those measures, adopted to achieve this end, and what the responsibilities devolving on the Islamic state in this behalf. Let us study some of the Quranic verses relating to the injunctions regarding Infaq and inducement to it:

> And those in whose wealth is a recognized right for the needy who asks and him who is prevented (for some reason from asking,); (Al Quran LXX:24-25)

> And in their wealth and possessions (was remembered) the right of the (needy), him who asked, and his who (for some reason) was prevented (from asking).
> (Al Quran LI: 19)

> And establish regular prayer and pay Zakat regularly, and loan to God a beautiful loan.
> (Al Quran LXXII: 20)

In Surah Baqarah (II) after saying "It is not righteousness that ye turn your faces East or West," God goes on to say:

> (Righteousness in this that) you spend of your substance, out of love for Him, for your kin, for orphans, for the needy for the wayfarer, for those who ask, and for the random of slaves; to establish regular prayer and pay Zakat regularly. (Al Quran 11:177)

The order of injunctions in this verse is worthy of note. Among the conditions of belief enumerated herein spending one's cherished goods has come up even before the establishment of prayer. In the same Surah, it occurs again:

> They ask thee what they should spend in the way of Allah Say:
>
> Whatever you spend that is good, is for parents, kindered and orphans and those in want and for way-farers. (Al Quran 11:215)
>
> They ask thee how much they are to spend; Say: What is beyond your needs. (Al Quran II: 219)

Explaining undue stress on Infaq the Quran says:

> In order that it (Wealth) may not (merely) make a circuit between the wealth among you.
> (Al Quran L1X: 7)

And then, to ease man's mind in connection with the dread of diminishing one's good and coming to poverty through Infaq, it was said:

> Whatever goods you spend in the way of Allah benefits your own souls, and ye shall do so seeking the countenance of God. What ever goods you spend in the way of Allah, shall be rendered back to you, and shall not be dealt with unjustly. (Al Quran 11:272)

And further on it has been said:

> (Those who spend of their goods in the way of Allah, by night and by day, in secret and in public, have their reward with their Lord:) On them shall be no fear, nor shall they grieve. (Al Quran II: 274)

The Quran tells us that spending one's goods in the way of Allah does not diminish it but there is an increase in it. This is a dealing altogether profitable and not one of loss. This is not an obligation to the receiver of the goods, but to the person who spends, since it will return to him with manifold profit. And then in the Hereafter, becoming the means of the pleasure of God on his own honour, shall make him deserving of that great reward of the eternal peace and satisfaction which is the real goal of a Muslim's life contrarily, if the goods of this world is hoarded, it will become a means of ruination in this world and in the Hereafter. Below are given some Quranic verses on this theme:

> And they feed, for the love of God, the indigent, the orphan, and the captive—(Saying), we feed you for the sake of God alone: no reward do we desire from you, nor thanks. We only fear a day of distressful Wrath from the side of our Lord. But God will deliver them from the evil of that Day, and will shed over them a light of Beauty and a (blissful) Joy.
>
> (Al Quran LXXVI: 8-11)

> The parable of those who spend their substance in the way of God is that of a grain of corn; it groweth seven ears, and each ear hath a hundred grains. God giveth manifold increase to whom he pleaseth: and God careth for all and He knoweth all things.
>
> (Al Quran 11:261)

> And the likeness of those who spend their substance seeking to please God and to strengthen their souls, is as a garden high and fertile heavy rain falls on it but makes it yield on double increase of harvest, and if it receives not heavy rain, light moisture sufficeth it. God seeth well whatever ye do. (Al Quran II: 265)

> Who is he that will loan to God a beautiful loan, which God will double unto his credit and multiply many times? It is God that giveth (you) want or plenty, and to Him shall by your return. (Al Quran 11:245)

> And there are those who hoard gold and silver and spend it not in the Way of God: announce unto them a most grievous Penalty—On the Day when heat will be produced out of that (wealth) in the fire of Hell, and with it will be branded their forehead, their flanks, and their backs....This is the (treasure) which ye hoarded for yourselves: taste ye, then, the (treasurer, ye hoarded! (Al Quran IX: 34-35)

> And let not those who covetously withhold of the gifts which God hath given them of His Grace, think that it is good for them; nay, it will be the worse for them:

> soon shall the things, which they covetously withheld, be tied to their necks like a twisted collar, on the Day of Judgement. (Al Quran III: 180)
>
> Who pileth up wealth and layeth it by thinking that his wealth would make him last for ever! By no means! He will be sure to be thrown into that which Breaks to Pieces. (Al Quran CIV: 2.4)

Along with extraordinary emphasis on Infaq and instructions to keep away from miserliness. God has also determined for the Muslims the moderate course of spending also, so that they may be spared from excess either way:

> O Children of Adam; Wear your beautiful apparel at every time and place of prayer: eat and drink: but waste not by excess, for God loveth not the wasters. (Al Quran VII: 31)

Here adornment or wearing one's beautiful apparel means proper dress which not only covers the nackedness but is also neat and clean. And the natural urge of food and drink must also be satisfied. However, there should be no wastage due to excess in the matter of dress, food and other needs of man's life. For wastage of the bounties, conferred on man by God, is most detestable in the sight of God. And in the immediately following verses, the negative attitudes of asceticism and Monasticism have been discouraged:

> Say: Who hath forbidden the beautiful (gifts) of God, which He hath produced for His servants, and the things clean and pure, " which He hath provided for sustenance? Say: They are, in the life of this world, for those who believe, and purely for them on the Day of Judgement. (Al Quran VI 32)

Along with the general commandments and instructions, the practical measures adopted for the economic security and prosperity of the individuals of the society are briefly these:

1. Every man has been instructed to take part in the economic struggle, so that he may not be a burden to others.
2. That man can have nothing but what he strives. (Al Quran LIII 39)

3. Determining the limits of approved and forbidden and proper and improper the sphere of striving and action was defined. By imposing restrictions on the sources of income such as interests, liquor, gambling, bribery, shameful pursuits and maintaining houses of ill-repute, purchase and sale of prohibited articles, adulteration, giving short measure or weight, black-marketing, hoarding and such other fraudulent practices, plundering of the society was eradicated, and economic exploitation was stopped.
4. Through prohibition of spending the earned income in ways not allowed by the Shuraih. Squandering and immoderation, luxuriousness and show of pump and pelf, and destruction of goods, the drain of wealth into the wrong channels was stopped, and burning its now in the right direction towards the really deserving individuals, they were saved from deprivation of their rights.
5. By determining the rights of other individuals in the earnings of every individual, is and has been enlisted for the collective system of maintenance of the Islamic state. According to the Islamic Shariah the individual's responsibilities are the following:
   (a) The obligatory maintenances or the responsibility of the support of the parents, wife and children, grand-fathers, grandmothers, both paternal and maternal, grandchildren (offspring of both sons and the daughters), brothers, sisters, aunts (father's sisters), nieces, and other blood relations.
   (b) Zakat which is to be spent on the maintenance of the general run of the needy which have been defined in the Quran. The income from this source shall go towards the support of the needy who ask, and those who don't and also those deputed for the realization of Zakat. Also a part of it will go to encourage and to win the hearts of the fresh converts to Islam, and for the freedom of the slaves and the Muslims in the clutches of the enemies, for the paying the debts of the indigent or the deceased persons, also for maintenance of those fighting in the way of Allah, the

students and other people engaged in the cause of Allah (in such a way that they don't find time to earn their livelihood Tr.) and to help the travellers who have been stranded and have no place to stay and maintain themselves during sojourn.

(c) Additional spending of one's goods or that even after providing for maintenance of family and blood relations, and paying of Zakat, it is incumbent on the individuals with plentiful resources, to go on spending on the support of the, indigent and the needy in the charities. The Prophet says:

> There is a share of the deserving in your goods besides the regular payment of Zakat.
>
> (Musnad-e-Darima, Tirmidhi, Muslim)

The reporter of the tradition, Fatima, bin-e-Qais, also adds that the Prophet quoted those verses of the Surah Baqara (Alquran 11-177) in which it has been said that "It is not righteousness that you turn your faces towards the East or the West, but true righteousness lies in spending one's cherished goods and possessions in the cause of Allah."

In this behalf there is a definite Quranic injunction that whatever one has beyond one's own needs (within the approved limits) should be given over to other needy persons:

> (They ask thee how much they are to spend;) Say: "What is beyond your needs. (Al Quran II: 219)

Under additional Infaq (spending in the way of Allah), three categories of persons have priority, even obligatory rights: The travellers who asked "for food, the needy who asks and one under conditions of emergency, a ravenously hungry or a very thirsty or a naked person, one in need of shelter from heat, cold or rain or in need of medication in case of being ill.

The Quran has granted this right to a disabled or a hungry person:

> It is no fault in the blind, nor in one born lame, nor in one afflicted with illness, nor in yourselves, that ye should eat in your own houses, or those of your father,

> or your mothers, or your brothers, or your sisters, or your father's brothers, or your father's sisters, or your mother's brother's or your mother's sisters, or in houses of which the keys are in your possession, or in a house of a sincere friend of yours: (Al Quran XXIV:61)

According to this Quranic verse to every blind, cripple, ailing and every such person who is incapable of earning his livelihood, every Muslim's house is open where he asks for food. To a common citizen too; not one but many doors are open where he may eat. Besides his own house, he can eat at his parents, grandparents brother's and sisters', uncles', aunts' or a friend's and at the house of those people who have given him keys of their houses, as freely as at his own house. So that it can be said that in the Muslim society it is not possible for any person to go hungry, naked or remain deprived of shelter and medication.

(d) Loan and allowing temporary use of the articles of daily use:

The wealthy persons have also been instructed by Islam to give loans to the needy freely and not to refuse temporary use of ordinary articles of daily use by those in need of them:

> It is not proper for a servant of Allah to disappoint his brother coming to him for a loan, if he is in a position to do so. Kanz-ul-amal, Vol. III, Tradition No. 3581 To give a loan is an act of charity.
>
> (Tabrani, Al-Mojim-al-Sagheer, p. 89)

Surah Ma'oon (CVI1) has been quoted earlier in which even those who are regular in their prayer but refuse temporary loans of articles of daily use to the people in need of them, have been warned with total ruination.

(e) Inheritance, will and alimony to wife and children in case of divorce, and other things. The legacy of a person after his death shall go to meet the requirements of inheritance, will, power and alimony to the wife and children for an appointed term in case he has divorced the wife, according to the law of the Shariah. And from the one third of his bequest that he willed, as permitted by the Shariah, will go to those named in his will.

The number of persons benefited by an individual's earning including those directly under his support, those related by blood the indigent and the needy of the society and the inheritors approaches thousands. And in this way the earnings of an individual in the Islamic Society became a source of beneficence for countless individuals. And he himself in turn must be benefited by such other fountains of benevolence.

Where there exists an economic system in which every individual is looking after the support of dozens of people and they themselves are supporting one another, how many people can remain deprived of board, lodge, clothing and medication in such a society.

The collective support and maintenance in Islam is not that the government taking over all the resources and the properties of the people entirely under its control, and reducing every individual of the nation to the position of a salaried servant, and depriving them of all freedoms, put them to work as it is pleased to do, and in return for this slaving or forced labour, provided them with food, clothes and shelter. As against this, collective maintenance or social justice here takes a different form altogether. Every individual is required to earn as much as he can within the limits of the Shariah, spend the barest minimum to meet his own needs, and what remains after that must go to the comparatively backward and indigent people to help them rise above poverty and indigence, so that gradually the economic disparities may come to an end, and moderation and equilibrium may be established in the society. The Prophet has termed this type of economic striving equivalent to Jihad. He says:

> Striving for charities to sees the countenance of Allah is like Jihad (armed struggle) in the way of Allah.

Before taking up the responsibilities of the state relating to economic security, a detailed discussion of the individual efforts and responsibilities was necessary since in Islam like other rights, this right too is not limited to the sphere of the mutual relation of the individual and the state, but right from an individual the families brotherhoods, small and big organizations and the government, this obligation devolves on every one according to the resources and powers at one's command.

Now let us take stock of the responsibilities of the state in this matter:

> The first and foremost responsibilities of the state is to completely close the doors on the illegal earnings in the society, open up the avenues of earnings and through its economic and educational schemes provided for every individual the necessary education and training for earning honest livelihood so that he may be capable of striving in the economic field.

The second responsibility of the state is that it must help in the fulfilment of all those rights determined by Allah. If a son refuses to support his father it must bring him to comply with the Divine injunction. If a husband denies his wife and children their maintenance charges, it must force him to pay their dues. In short, whatever is due to any one from any body else it must make its payment certain.

The third responsibility of the state is this that it must establish the system of Zakat and realizing the dues of the deserving from those who owe it to them. Take it to them or spend it collectively for their well-being. The fourth responsibility of the state is that it must support those who have no other people to support them. The Prophet has said:

> One who has no guardian or supporter can look to Allah and His Prophet for his support. (Tirmidhi)

Similarly, the Prophet prescribed the responsibility of the state to pay the debts of the deceased and the support of those left behind by him.

> The Muslim who dies leaving behind debts, their payment is my responsibility and the assets left by him shall go to his inheritors. Bukhari, Muslim, Abu Daud, Nasai. One who leaves behind goods, is for his dependents, and he who leaves them without support, their support is my responsibility.
>
> (Tirmidhi, Abu Daud.)

When sending out Ma'az bin Jabal to Yemen (as the governor), the Prophet stated the following principle in connection with the economic responsibilities of the Islamic state:

> Tell them that Allah has imposed on their goods, Sadqah (Zakat) which will be realized from their haves and distributed among their have-nots.
> (Bukhari, Mo'atta, Maslaq, Abu Daud, Nasai, Tirmidhi.)

This economic security is not limited to the Muslims alone but the non-Muslim subjects of the Islamic state have an equal right to it. When 'Umar found a Jew begging, he took him to his own house gave him something to meet his immediate needs and then calling the treasurer of the Bait-al-Mal and instructing him to dole out to him and all others in his position, their daily needs, he said:

By God! It is far from justice and fair play that we realize from them Zizya when they are young (capable of earning) and leave them to fend for themselves when they get old and infirm.

'Umar, during his period of caliphate, has imposed on the Islamic state the provision of the following needs in connection with the economic rights of the citizens:

> (a) The necessities relating to food (b) Clothes for the winter and summer seasons, (c) Conveyance for normal movements and Hajj and Jihad.

So during his ('Umar's) period, stipends were given to the common citizens, even the new born babies, from the public treasury (Bait-al-Mal), and they were totally rid of their economic needs. This use of the Bait-al-Mal continued during the periods of 'Uthman and 'Ali too.

The Islamic state of today, can, on the basis of this principle, keeping in view its own resources and the minimum needs of the citizens, determine their economic rights. Islam has also empowered the state to make additional provisions by further taxation if the normal revenues of the state fail to meet its responsibilities in connection with the collective welfare and social justice in the economic field.

The temperament and the character and the sense of responsibility of the Islamic state relating to the economic security can be judged from a speech of 'Umar the second caliph and from the correspondence of 'Umar bin-e-Abd-ul-Aziz. 'Umar said in connection with his responsibility relating to the distribution of the resources:

> By God! If I live long enough, a herds man looking after his cattle on a hill in Sura (in far off Yemen Tr.) shall get his share out of the goods coming to us (Bait-al-Mal) at his own place, without reddening his face (running about so much that his face gets flushed before he can have his due).

And we come across the following correspondence between 'Umar bin-e-Abd-al-Aziz and the governor of Iraq province relating to the economic rights of the common people to the Bait-al-Mal:

> 'Umar bin-e-Abd-al-Aziz wrote to the governor of Iraq, Abdul Hameed bin-e-Abd-al-Rehman: Give the people their stipends.
>
> Abdul Hameed wrote back in reply:
>
> I have already paid the stipends of the people and still there is enough left as balance in the Bait-al-Mal.

At this, 'Umar bin-e-Abd-al-Aziz wrote the following reply:

> Now look for those who are indebted, and if they have not taken these loans for extravagance and dissipation, pay up their debts from the balance in hand at the Bait-al-Mal.

Abdul Hameed once again wrote to him:

> I have paid such debts, but still there is a balance with us at the Bait-al-Mal.

Umar bin-e-Abd-ul-Aziz wrote the following reply to this:

> Now look for such unmarried people who are poor and would also like that you get them married. Get them married then, and pay the dowers from them to their wives.

Abd-al-Hameed said in his written reply:

> I have got married all such unmarried men whom I could find and yet there is a surplus reserve at the Bait-al-Mal.

Umar bin-e-Abd-al-Aziz then wrote to him:

> Now look for all those that have to pay Zizya and they

> are unable to manage their lands (for want of funds for the inputs). Give all such zimmis enough to enable them to manage their lands, since we don't have to deal with them temporarily for a year or two.

***Right to Abstain from Sin :*** Islam has granted every citizen living within its boundaries to refuse to obey any laws involving transgression and sin. Such refusal to obedience is no crime in the sight of the Islamic law. Rather, obedience to such orders shall be deemed aiding in the crime, since the authority issuing such order shall itself be liable to prosecution for the violation of the commandments of the Sovereign. Recourse to legal action in a court of law against such orders is permitted, which will not only provide legal protection to the person refusing to obey sinful orders, but shall also mete out appropriate punishment to those issuing such orders. In this connection the Quranic verses and the saying of the Prophet have been profusely quoted under elucidation of the heading "Limits of Obedience". They have been summed up in the following two traditions:

> No obedience to the created beings where transgression against the creator comes in.
>
> (Kanz-ul-amal, Tradition No. 294)

> Obedience to the Amir's, is obligatory so long as they do not order things involving transgression against God and disobedience to His Prophet. But when it comes to orders in contravention of loyalty and obedience to God and His Prophet, one is neither bound to hear nor obey. (Bukhari)

***Freedom of Organisation and Assembly :*** The citizens in the Islamic state shall have the right of organization and assembly, conditional to the basic condition of enjoining good and forbidding evils. The aim of the existence of the Muslims has been fully explained in the following verse of the Quran:

> Ye are the best of People, evolved for mankind, enjoining what is right, forbidding what is wrong', and believing in God. (Al Quran 111:110)

This is the mission assigned to the Muslim Ummah as a whole. But if all the Muslims are not devoted whole-heartedly to this mission and lacking in sympathy and an internal urge to strive for this cause, even then there must remain a powerful and duly conscious group among them which remains devoted to it. The Quran says:

> Let there arise out of you a band of people inviting to all that is good, enjoining what is right, and forbidding what is wrong: (Al Quran 111: 104)

So if some people in the Islamic state wish to organize themselves into a party to discharge the duty of enjoining what is right and forbidding what is wrong, and for this purpose they want to assemble for organizational needs or contact people, they shall be entitled to do so. This principle shall also apply to the organization established for the protection of their lawful rights, redressal of grievances and solution of problems, and it shall also apply to the meeting of such an organization, provided the establishment of the organization audits gathering are for the purpose of enjoining good and suppressing evil.

***Right to Participate in the Political Life :*** Since, according to Islam, the vicegerency on earth, has been conferred on the Muslim Ummah as a whole and not any particular individual, group, family, race or a party, every Muslim as a vicegerent has a right to participate in the affairs of the state. It is for this reason that to run the administration of the Islamic state the Quran has laid down the following principle:

> Who (conduct) their affairs by mutual condition.
> (Al Quran XXII:38)

Even the Prophet, who, being guided at every step by revelation, needed no consultation, was commanded:

> And consult them in affairs (of moment).
> (Al Quran 111:159)

In this sense of Shura are included the following political principles of the Islamic state:

1. The Amir and his advisory body be elected by the free will of the people.
2. The people and their representatives should be tree in the matter of criticism, contention and expression of opinion.

3. A true picture of the circumstances and problems confronting the country must be presented to the people so that they may have a correct idea of and opine correctly on them.
4. The people should have the right that only the person enjoining their confidence should rule and one who loses that confidence must be deposed.

***Freedom of Movement and Residence :*** Every citizen of the Islamic state shall have freedom to reside anywhere in the country he likes and move about within the country, and under normal conditions, anywhere in the world outside his own country. The Quran has declared it a crime to oust people from their homes. Commenting on the betrayal of trust on the part of the Israelites and other crimes committed by them, it was said:

> ....And banish a party of you from their homes; supporting one another against them by sin and transgression—and if they come to you as captives, ye ransom them, though their expulsion itself was unlawful for you. (Al Quran, I:85)

Similarly, freedom of migration and moving about has also been conferred by God on His servants:

> Was not the earth of God spacious enough for you to move yourself away (from evil). (Al Quran IV: 97.)
>
> He who forsakes his home in the cause of God, finds in the earth many a refuge, wide and spacious: (Al Quran IV: 100.)
>
> Islam has prescribed banishment for mischief-makers and rebels only. The citizens in general cannot be punished in this way. In Surah Al Maidah (V), along with execution crucification and the cutting off hands and feet from the opposite sides, this punishment was also prescribed for waging war against God and His Apostle, and striving with might and main for mischief through the land: Or exile from land: (Al Quran V:33)

During the period of Ali's caliphate, the headstrongness,

mischief- making, creating tumult had crossed all limits. But All gave them the right of moving about freely in the land and living where they liked. And in his message, giving them assurance of this right he said:

> You are free to move about where you like. However, there is a covenant between you and us that you will not shed anybody's blood unlawfully, not create breach of peace and not oppress anyone. If I find you guilty of any these crimes I shall declare and wage a war against you.

***Right to Wages and Compensation :*** The workers, peasants and other toilers shall have the right that they should not be made to work as slaves (forced Labour, not paid any wages for the work done by them) in the Islamic state. They should be adequately paid for the labour they put in. Compensation should be paid for monetary loss or physical injury. They should not be burdened with harder or greater amount of work than they are physically capable of. And they should be treated benevolently.

Along with this, the Quran has imposed the obligation on the persons receiving the remuneration for service (workdone) that they must put in the best service in return for the wages mutually agreed upon, put in all the energy they can in their work and whatever material, they are given to work with, they should treat it as a trust and should not waste it through misappropriation, unlawful use or in any other form. In connection with a good servant the Quran says:

> Truly the best of men for thee to employ is the (man) who is strong and trusty. (Al Quran XXVJ1I-.26)

Shoaib, (the father in law of Moses), after offering Moses the conditions of service, gave him assurance about his own responsibilities in the capacity of his employer:

> ......But I intend not to place thee in difficulty: Thou will find me indeed if God wills, one of the righteous.
> (Al Quran XXV1I1:27)

What he meant to say was that he on his part would abide by the terms agreed upon between them and would not demand more work from him, and pay in full the remuneration settled. And that he would find him (Shoaib) a true a righteous person.

The first right of the workers among those determined by the Prophet, is that they should not only be paid full wages for the work done, but should also be paid with due haste. He said:

> The wages of a worker should be paid before the sweat of his brow dries up. (Baihaqi, Ibn-e-Majah.)

In another tradition he said:

> God says that he would be the enemy of three persons. One of them would be the person who made a promise in my name and then went back upon his plighted word. The other person would be the one who sold free man or woman (as slave) and consumed the price he got for it. And the third person would be the employer who took full benefit of the labour of a worker and denied him his wages. (Bukhari)

Anas says,

> The Prophet never underpaid a worker. (Bukhari)

The Prophet has also directed:

> Do not employ a worker without first setting the wages for the work to be done. (Baihaqi, Kitab-ai-lyarah)

What he meant to say was that so long as the worker is satisfied with the offer of wages for his work and accepts the terms gladly, he should not be put to work forcibly.

The Prophet has also instructed us to pay the worker a share out of the profit we make through his labour:

> Let the worker have his share out of the profit gained through his labour for God's agent is not to be deprived. (Musnad-e-Ahmad)

*Hidayah*, the well-known book on Muslim jurisprudence, explaining the reason for the share of the worker in a business, says:

> The capitalist is entitled to the profit for the capital he invests in the business and to his working partner, the worker, it accrues because of the labour put 'in by him in that business. (Hidayah, Kitab-al-Mazaribah)

For determination of the wages and conditions of working, the Prophet gave us the following rule:

> The workers should be provided proper food and clothing according to the existing standards at a particular time and they should be burdened with only as much work as they can easily cope with (without totally exhausting him or affecting his health adversely).
>
> (Moatta Imam Malik)

What the Prophet meant to bring home to the employer is that the worker should be paid wages at the rate appropriate to the existing conditions at any particular time or place and the wage earner may be able to provide himself and his dependents with food, clothing, a place to live in, medication, education and other basic needs with what he gets for his work. It is the same as to say that the employer is responsible for the complete support and maintenance of the workers employed by him. And along with that he imposed this condition on the employer that in return for this total support of worker, he should not burden his workers and salaried staff with more work than they can easily put up with. Mawardi stating the responsibilities of the state in this behalf says:

> The Muhtasib should, in case of the men and women workers or salaried staff being harassed by the employer, take him to task, and order them not to take work from them harder than they can endure. Similarly, if they do not provide adequate food for the working animals or put them to work harder than their normal capacity they should take proper action against them.
>
> It was customary with 'Umar to go to the hamlets around midnight on Saturdays, and if he noticed any body burdened with work heavier than his capacity, he managed to lighten the burden on him.
>
> (Moatta Imam Malik)

The incident relating to the Abbasi caliph Mansur has already come for mention under accountability through the judiciary, in which Mansur had been summoned by Muhammad bin-e-Imran, the Qadi of Medina, all the way from Baghdad and compelled to pay the camel owners the freight for the transport of luggage, during the Hajj season, agreed upon mutually, but not paid.

Similarly, a peasant complained to 'Umar bin-e-Abd-al-Aziz that he had sown his field, but the Syrian armies passing that way trampled and ruined it. The peasant was paid ten thousand dirhams by him from the Bait-al Mal.

In connection with the compensation for the acquired properties, it has already come for mention under the right of ownership, that the state cannot acquire the lawfully gained properties of an individual without paying due compensation for them. It can certainly acquire them against his will, in public interest, but cannot deprive the owner of his right to compensation.

***Muslims' Rights***

The fundamental rights that have come ıor mention so far are enjoyed by the citizens irrespective of belief and faith. Now we are going to take up the rights exclusive to the Muslims. We have thrown ample light on the causes of this distinction in the chapter dealing with the "Islamic Concept of the Fundamental Rights."

According to the concept of the Fundamental Rights given to us by Islam, all the rights determined by the Quran and the Sunnah shall be deemed fundamental rights for the Muslims. They include the rights of inheritance, ownership, alimony, dower, Nikah (Wedlock), divorce, Khula or obtaining of divorce by the woman, sale and purchase and all those rights relating to other affairs of human life determined by the Shariah externally, and which are inviolable in as much they cannot be amended or cancelled through Legislation.

Besides, these rights, where in the matter of civil rights all the citizens enjoy equal status, in that political rights there shall be distinction between the Muslims and the non-Muslims. Since the non-Muslims not believing in the Quran and the Sunnah, do not fulfil the condition of allegiance to the principle on which is based the entire system of government, nor are they committed to any covenant with the Sovereign for the practical enforcement of their principles. It is for this reason that Islam does not approve of their heading the Islamic state or appointment to the key posts which are concerned with the shaping of policies. They can however be appointed to high ranking posts where the machinery responsible for the execution of these policies is concerned. In this connection defining the position of the Zimmis, Mawadi has written:

> A Zimmi may become a minister of enforcement, but not a minister with executive and judicial powers. The way these two posts differ in their powers, the condition pertaining to them are also different. This difference is apparent in these four aspects. The first difference is that a minister with executive and judicial powers can himself issue orders and can judge criminal cases but a minister with only the powers of enforcement does not have these powers. Secondly the minister with executive powers can appoint government servants, but not so the minister with powers of enforcement only. Thirdly the minister with the executive powers can take administrative steps in matters pertaining to the army and warfare, while the minister with the powers of enforcement only cannot. Fourthly, the minister with executive powers can realize the dues of the state and pay whatever is due from the state, but the minister with powers of enforcement alone cannot do that. Besides these four conditions there is no other thing barring Zimmi from being appointed to this (key) position.

Dr. Hassan Ibrahim Hassan also concerning with Mawadi writes:

> A Zimmi cannot be appointed to the post of a minister with executive and judicial powers or that of the Prime Minister, since for these posts the condition pertaining "Imamat" (Leadership of the Islamic State) are essential. Bin-e-Taimiyah, Nizam-ul-Mulk and other Muslim political thinkers have also expressed the same opinion concurrently. Under this principle the Muslims shall have the following political rights:

1. The President and the Prime Minister must be Muslim.
2. They shall be elected by the Muslim votes, and the voting right shall also be limited to the Muslims in their election.

3. Since the Quran has laid down the condition for "those in authority" of being from "among you", all the key posts shall go to the Believers, so that they may frame the guiding principles of their policies according to the dictates of the Quran and the Sunnah, and in the capacity of those in authority may enforce them with the cooperation of the Muslims. So under this principle the Chief Justice, Judicial Minister, Commander-in-Chief, Defence Minister, Finance Minister (Nazim-e-Bait-ul-Mal) and other officers having similar importance shall be appointed from among the Muslims.
4. Since the Quran has imposed the condition of "mutual" (consultation) for Shura or the advisory council, (Who conduct their affairs by mutual consultation Al-Quran XLII 38), the members of the advisory council or those of the parliament shall also be elected from among the Believers. This is the Central and most important policy-making institution of the Islamic state. All the affairs of the state shall be conducted in the light of the Quran and the Sunnah. So in this institution only those can do justice to counselling, who not only believe in the Quran and the Sunnah, but have an insight into their teachings, and have also been endowed with the capability to solve problems with reference to them. Besides these rights there are no others in which any distinction is permissible between the Muslims and the non-Muslims.

### *Dhimmis' (Zimmis) Rights*

In connection with the rights of the Zimmis, first of all it must be clarified that the way the Islamic state is committed in connection with the enforcement of and respect for the rights of the Muslims determined by the Quran and the Sunnah, so also it is bound by the limits prescribed by them relating to the rights of the Zimmis. That is to say that the rights of the Zimmis too are inalienable. The Muslims have no power to amend or cancel them. The Islamic state cannot curtail the rights determined by the Shariah. However, it can grant them additional rights provided such additions are not in contravention of the Islamic principles. It comes to this then, that as regards the determination and protection of the rights, the position of the Muslims and the Zimmis is the same in the Islamic state. The rights of both have been guaranteed by the Quran and the Sunnah. The constitutional and legal safeguards enjoyed by the Muslims are also enjoyed by the Zimmis. Rather, from this point of view of safeguards, they are better placed than the Muslims. The Islamic state, in view of the exigencies and the demands of times, can levy additional taxes on Muslims and can acquire their properties in public interest. But it can not put any additional burden on the Zimmis beyond the conditions of the agreement. If the Islamic state fails to protect the lives and properties of the Muslims, and in case of a foreign aggression, are unable to make proper defence of them, it is not bound to return the taxes received from them. But under the similar conditions, they will have to return the amount of zizya realised from the Zimmis. Abu Ubaidah, the Muslim general, had returned the amount of zizya realised from the Zimmis of Hams and Damascus on the occasion of the battle of Yarmuk, since he was not sure they would be able to fulfil their responsibilities of their defence, (engaged as they were in an all-out war against the Christian world Tr.).

Islam has divided the Zimmis into three categories according to their position:

1. Party to a treaty or covenant: Those who agree to live as Zimmis in the Islamic state under a treaty or agreement, during a war or even without it. They are called Muahids or those who are a party to a treaty.
2. The subdued Zimmis: Those who have been fighting up to the last and defeated in a battle might have come under the domination of the Islamic state as subjects. In the terminology of the Islamic Fiqh (jurisprudence) it is also known as All-al-Janwah (those taken by force).
3. Zimmis who have come to be citizens of the Islamic state in some way other than through a peace treaty or during a war, like non-Muslim citizens of Pakistan who opted for Pakistan on partition of the Indian subcontinent. The basic law of the Shariah relating to the Zimmis under an agreement, is this that they shall be treated according to the terms of the agreement, which shall be strictly adhered to, and shall not change with the change in the government

of Islamic state. Their position is eternal, save where the contracting party itself requests certain changes and they are mutually agreed upon. The Islamic state shall not have the power to make alteration in the contract as they please. The Prophet says:

> Take heed! Whoever oppresses a Muahid, or a zimmi covered by an agreement or curtails his rights or burdens him with a heavier burden than he can bear, or acquires something from him against his will, I shall stand up against him as a complaint on the Day of Reckoning. (Abu Daud, Kital'-al-Jihad)

Similarly, he has said in another tradition:

> If you happen to fight against a people and vanish it in a combat, and they agree to pay you tribute to save their own lives and those of their children (in another tradition it was said They enter an agreement with you), do not demand later, a grain more than agreed upon, since it will be unlawful for you to do so.
> (Abu Daud, Kitab-al-Jihad)

Qadi Abu Yusuf explaining the Islamic law in this behalf, says:

> They shall pay only what has been mutually agreed upon to the treaty. The terms of the treaty shall be fulfilled and no enhancement made in the amount of the tribute.

The vanquished non-Muslim subjects of the Islamic state shall have the following rights:

1. Once they agree to pay Zizya, the Islamic state shall become committed to provide them protection (both internally and against outside aggression). Their lives and properties shall be sacred. Neither their properties and possessions can be confiscated nor they can be enslaved.
2. The Zimmis shall have proprietary rights over their properties and they shall be transferred to their inheritors. They shall have perfect authority to sell, gift or mortgage them as they please. The Islamic state shall have no right to oust them.

3. The amount of Zizya shall be determined according to the state of the person concerned—more from the wealthy, less from the middle class and a minimum from the poor. Those having no source of income of their own and dependent on others for their livelihood, shall be exempt from Zizya.
4. Zizya shall be imposed only on the combatants. It shall not be realized from women, children, old and infirm individuals, disabled persons, monks, those engaged in the service of the houses of worship, those permanently ailing and the slaves.
5. The places of worship of the Zimmis shall be allowed, to remain untouched. During the period of 'Umar's caliphate not a single church or synagogue was touched. Qadi Abu Yusuf writes:

   They (the churches and the synagogues) were left alone. They were neither demolished nor tampered with in any other way."

During the period of the Prophet and that of the rightly guided caliphs, the Muslims unexceptionally gave assurance of the protection of their places of worship in all their treaties with the Zimmis, and the later day governments also remained committed to this practice. Besides these special rights of those under a treaty or conquered people, all the three types of Zimmis shall also have the following rights:

1. The Penal Laws of Islam are, generally speaking, the same for the Zimmis and the Muslims. But the Zimmis are exempt in the matter of wine and drinking. According to Imam Malik they are exempt in the matter of fornication and adultery also. He argues from the decision of 'Umar and 'Ali that if a Zimmi is found guilty of fornication, his case should be left to his own millat (people).
2. The civil laws too are the same for the Zimmis and the Muslims. In the matter of proprietary rights and restrictions relating to their possessions. The methods and trade and commerce prohibited for the Muslims are also prohibited for the Zimmis. The dealing involving interests are also

equally prohibited for the Muslims and the Zimmis. However drinking and eating of pork is an exception in the case of the latter. The Zimmis have the right to prepare alcohol, drink and sell it also in their own community. They also have the right to breed pigs, eat its flesh and sell it to their own people. If a Muslim destroys the liquor or a pig belonging to a Zimmi, he will be forced to pay compensation for it.

3. The contract with the Zimmis is eternally binding on the Muslims. Once entering it, they can never walk out on it. But the Zimmis have a right to break this tie whenever they like. However great the crime of a Zimmi against the Muslims their commitment of protection to the Zimmis remains intact. Even if they stop paying Zizya, under a Muslim, make disrespectful remarks about or indulge in destructive criticism of the Prophet, are guilty of molestation of a Muslim women, the tie does not snap. The criminal shall certainly be punished according to the law but shall not be excluded from the protection of the state. Only in the exceptional cases of a Zimmi's joining hands with the enemy of the Islamic state and openly rebelling against it creating mischief and resorting to sedition will make him liable to be dropped out of the contract.

4. The personal affairs of the Zimmis shall be decided according to their own Personal Law. For example, if their Personal Law allows Nikah or marriage contract without witnesses, marriage without dower, second marriage within the period of Iddat or waiting (after divorce or death of the husband), or incest marriage with the eternally prohibited ones, all these shall be deemed allowed for their sake. To a query of Umar bin-e-Abd-al Aziz, Khowajah Hassan Bash had issued the following edict:

   They have agreed to pay Zizya only after the freedom to live according to their belief and faith. Your business is to follow the usage of old and not invent anything new for yourself.

5. The Zimmis shall be perfectly free to observe their religious ceremonies and national symbols in their own localities

and towns. However, they shall not be allowed to openly observe their religious symbols in the Muslim localities. In their own places of worship they shall any way be perfectly free to do as they please. The government shall not interfere with it in the least.

The places whose land belongs to the Muslims and they have specified those places for the observance of their religious symbols, if any old standing places of worship of the Zimmis exist in such exclusive Muslim lands, they shall not be tampered with. If they get demolished, the Zimmis shall have the right to rebuild them. At other places which are not exclusive to Muslim's religious observances, the Zimmis can even build new places of worship.

6. The Zimmis shall have perfect freedom to make arrangements for the religious education of their children, building and running schools for them and preaching and teaching of their own religions among their own community. They shall also be free to state the merits of their religions. However, they shall not be allowed to attack Islam in an antagonistic way (levelling destructive criticism against it and reviling the religious leaders Tr).

An important problem in connection with the Zimmi is how to accommodate them in the Islamic state of today. Where local bodies are concerned they can be allowed all the rights of representation in them. However, their representation in the central and provincial advisory councils or assemblies is an intricate problem. Two courses can be adopted for this purpose.

1. On the basis of separate elections, the Zimmis should be allowed proportional representation. But in the Parliament they would have to remain committed to the legislation according to the dictates of the Quran and the Sunnah. However, in those matters where Quran has itself allowed freedom to exercise their right to act, in such situations they would be perfectly at liberty to express their opinions and put up their suggestions.
2. A separate representative institution be created for the Zimmis where they can solve their own problem as they

please and the government should aid them in giving their recommendations as practical shapes. They should have the authority to legislate and amend the current laws to the extent of their own personal affairs, and their suggestions and recommendations may become enforceable after the approval of the head of the state. They may present their suggestions, complaints and objections concerning administrative affairs and the decisions of the Parliament and the government may consider them sympathetically under the demands of justice and remove the complaints as far as possible.

In this behalf we have no fixed and accepted principle before us. Any appropriate course can be adopted to meet the situation. What Islam aims at and has at heart is that the non-Muslim subjects of an Islamic state should not interfere with the way Islam likes to be demonstrated as a way of life. At no stage in its working and rule in an Islamic state the non-Muslim subjects should become a strongly resistant force. Islam stresses benevolent treatment of them, safeguards their rights more indulgently than those of the Muslims, offers them the shade of its blessings and makes them a partner in its fruits and blessings, but cannot allow them to become a stumbling block for itself. That is why it keeps them away from such positions which are concerned with the leadership and guidance in the interpretation and elucidation of the Shariah and the formulation of policies and laws in its light.

# 4

# Rights in Islam

Anyone who undertakes to speak of 'Islam and Humanity' in an age in which, the universal respect for and observance of human rights and fundamental freedoms for all, without distinction as to race, sex, language, or religion, has been highlighted by the Charter of the United Nations (Art. 55), followed by the Declaration of Human Rights of 10th December, 1948 and by the two Covenants that have been subsequently drawn up on social and cultural rights and on civil and political rights, ought to provide the contextual framework of human rights as understood both in the West and in Islam.

In this way, we will throw into better relief those aspects of human rights as conceived by Islam which may be radically different from those normally associated with a modern approach. At the conclusion of the Second World War, when thought was again turned to the orderly functioning and reconstruction of the international community of mankind, the primary purpose which inspired the founding fathers of the United Nations was undoubtedly 'to save succeeding generations from the scourge of war, to maintain international peace and security.'

But the indispensable means for the realisation of that purpose in their thinking could only be the recovery of the individual from the super-incumbent weight that had been imposed on his freedom, initiative and growth by totalitarian regimes. Hence, the emphasis in the United Nations Charter on 'Human Rights and Fundamental Freedoms.'

The full extent of that crisis which had brought about a disruption in the soul-life of the modern man had never been fully appreciated by those publicists who in the mid-twentieth century had set out to make a general survey of the political, economic, social, cultural or humanitarian implications of human rights and fundamental freedoms that had to be guaranteed to the people of United Nations, since, the unhappy predicament of modern man had not as then been fully comprehended.

The forces of modern history have been virtually at war with the harmony of human life. This generation which has been actually involved in the chaos and the crises that have overtaken human civilization is not able to appreciate the extent to which the individual had been made subservient to the authority of totalitarian states that have emerged in the wake of mass society. Ortega de Gessa in The Revolt of the Masses speaks of the characteristics of such societies.

In the welter of contending voices that are even now being heard from the protagonists of the philosophy of enlightenment, and the pioneers of secularist liberalism and Marxist socialism, we have not as yet been able adequately to appreciate the extent of the disruption that has taken place in the contemporary value system.

On the one hand, thanks to the technological and scientific revolution of our times, the social environment of modern man, on a world-wide scale, has become much more integrated, in the sense that the days of isolated civilizations and localised cultures are gone never to return. There was a time when diverse cultures and civilizations could coexist and grow side by side without interaction or interference one with the other. Now, largely due to the application and transport, modern man, no matter where he may be, is involved in the total life of humanity as never before.

On the other hand, although the overall external shell in which the snail of humanity is living has been woven into a more or less homogeneous pattern through the interplay of all those factors which go to define the social and cultural environment of modern man, the springs of modern man's actions are ruled by the most contradictory philosophies of life.

There is, to begin with, the religion of love and universal brotherhood brought to us by the Prophets of universal religions and a great deal of our life, at least in Asia and Africa, is lived as though religious norms even today were the decisive criteria in evaluating the worth of man's activities.

Then .there is the philosophy of life founded upon the secularist approach which, in the name of liberalism, places a high degree of emphasis on the value of the dignity and freedom of the individual and upon the gospel of tolerance, mutual discussion and debate as a means of organising political institutions with a view to securing the development of human personality.

This approach had been countered by the challenge from the Marxist socialists who are prepared to surrender the value of human individuality at the altar of new gods who must be worshipped in the temple of dialectical materialism. Their claim for social justice, security and a planned social order as prime movers of social change in the requisite direction are well known.

The arrogance of race and of power, the worship of the cult of saviours and of heroes who applaud the military virtues of conquest, total discipline and blind obedience, seem to triumph precisely because of the confusion in thinking which is reflected by this western secularistic approach to life. Modern man is so completely caught up in this confusion that he is prepared to sell his soul to anyone who offers him the chance to enjoy what he considers to be the good things of life—the ability to 'eat, drink and be merry.'

## Human Relations

There is a fundamental difference in the perspectives from which Islam and the West each view the matter of human rights. The Western perspective may by and large be called anthropocentric in the sense that man is regarded as constituting the measure of everything since he is the starting point of all thinking and action. The perspective of Islam on the other hand is theocentric-God conscious.

Here, the Absolute is paramount and man exists only to serve his Maker, the Supreme Power and presence which alone sustains his moral, mental and spiritual make-up, secures the realisation of his aspirations and makes possible his transcendence. It is this which constitutes the decisive distinction between the two attitudes.

The Western tradition of liberty is evidenced by the most notable of its charters of rights: the Bill of Rights consequent on the English Revolution of 1689, the Bill of Rights promulgated by the State of Virginia in June 1776, the Declaration of Independence issued by the thirteen American States Constitution of 1789. The Declaration of Rights of Men and Citizenship issued by the Constituent Assembly of France in 1789, and later incorporated word by word in the Revolutionary Constitution of 1791 and again more recently in our own time in the Soviet Constitution of 1939, are in the same tradition.

Here, the rights of man are seen in a setting which has no reference to his relationship with God, but are posited as his inalienable birthright. The student of growth of Western civilization and culture notices throughout that the emphasis is on human rights within the framework of an anthropocentric perspective of human destiny. Each time the assertion of human rights is made at, it is done only to secure their recognition from some secular authority such as the state itself or its ruling power.

In marked contrast to this approach the strategy of Islam is to emphasize the supreme importance of our respect for human rights and fundamental freedom as an aspect of the quality of religious consciousness that it claims to foster in the heart, mind and soul of its followers. The perspective is 'theocentric' through and through. Man has first to believe in the cardinal doctrine:

> "There is no God but God and Muhammad is His Prophet."

Before he can hope to do good deeds, the emphasis in the Holy Quran is on securing the transformation of the quality of man's consciousness. Man is asked to live and work in full awareness that he must show obedience to the Will of God.

Islam in its turn affirms the grand tradition of the development of the institution of universal religions, whose tradition, according to the Holy Quran, was consummated in the mission of the last

Prophet by means of the revealed word communicated to him by process of divine revelation.

It seems at first sight, that there are no human rights or freedoms admissible to man in the sense in which modern man's thought, belief and practice understand them; in essence, the believer has only obligations or duties to God since he is called upon to obey the Divine Law, and such human rights as he is made to acknowledge stem from his primary duty to obey God.

Yet paradoxically, in these duties lie all the rights and freedoms. Man acknowledges the rights of his fellow men because this is a duty imposed on him by the religious law to obey God and the Prophet and those who are constituted as authority to conduct the affairs of state.

In everything that a believer does his primary nexus is with His Maker, and it is through Him that he acknowledge his relationship with the rest of his fellow men as even with the rest of the creation. In the words of the Quran:

"Man has been created only to serve God."

And further he alone is acceptable who has acquired nearness to God.

This distinction between the attitudes of Western man and a Muslim is implicit in the Quranic view of life which divides its functions into *huqoo qullah* or obligations to God-and haqoo qunnas or haqoo qulabad obligations to society. The former category embraces matters like prayers, the need for ritual purity of mind and body, etc., primarily the personal concerns of the individual; the latter category has a social aspect.

In both cases the foundation for 'righteous action' whether on the individual or social plane is no other than the quality of consciousness or niyyat which directs all man's actions to the sole purpose of obeying the will of his maker, in order to please his ever-watchful Lord and Master, who sees even the innermost thoughts and motivations that impel him to act.

He is eventually to return to his Maker and will have to render an account of what he did with the opportunities with which life provided him to do that which was demanded of him by the Divine

Law, and his accountability is absolute which constitutes the sanction which Islam provides to secure the believer's obedience to the demands that the Divine Law makes upon him.

The haqoo qunnas is obligations to society, in the last resort and come within the scope of the jurisdiction or authority of the state in Islam, and relate largely to what in our own time are treated by Western thinkers as constituting secular affairs and secular dealings or relationships between man and man.

It was in relation to this aspect of enforcing obligations to society that the first four rightly guided Caliphs, in view of the nascent stage through which the Ummat in the early days of Islam had to pass, were forced to keep 'a mild form of patriarchal watch whenever necessary and even interpreted the religious injunctions in their application to new conditions of life in consultation with their companions.' But by doing this they did not claim 'spiritual leadership' of the community.

Indeed haqoo qullah and haqoo qunnas were as binding on the Caliphs themselves as on any other believer who was a member of the community. The Caliph was himself accountable directly to God no more and no less than the humblest citizen of the realm, and obedience to the Caliph so long as he conducted the affairs of the community according to the Book of God and the Practice of the Prophet was based on the divine injunction:

> "Obey God, obey the Prophet and those who are acting as constituted authority from amongst you."

This accountability, in the last resort, was owed to the Maker, and the believer knew that even if he erred in disobeying the order of the Caliph and escaped the punishment prescribed for such disobedience, he would eventually be punished on the day of judgment when his accounts would be audited with merciless severity in respect of those aspects of his conduct which injured the rights of others. This is the sense in which though man has no rights within a theocentric perspective, only duties to his Maker, these duties in their turn give rise to all the rights, including those contained within the modern understanding of human rights.

This mode of approach to the problem of human rights has the obvious advantage of dispensing with the need to provide and implement separate procedures for giving effect to human rights since, within the religious context of Islam, no one escapes the penalty for violating the rights of others, and state power is only an earthly agent of the divine power acting by virtue of delegated authority to enforce the Divine Law.

The ruler himself, if he betrays his trust, will also be punished. Since both are bound by the Divine Law, there can, in the strict theory of the Islamic law, be no conflict between the state authority and the individual.

This view is fully reflected in the very first address given by the First Caliph of Islam when elected to his office as Head of the Muslim State which had been founded by the Prophet:

> "My fellow men! I call God to witness, I never had any wish to hold this office; never aspired to possess it. Neither in secret nor in the open did I ever pray for it. I have agreed to bear this burden lest mischief might raise its head. Else, there is no pleasure in leadership. On the other hand, the burden placed on my shoulders in such as I feel I have not the inherent strength to bear, and so cannot fulfil my duties except with Divine help. You have made me your leader, although I am in no way superior to you. Cooperate with me when I go right; correct me when I err; obey me so long as I follow the commandments of God and His Prophet; but turn away from me when I deviate."

Even he who is called upon to handle the affairs of the state is within the grip of Divine Law, and cannot claim any special privileges or prerogatives or immunities.

The affairs of the people are to be run for the benefit of the people as a whole. No Caliph had any special privilege attached to his person. As Abdul Latif points out, he was at best only first amongst equals. When food and clothing had to be rationed in Medina he had but to receive his share just as any other ordinary citizen; every man and every woman had the right to question him on any matter touching the affairs of state; he must appear, as did not Caliphs Umar and Hadrat Ali, before subordinate judges appointed by them, to answer charges against them. The same author goes on to add:

> "The economic system of life formulated by the Quran, laying a special emphasis on the uplifting of the economically depressed, under which a state levy was to be collected from the rich for the relief of the poor, was rigidly enforced by the state. The exchequer of the state was considered to be the treasury of the people; the surplus, if any, accruing at the end of the year came back to the people in the form of annuities distributed on the basis of individual needs."

The Quranic injunctions governing the status of women, as independent economic units functioning in their own individual right, were scrupulously respected and upheld. Similarly, security of life and property and freedom of conscience were guaranteed to non-Muslim minorities who were styled Dhimmis. The Dhimmis were protected by the Prophet of God. The Prophet had proclaimed, 'I shall myself be the complainant against him greater than he can bear or deprive him of anything that belongs to him.' Indeed so mindful was he of their welfare that a few moments before he expired, the thought of the Dhimmi came to him. He is reported to have said:

> "Any Muslim who kills a Dhimmi has not the slightest chance of catching even the faintest smell of Heaven. Protect them; they are my Dhimmi."

In a moment of like remembrance, Caliph Umar, as he lay assassinated, exclaimed, "To him who will be Caliph after me, I commend my wish and testament—Dhimmi are protected by Allah and the Prophet. Respect the Covenants entered into with them, and when necessary, fight for their interests and do not place on them a burden or responsibility which they cannot bear."

Indeed, Islam went further in catering for the welfare of the human race by securing the consent of the believers to certain basic principles guaranteeing its preservation in times of war. These are the principles of justice and moderation laid down by Caliph Abu Bakr for the guidance of the first expedition into Syria:

> "Be just; break not your plighted faith; mutilate none; slay neither children, old men nor women; injure not the date-palm nor burn it with fire, nor cut down any fruit-bearing tree; slay neither flocks nor herds nor camels, except for food; per chance you may come across men who have retired into monasteries, leave them and their works in peace."

The foregoing illustration is typical of the emphasis on what man is not to do, yet the rights of others are implied even when the principles are formulated as prohibitions on the believers.

On the more positive side, the Prophet's last Khutba (congregational address) on the occasion of his final pilgrimage provides the earliest declaration ever made in the history of mankind of what might be called the obligations that were imposed upon believers:

> "Then the apostle continued his pilgrimage and showed the men the rites and taught them the customs of their hajj. He made a speech in which he made things clear. He praised and glorified God, then he said, 'O men, listen to my words, I do not know whether I shall ever meet you in this place again after this year. Your blood and your property are sacrosanct until you meet your Lord, as this day and this month are Holy. You will surely meet your Lord and He will ask you of your works. He who has a pledge let him return it to him who entrusted him with it; all usury is abolished, but you have your capital. Wrong not and you shall not be wronged. God has decreed that there is to be no usury and the usury of Abbas b. Abdul Muttalib is abolished, all of it. All bloodshed in the pagan period is to be left unavenged. The first claim on blood I abolish is that of b. Rabia b. al-Harith. Abdul Muttalib (who was fostered among the b. Layth and whom Hudhay killed). It is the first bloodshed in the pagan period which I deal with. You have rights over your wives and they have rights over you. Your have the right that they should not defile your bed and that they should not behave with open unseemliness. If they do, God allows you to put them

> in separate rooms and to beat them but not with severity. If they refrain from these things they have the right to their food and clothing with kindness. Lay injunctions on women kindly, for they are prisoners with you having no control of their persons. You have taken them only as a trust from God (bi amanatillah) and you have the enjoyment of their persons by the words of God, so understand my words, men, for I have told you. I have left with you something which if you will never fall into error—a plain indication, the Book of God and the Practice of His Prophet, so give good heed to what I say. Know that every Muslim is a Muslim's brother, and that the Muslims are brethren. It is only lawful to take from a brother what he gives you willingly, so wrong not yourselves."

## Universal Laws

Talking about the sum and substance of the various human rights and the fundamental freedoms which have been incorporated in the Universal Declaration of Human Rights of 1948, Syed Abdul Latif sums up the position as follows:

> "The twin aim of this Declaration is one the one hand to equip the individual to live a free life considered successively as (i) physical organism; (ii) a moral personality; (iii) a worker; (iv) an intelligent being and (v) a member of a community and of a polity, and on the other to help the individual so equipped to make his contribution to international amity or the peace of the world. For the student of the Quran not one word in the preamble or in the objective of the Charter, and not a single article in the text of the Universal Declaration of Human Rights, will seem unfamiliar."

Under a creed which places man next to God, and brushes aside distinctions of race, colour and birth, and calls upon all mankind to live together as a family of God or as a 'fold' every member of which shall be a shepherd or keeper unto every other and be accountable for its welfare,' the Universal Declaration of Human Rights must follow as a basic corollary, or an extension of the Quranic programme. But a mere declaration of them will not carry humanity far. Several questions call for attention from the Quranic point of view.

The questions he raises concern first the impulse underlying the Charter of the United Nations, and the Universal Declaration of Human Rights adopted in pursuance thereof. Is the scheme in the interest of or for the good of humanity as a whole, or is it a practice to serve the interest of a particular country or group of countries? Secondly, looking at the list of rights covered by the Universal Declaration, he asks if it is possible for any country claiming to be civilized at the present hour to say with confidence that all the rights are observed by it, or that it may serve as a pattern for the rest.

It is obvious that the initiative for implementing them must come from the government or legislature of each country. Is the system of political life in every country such as may place in high office the type of men who may have the urge and the high-mindedness to respect the Declaration and implement its provisions? Lastly, he considers the world order which is the aim of the two documents, and which argues a common purpose acceptable to all the countries of the world. As things stand, the world is divided, broadly speaking, into two camps—the Soviet and the American.

A world arrangement, whatever its form, will be possible only on the basis of some sort of reconciliation between the two contending ideologies, or by building a half-way house for mutual cooperation. Is such a reconciliation possible? He surveys possible answers to these disturbing questions, and records as his opinion that there is a vast discrepancy between the provision of these rights contained in the Universal Declaration and the actual practices of the people of the modern West. In the words of Professor Hitti:

> "Unfortunately during the last decade or two, in particular, the impact of the West has not been entirely for good. There is a striking contrast between the humanitarian ideas professed by Western missionaries, teachers, and preachers, and the disregard of human values by European and American politicians, and

warriors; a disparity between word and deed; and overemphasis on economic and nationalist values."

The behaviours of the so-called advanced nations during the last two wars waged on a scale unknown in history; the ability of Western man let loose those diabolic forces which are the product of his science and his machine and which now threaten the world with destruction; their intervention in the Near East, particularly in the handling to the Palestine problem by America, England, France, and other nations, all these have worked together to disillusion this man of the near-East who has been trying to establish an intellectual rapprochement with the West. It is these actions of the West which alienate him and shake his belief in the character of Western man and his morality on both the private and the public levels.

## Ideals in Islam

It is within the context of such evaluations of the negative impact in any practical terms of the Universal Declaration of Human Rights that we can point the excellence of the strategy with which Islam has enjoined upon its members the obligation to acknowledge and implement human rights. Islam is primarily interested in securing for its believers 'right belief and right conduct, but in accordance with its teachings the conduct is never right unless it is based on right belief and is consciously willed.

Islam is an enemy of all mechanical actions. One cannot in Islam perform prayers without forming conscious intention to pray; one cannot give Zakat (alms) without consciously intending to do so; one cannot fast without forming conscious intention to fast; you cannot go on pilgrimage and perform the prescribed rites without being aware of their significance and without the formation of conscious intention to do so. This 'conscious intention' is the core of the matter and the Prophet said that the niyyat (intention) of the Momin (believer) to do the deed, in obedience to the Law of God, was better than mere external conformity with the terms of the conduct prescribed by such law (Al-niyyatul Momin Khairun Mined Amalhi).

Since, it is in the inwardness of his being that such a conscious willing intention can be formed, Islam takes good care to insist that its primary purpose is to produce the Saliheen (righteous people), the Muttaqis (self-controlled people) and the Sadiqeen (people who adhere to truth). It is the transformation of the old Adam in man into an expression of the Divine that forms the essence, if not the quintessence, of the strategy of Islam.

The Western world believes that mechanical conformity to the pattern of conduct, prescribed by the law of the state or by some such authority, is sufficient to secure public order and universal peace. In other words, its procedure is to attempt to influence from outside the inner condition of man believing that social, political economic and other institutions are capable of influencing the individual character. It is submitted that this is a fallacious approach; only slaves can be thus handled, not free people.

Islam, on the other hand, begins by inviting man to accept the paramountcy of the power of the Lord, his own servitude and bondage to the will of his Master who is the Sovereign Ruler of the universe; in the last resort it redeems him by prescribing norms of behaviours by which he is to regulate his life. In the words of Professor D. De Santillana:

> "We may agree with the Muslim jurists when they teach that the fundamental rule of law is liberty...God has set a bound to human activity in order to make legitimate liberty possible for all; without the 'bounds of God,' liberty would degenerate into licence, destroying the perpetrator himself along with the social fabric."

This 'bound' is precisely what is called law, which restrains human action within certain limits, forbidding some acts enjoining others, and restraining the primitive liberty of man so as to make it as beneficial as possible either to the individual or to society. Whatever their form, these rules tend to the same end and have the same purpose, that is, the public weal (maslahah). Accordingly, law, divine in its origin, human in its subject-matter, has no other end but the welfare of man, even if this end may not at first sight be apparent; for God can do nothing which does not express the wisdom and mercy of which He is the Supreme source. The Quran itself provides clear justification for such a thesis:

> "In the name of Allah, the Beneficent, the Merciful. Nay, I swear by this city—and thou art an indweller of this city—and the begetter and that which he begot, we verily have created man in affliction: thinketh he that none hath power over him? And he saith: "I have destroyed vast Wealth" thinketh he that none beholdeth him? Did we not assign unto the parting of the mountain ways? But he hath not attempted the Ascent-All, what will convey unto thee what the Ascentis! It is to free a slave, and to feed in the day of hunger an orphan near of kin, or some poor wretch in misery, and to be of those who believe and exhort one another to perseverance and exhort one another to pity. Their place will be on the right hand. But those who disbelieve our revelations, their place will be on the left hand. Fire will be an awning over them."

The title of the Surah is Al-Balad or 'the City,' and it represents the condensed essence of the wisdom upon what may be called the subject of civic rights in the context of the development of monotheistic religion. By the word 'City', by which the verse begins, is meant Mecca. The Surah is in the nature of a 'charter of freedom' given to man after the prayer of Ibrahim for the foundation of a city by one of his descendants—the Prophet of Islam—had been answered.

It draws attention to the evolution of religion and man from Ibrahim to Muhammad—the entire period of Semitic civilization—and Mecca as its place of birth and completion.

Man has been created to face difficulties, and to help him confront these trials with fortitude he has been reminded that there is some 'power' that is an overseer of his deeds, namely his Lord and Master who sees him through and through. The surah goes on to recount the grace of God to man evidenced by the conferment of powers of sight and of speech.

Furthermore, man has been shown two conspicuous ways and now the choice is his, either to elect to negotiate the way of truth or of falsehood to choose the good or evil deed. Of these two possible choices the path of righteousness consists in siding with the truth and of doing good deeds. This is the uphill or higher way, and the highest deed available to the believer is to 'free a slave'. This constitutes not only physical freedom, but moral, mental and spiritual freedom, as much from other human beings as from one's lower self. It is this freedom from necessity that 'freeing the slave' expresses. This amounts to securing the emancipation of man from virtually all manners of servitude.

It imposes on man a whole range of social duties—freeing the slave, feeding the orphan, caring for 'the poor wretch in misery'—and these duties which confer corresponding rights on all. Over and above these are the duties to believe, and exhort one another to patience and to mercy. Man must believe in the 'Unseen', he must believe in 'all the Prophets' in 'the Angels', in all the 'revealed books' including those that have preceded the Quran. Man's ultimate return is to God who is his Creator, and his liability to render account is absolute.

While facing the tests and trials of life, a believer is called upon to be 'patient and to pray' and to show 'compassion and mercy to others'. Those who can adhere to this way of life and exercise their power of choice in conformity with the tenets of the Divine Law are declared to be the 'people of the right hand' and those who disbelieve are characterised as the 'people of the left hand.' It is this distinction which is vital.

Islam presents man with a charter of human liberty within a religious framework which emphasizes the necessity of his being aware of his responsibility and accountability. In the earlier forms of religious belief and practice, the injunctions prescribed to regulate man's conduct were conched as 'absolute commandments', as for instances in the Ten Commandments given by Moses.

In those cases the obedience of the believer was complete if he conducted himself in accordance with the law; at worst even mechanical conformity was enough. But the Quran is also the furqan. That is to say it is book that makes exercise of discretion and discrimination possible for man, in that it outlines for him the possible courses of conduct that are open to him as a free agent and invites him to choose the difficult uphill way; to choose the right side with truth and to stand steadfastly against all odds.

Islam makes the believer his brother's keeper, particularly if the brother is helpless, uncared for or unprotected. It extends the sphere of his responsibility by commissioning him to believe, because without proper belief there is no proper conduct. He is, therefore, asked to base his conduct on right belief taught through the revealed Word of God contained in the Quran. He is also invited to be a missionary in the cause of Islam, to become a diligent crusader in the cause of inviting his fellow men to the way of patience, to show fortitude and compassion so long as his earthly life lasts.

Should he do all this, he is rightly guided and will be duly rewarded by the grant of Eternal Life; real life as opposed to this life which is only the seed-bed of the Hereafter. That life which is to come is better and eternal; this life exists only to provide the opportunity to win the reward of that life. If he uses this to its full advantage, not only will the believer achieve success here and now, but will also gain the reward of Eternal Life in the Hereafter. If the life of man is to be located in the conceptual framework which results from close study of the Holy Book, the position of man in the scheme of things must be viewed not as though he were a finished product, but rather as an evolving being, in a state of transition.

Broadly speaking, man is to be regarded as one who is here on the earth to spend his time as though it constituted a transitional phase which will one day be brought to an end by the most certain of all events, namely, his death. During this interim phase he cannot, on his own, hope to know the path he should pursue in order to enable himself to reach higher levels of his being.

Just as it is inconceivable, seeing the rose bush embedded in manure and covered in thorns, to imagine the beauty of the rose it will one day produce, it is equally impossible to envisage the final phase of man's evolution in which he is destined to reach his highest fulfillment and expression. As the gardener prunes the rose to encourage yet more beautiful blooms, so process of taqwa in the life of the believer.

Instead of abandoning himself completely to the animal impulses within him he must learn to acquire self-control so that the energy available within him does not exhaust itself on the animal plane of his existence, but is transmuted into higher forms of being capable of surviving the ravages of death and of enjoying the reward of higher, better and eternal life.

Human rights conceived from the anthropocentric perspective are treated by Western thinkers as thought they were no more than an expedient mode of protecting the individual from the assaults that are likely to be made upon him by the authority of the state's coercive power by the unjust laws that may be imposed by the power of the brute majority to deny man the possibility of self-development.

Islam, on the other hand, formulates, defines and protects these very rights by inducing in the believers the disposition to obey the law of God, the practice of his Last Prophet, and to show obedience to those constituted authorities within the realm who themselves are bound to obey the law of God and the practice of the Prophet and conduct man's affairs accordingly.

Furthermore affirmation of those rights is to enable man not only to secure the establishment of those conditions in terms of which the development of man as an individual on the earth may be possible, but also to enable man to so conduct himself inwardly as well as outwardly, that he may be able to obey the Divine Law, that only his Maker is qualified to impose on him. By accepting to live in bondage to this Divine Law, man learns to be free.

Islam terminates the era of revealed religions, declares man free by telling him that no other Prophet hereafter would come, indicates the straight road to be traversed by him, and in the Holy Book provides sufficient guidance to enable him to choose. It is now for him to choose. Depending on the choice he makes, the road he takes will lead him either to Heaven or to Hell.

It is quite impossible within the scope of this chapter to do full justice to all aspects of our subject. But before concluding, there is a question which must be answered. The question so frequently asked by Western scholars is why Islam has insisted so strongly on rewards and punishments? Why the emphasis on Heaven and Hell? The answer to their question turns on the interpretation of freedom.

Islam, a religion of mature minds, gave man complete freedom in the conduct of his life for the first time in history. To this freedom were annexed the consequences of his choice. Given the particular nature of man, true freedom lies only in obedience to God's law; only when he disobeys this law and submits to the rule of the lower passions that stem from his animal nature is man condemned to bondage. It is with this in mind that the Quran asks, "have you seen that person who has taken his lower patience as his gods?"

In disobeying God man acts counter to his own nature and reduces himself to slavery. It is too his obedience to God which itself ensures that he shall retain the capacity to be free and responsible. Heaven and Hell are not locations, but merely names for the states of man's being:

> He makes heaven or hell for himself by the way he conducts his life. Rewards and punishments are not imposed from outside but follow as natural consequences of what a man does with his life here below.

God is not some kind of policeman who enforces the law, but His Prophet sent down to help humanity is the warner and guide. He, through the revelation from God, has told us what we must do if we wish to avoid the many pitfalls along the way and make the most of the opportunities which life on earth offers. According to Islam, human action has an objective quality inherent in it, and it is this which overtakes man either as punishment if his conduct be bad, or as reward if it be good.

***The Solution :*** How can we best sum up the contribution Islam can make to the world today? In a lecture delivered by Arnold Toynbee in 1948, under the title "Islam—the West and the Future," he observed that Islam could provide the solution to two of the main problems of the present day, family those of racial discrimination and of alcoholism. But these are no more than symptoms of a far deeper malaise.

There is neither spiritual nor practical reason why Islam should confine itself to the solution of these issues rather than to other far more deeply-rooted problems now confronting mankind. The mission of Islam is to face all such problems and to offer a solution by showing mankind the true path he should follow to gain salvation in this world and the next.

Let us determine the solution by first of all defining the need. What is mankind's greatest need today? How can Islam meet this need? According to Holy Revelations the basic issue in man's life has been, and will be till the Day of Judgment, the question of worship. Who is to be worshipped and how is He to be worshipped? Let us deal with the first question:

> "Who is to be worshipped? Writers and thinkers in the West during the Age of Enlightenment and the Age of Materialism in the 18th and 19th centuries when these ideas were first raised, sought to solve the problem by making it disappear."

Their advice was 'Forget about this issue, it is of no concern whatsoever; live life and enjoy it, if you choose, do not worship anything at all.' By freeing man from the bondage of religion they thought to offer him an unprecedented opportunity of finding happiness on this earth. But their thinking was based on two major illusions. The first illusion was the belief that humanity would attain happiness, and would experience constructive development when it rejected religion.

Indeed the West has progressed tremendously, both technologically and scientifically, since it rejected religion. This very progress fostered the illusion in the hearts of men. They forgot that religion in itself was not the force that held them back, but their own interpretation which, since the Middle Ages in Europe, had obstructed their progress.

However, they overlooked a more important factor—that the scientific and technological progress achieved by Europe after neglecting its religion was not the first, nor even the fundamental ingredient of life. It cannot by itself establish a sound human life.

Only now is the West coming increasingly to realise this, as they recognize that the absence of spiritual values is the main reason behind the anxiety, confusion, madness, suicide, many other psychological and nervous disorders, and the feeling of perplexity and illusion among youth, all of which constitute a threat to the security, peace and welfare of humanity, despite all the material progress achieved during the last two centuries.

The second illusion is the related thought that man can do without worship altogether. This naive illusion is not borne out by our knowledge of man's history from his earliest known origins up to the present time. Whether in the ancient or the modern world 'worship' in some form or the other has never ceased to exist in man's life.

When man says to himself 'I will worship nothing whatsoever', he does not, as he imagines, rid himself of the problem of worship. He merely changes the object of worship, and proclaims himself or his interests as the God to be worshipped and to govern his whole life. Worship is not confined to the offering of prayers, devotions or the submission of offerings, as people appear sometimes to imagine when talking of the subject.

This is a matter of form only. Worship itself is essentially obedience and acquiescence to a certain Being, and the belief that it is our duty to obey that Being. Worship in this sense is an integral part of every man's entirety and existence because it is a component part of himself. Within this context there can be no one who does not worship even man's entirety and existence because it is a component part of himself. Within this context there can be no one who does not worship even though he claims otherwise.

Man is an instinctive worshipper whether or not he chooses or is aware of it. It is only in the nature of the worshipped deity or the way he is worshipped that one man differs from another. Either he worships God, or he worships some other deity or deities by whatever name. His worship of God is either true or deviant, and no sensible man would make false deities the object of his worship.

Having established this fact, the Quran proceeds to the other part of the question, namely the explanation of the right way to worship God. It stipulates the uniformity of worship just as it stresses the Unity of God. The correct worship of God is represented in two integral indivisible aspects, namely the maintenance of the rites of worshipping God to the exclusion of any other, and the following of God's revelation in establishing a point of reference for guidance in life. To pray or present offerings to an idol, an object, or a person, is corruptive of religion as well as of worship. The same corruption results from the adoption of a non-godly attitude and practice in life.

There must be unity between man's worship and his attitude towards life. The deity addressed by man in his prayer and devotions is the same deity addressed while studying, earning a living, attempting to better conditions on earth, eating, drinking, copulating, as well as while communicating with his family, with other individuals, with other societies, peoples and states, whether in peace time or during war. Say:

> "Lo! my worship and my sacrifice, and my living and my dying, are for Allah, Lord of the Worlds" (VI. 163).

In all that he does, the constant reiteration of God's name in his heart had the practical effect of recalling to him God's commands, so that he may obey them. In Islam God's commands deal with all such matters and indicate the permitted as well as the prohibited.

When this happens something of considerable significance occurs in man's life. To being with man will be giving due worship to His Creator. Man would never appreciate God as he truly should if he worshipped Him in prayer once during the day and considered this to be the end of it. God says:

> "I created the Jinn and humankind only that they might worship Me"(LI:56).

Meaning by this the wide range of worship which comprises prayer and devotions, living and dying. To do otherwise would be to worship two deities, one in the holy shrine through prayer and devotions, the other (or others, though eventually they culminate into one), through obedience in affairs of everyday life. Allah hath said:

> "Choose not two gods. There is only one God. So of, he only, be in awe." (Al-Nahl IXVI:51).

The ability of the human heart to sense the glory of God and His miraculous powers revealed in the creation of a universe which is such a wonderful model of accuracy, order and uniformity, as well as in the creation of all living objects, will or should lead man to worship this Almighty God in due veneration of His glory and power.

This could never occur through a worship that is pursued from moment to moment and relinquished for the remainder of man's day-to-day living. Regardless of God's reward for this worship, a sense of duty demands that it should be followed as a means of paying others what is due to them.

Lo! Allah commandeth you that ye restore deposits to their owners. (IV. 58), and who except this Omnipotent God serves disinterested and constant worship?

Yet of His Mercy God is bounteous to those who give Him His due, namely worship in its wider or uniformly comprehensive sense, for He will reward them by eternal life in paradise, and secure their future after death, which, since it is the longer period of man's life, is the worthier to be preserved.

The uniformity of worship during man's span of life influences many important aspects of his living. It gives him first of all an inner security which is nowhere to be found outside the frame of faith. It cannot be obtained either through drugs, drinks, narcotics, leisure or sensual pleasure. All these confirm the state of mind which man wants to evade, but they neither remove nor cure it. Security emanates from faith and the mention of God's name.

As the Quran puts it:

> "those who believe, and whose hearts find satisfaction in the remembrance of God: for without doubt in the remembrance of God do hearts find satisfaction."

This security is not a placid resignation to events. Rather, it is the search for the good life wherever it is to be found; the Jihad under God's name to instal God's justice in the world; the opposition to all forms of injustice abhorrent to God; the search for knowledge and instruction. In all these activities the believer will rely on God because everything is moved by and returns back to Him.

The believer, moreover, is confident that God promises only goodness to him, and this is why no anxiety overshadows the earning of a living, the pursuit of study, the Jihad, and the establishment of a civilization, a fact that was once apparent in the early Muslim period.

Until recently, there were writers who acclaimed the present age as the 'age of anxiety', calling it the age of creative anxiety. But they came to realise that it was now more in the nature of a poisonous drug even though taken in the smallest doses. They also realised that the impetuous frantic activity was neither a real nor creative activity. It was only symptomatic of an illness that would soon lead to other consequences, causing man to lose his sense of security and psychological balance. Other writers have said that anxiety is a necessary accompaniment of civilization however damaging or beneficial.

This interpretation lacks scientific precision, since, anxiety goes hand in hand only with a civilization thriving on materialism and neglecting the spirit. This type of civilization lacks the basis for inspiring a true sense of security, and it is this civilization which is responsible for tearing the human soul between two deities, the other who dominates the realities of day-to-day life. This latter deity who accompanies man is more often than not a tough and ruthless one who does not inspire security and stability in his worshippers.

As history shows this was once a flourishing civilization that sensed no pangs of fatal concern because it was secure in the name of God. Uniformity of worship brings together many aspects of man both within his inner self or in his life generally, which present-day deviations have, without justification, torn as under.

It brings together spirit and matter, body and soul. It brings together religion and science, piety and material development, religion and life. Finally, it brings together this life and the Hereafter.

Let us look briefly at each of these unities brought about by Islam. Soul and body or spirit and matter are both or genuine authenticity in the human make-up.

"Behold, thy Lord said to the angels: I am about to create man from clay. When I have fashioned him (in due proportion) and breathed into him of My Spirit, fall you down in obeisance unto him."

They were brought together inseparably at the birth of man,

and the whole of his history is a living confirmation of this fact. But in periods of Jahiliyyah, there is always a tendency to set them apart by directing each on a separate course of its own, and by the exaggeration of one at the expense of the other.

Some pre-Islamic periods emphasised the spirit as the real essence of man and despised the body as an impure object unworthy of veneration. Such an object was entitled only to degrading and tortuous acts. The material aspect of life was also despised as it was nearest to the body, to clay. Other pre-Islamic periods exaggerated the body and sensual pleasure. They considered the body to be the real thing, and the soul only a beautiful shadow that lacked substance. They saw it as a secondary object in man's life or as an inhibitor.

As a result these years of history dedicated a great deal of their interest to material produce and construction and almost completely neglected the spiritual make-up of man. Both attitudes base themselves on a false premise, namely that there is a deep-rooted contradiction between body and soul that can be only conciliated by suppressing one in favour of the other. One either suppresses the body to free the soul, or suppresses the soul in order to attain material emancipation.

But, in reality, in neither case does suppression lead to goodness. The suppression and devitalization of the body runs counter to instinct, resulting in the obstruction of man's energy, material and cultural retardation, poverty, misery, depression, pessimism and despair.

Alternatively, the suppression and blackening of the soul lead to inner worries that can never be satisfied even by the deepest immersion in earthly pleasures which necessarily result in conflict between individuals, communities, states and peoples. These are signs that something counter-instinctive has occurred; the result is a loss of equilibrium in man's life.

Islam, on the other hand, provides the balanced alternative which harmonises soul and body and disposes of any contradiction and conflict between them. Islam never accepted the idea of an irreconciliable situation between these two entities.

It is true that the body and the soul are two different elements but they are integrated in man. Their lack of cohesion is not caused by their mutual existence in the human-being, but by the domination of one by the other, and the consequent loss of the instinctive equilibrium which God bestowed on him:

> "O Man! What has seduced thee from Thy Lord Most Beneficent? Him who created thee, fashioned thee in due proportion, and gave thee a just bias." (V:7).

Moderation or equilibrium lies at the basis of God's creation. But man in his ignorance disturbs this equilibrium. As a result disturbance occurs in the soul well as in the actualities of life, as is testified by events. This idea is expounded in L' Homme Get Inconnu by the scientist-physician Alexis Karel. He indicates:

> "put serious ignorance of the nature of man as well as our neglect of his spiritual aspect, and our setting up of economic, social and political systems based on ignorance, lie at the root of our scientific and cultural progress."

And it is Islam which restores to man the balance and moderation with which he is endowed by God. It puts into effect a simple and realistic though far-reaching measure, namely an invitation to the soul and body to take part in the whole of life.

Prayer is not only a spiritual hymn, it is also a set of movements performed by the body through standing, kneeling and prostration, combined with a conscious mental concentration on the verses recited in prayer. Food, drink and sex on the other hand are not pure body movements, but also represent spiritual aspirations made permissible by mentioning God's name, and performed in strict observance of what is lawful and what is forbidden. In this way, such acts invariably lie between these two poles and is thus included in the integrating system which brings together soul and body, spirit and matter, earth and sky.

A similar split occurred between religion and science. Man has an instinctive disposition to know the secrets of the material world around him, and to subject these to his power. Both dispositions are instinctive and authentic; both are innate. No necessary contradiction, split or conflict exists between them.

Divine Revelation provided no grounds for it, but man's errors have created conflict and dispute between them. This dichotomy occurred in Europe at the beginning or the Renaissance when the Church opposed science and scholars, and threatened to bury, torture and kill people of science such as Copernicus, Galileo and Jordan Bruno.

As time passed, the gap widened and the conflict deepened, until the mere mention of God's name in scientific research was tantamount in the ordinary European's sense to a violation of the spirit of that research and an unwarranted attempt to integrate two irreconciliable attitudes. As Darwin put it:

> "The interpretation of evolution with reference to Providence is an introduction of a metaphysical element into a purely mechanical situation."

This misinterpretation of the nature of the relationship between the two subjects could not help but disturb man's balance and security. It aroused conflict in man's inner self between two genuine elements each requiring satisfaction. When one feels that the satisfaction of one's spiritual needs lies outside the frame-work of science, and that the satisfaction of scientific needs lies beyond the reach of religion, and if at the same time feels that these needs proceed in two separate and diverging directions, one ends by worshipping two irreconciliable deities, each demanding from his worshipper a differing attitude, behaviour and point of view.

For the time being, there is no choice other than to worship the two. Again, man is torn apart, whether consciously or unconsciously. His anxiety is reinforced, and when, as frequently happens, he is forced to choose between them, he succumbs to the deity of science as being more able to satisfy his immediate needs, and abandons the deity of religion as belonging to a world altogether less real and tangible whose existence in any case, he doubts.

Islam in its simplicity eliminates this contradiction again by means of a realistic and simple procedure. The God who man worships in his prayers is the same God who gave man knowledge for the first time, and the same God who invites man still to learning and knowledge.

"He taught Adam the nature of all things" (p. 31). Read in the name of the Lord who createth. Createth man from a clot.

Read; And thy Lord is the Most Bounteous, who teacheth by the pen. Teacheth man that which he knew not." (XCVI. 1-5).

God invites man to contemplate the secrets of the universe:

> "Behold in the creation of the Heavens and the Earth; in the alteration of the night and the day; in the sailings of the ships through the ocean for the profit of mankind; in the rain which God sends down from the skies, and the life which he gives therewith. To an Earth that is dead, in the beasts of all kinds that he scatters through the Earth, in the change of the winds, and the clouds which they trail like their slaves between the sky and the earth; (here) indeed are signs for a people that are wise." (II. 164).

God taught that He was all that is between the sky and the earth:

> "And hath made of service to you whatsoever is in the Heavens and whatsoever is in the Earth."(XLV. 13).

In order to exploit what is in the Heavens and on Earth by his physical and mental efforts, all that man has to do is to learn the universal law by which God administers this universe:

> "It is He who has made the Earth manageable for you, so traverse ye through its tracts and enjoy of the substance which He furnishes (But unto Him is the resurrection)."

Thus will come the unity of orientation through the Oneness of God.

Human knowledge is not stolen from God despite His will as in the Greek myth of Prometheus. It is a divine gift bestowed on man. Man does not need to disobey God in order to learn. It is God who instructed mankind to learn and to seek knowledge. The Prophet says:

> "The quest of knowledge is an obligation."

Man should not have any sense of guilt when he exploits the resources of the Heavens and Earth for his benefit, nor should he think that he is doing so in rebellion against a Divine Will which seeks to crush and oppress him in the way the relationship between man and God is portrayed in the Greek myth. It is God who harnessed the resources of this universe for the benefit of man and instructed man to settle on the earth.

"It is He who produced you from the earth and settled you therein."

There is thus no need for man to feel that he is worshipping two opposed gods, each one with conflicting demands on him. In all that man does there is only one God. When man seeks knowledge Allah demands him not to use the fruit of this knowledge in wrongful tyranny over the earth. Man does not feel that he is surrendering to God only out of ignorance of inability, as Julian Huxley claimed in Man in the Modern World. According to Huxley:

> "When man gains knowledge and control over his environment, he rebels against God, making a god of himself."

On the contrary, the more man learns the nearer he becomes to God and to the fear of God.

> The erudite among his bondsmen fear God alone."
> (XXXV:28).

Man prays to God of give him more knowledge:

> "Oh My Lord. Advance me in knowledge." (Taha 114).

Thus even when he is seeking knowledge, man is in his heart always thinking of Allah. He will conduct his life in exploiting the fruits of science for righteous ends with the same assurance and confidence he has in Allah when he offers Him his prayers. In this way, Islam establishes a unity between religion and science and learning, as between religion and life.

In Europe, life was excluded from the sphere of religion through particular circumstances which were not inherent in religion itself. Western man thought of religion as a spiritual relation between man and God, and of life as human endeavour with no relation to God. This is invented by the West, and not revealed by God.

It is inconceivable that such a concept could be supported by the words ascribed to the Messiah:

> "Render therefore unto Caesar the things which be Caesar's and unto God the things which be God's."

This is contradictory to the entire concept of religion according to which Allah is the Lord of the heavens and the earth, and Caesar and all men must surrender to the judgment of Allah.

These words should be seen as an instruction by the Messiah to his followers not to declare war against Caesar, but to pay the taxes, he required, till the establishment of a state that would enforce what Allah had revealed, and would subject Caesar himself to the judgment of Allah. There is a similar case in Islam.

Allah told the Muslims in Mecca before the establishment of the Muslim State:

> "Withhold your hands establish worship and pay the poor due." (IV. 77).

No Muslim has understood from this instruction that religion is only a spiritual relation between man and Allah, and that the daily affairs of life should be administered by Caesar or other nonbelievers in the way they choose. This instruction was for a period of time only, and was followed by the establishment of Muslim society and the Muslim state, thus making life in its entirety subject to the judgment of Allah. This was accompanied by the revelation of detailed legislation governing all aspects of life.

As a result of this wrong interpretation of the scope of religion in the West, life increasingly moved away from religion, until in modern times it was finally excluded completely from its ambit. Politics followed the principles of Machiavelli who justified lying, deception, hypocrisy, dishonesty, killing, murder, fraudulence and trickery, all of which were forbidden in Islam.

Economy was based on the usurious system which is also forbidden in Islam. Social relations were based on social hypocrisy and the hideous isolation of individuals described by Aldous Huxley in Texts and Pretexts, where every man had become an island in itself without any connection with other islands scattered in the ocean of life.

Karel considers that the contravention of innate laws cannot take place without severe punishment, as these laws are as crucial as the Law of Nature itself. The chaos and turmoil now rampant all over the world is the heavy price man has paid for the contravention of the innate laws created by Allah. It is Allah and not man who knows human nature.

How ignorant man is of his nature, as Karel again so rightly observes. Though he has learnt a great deal about the universe surrounding him, his ignorance of himself is profound, since, he sees himself only through his passions and desires. Allah alone knows the innate human nature; He knows what is suitable for it and what is not. He has revealed this religion to guide the life of man as well as his relation with Allah. In a simple yet far-reaching way, Islam establishes the connection between religion and life, and extends this to embrace the hereafter.

Islam presents the true concept of religion. Religion is faith and laws; a faith governing spiritual relations with God, and laws administering the affairs of life in the name of God. In both cases, we are seeking the same God, we worship one God. The Shariah as revealed encompasses the whole range of human activity, as well as international relations whether in peace or in war. Thus, politics becomes Islamic politics; economics becomes Islamic economics, social relations become Islamic relations and relations between the two sexes will be organised according to Islam, thought and art become Islamic activities. Islam embraces the whole of life.

Allah who revealed the Shariah knows that in man's life there are permanent elements, and others that develop and change. Allah does not want these latter to be petrified or stunted in their growth, therefore, he enacts in his Shariah comprehensive and constant principles which, without themselves altering, allow for the process of continuous change through the right interpretation of these laws in their detailed application to new circumstances. This had been the endeavour of Muslim scholars throughout history.

In this way, a constant interconnection is maintained between religion and life. Life will neither be petrified in one form, nor will its development contravene the scope of religion. As Khalifah Umar Ben Abdul Aziz said:

> "The more new problems people have, the more new rules they will find."

It is through this fusion that unity of this life and the hereafter will be achieved. The dichotomy between religion and life led to a separation in the awareness of people of this life and the hereafter. In pursuit of these separate ends they developed two completely unconnected sets of actions, one bearing no relation to the other.

> Islam establishes a unity between this life and the hereafter and considers them as a continuous process. Together they constitute one path, the beginning of which is this life and its end the hereafter.

"But seek, with the (wealth) which God has bestowed on thee, the home of the Hereafter, not forget thy portion in this world". (XXVIII. 77), and "Say who hath produced for His servants and the things, clean and pure, (which he hath provided) for sustenance? Say they are, in the life of the world, for those who believe, (and) purely for them on the Day of Judgment."

In Islam, there is not a single deed which is concerned exclusively with worldly life or with the Hereafter; its purpose is always two fold. Offering prayers, for example, which people may think of as a deed motivated solely by concern for the hereafter, also has its purpose in the worldly life. As God says in the Quran,

> "Prayer restrains from shameful and unjust deeds."
> (XXIX. 45).

Prayer is intended to be offered in the worldly life, and be rewarded in the hereafter. Even the relationship between the sexes, which might be thought of as an exclusively worldly affair, is linked in the consciousness of Muslims with the hereafter. Muhammad said: "You will be rewarded by Allah for copulation with your wives." He was asked: "We do that to satisfy our desire how can we be rewarded for it?" Muhammad replied: "If you satisfy your desires in a forbidden way, wouldn't you be punished for it?" They answered:" Yes we would." Muhammad then said: "If you then satisfy your desire in a permissible way, you must be rewarded."

The result is that this world and the hereafter are interconnected in the awareness of the Muslim individual. In everything he does he commits himself to act in accordance with the revealed Will of Allah. While he conducts his worldly affairs in this life, he will be looking forward to God's reward in the hereafter.

This full integration in the structure of Islam is clearly expressed in a way which has roused the interest of many Orientalists writing about Islam. The English Orientalist Gibb says,

"The kind of society that a community builds for itself depends fundamentally upon its beliefs as to the nature and purpose of the universe and the place of the human soul within it."

This is a familiar enough doctrine and is reiterated from Christian pulpits week after week. But Islam is possibly the only religion which has constantly and consistently aimed to build up a society on this principle. The prime instrument of this purpose was law.

The Canadian Orientalist Wilfred Cantwell Smith remarks:

> "Observers have noted the paramount position of the community in Islam. Less thought has been devoted to its significance in Islamic history, which is that community in motion, it is well known that Muslim society has a remarkable solidarity, that the loyalty and cohesion of its members are intense. Many have recognised that the community is not only a social group but a religious body; that the 'church and state' are one, to use the inappropriate language of the West."

We would go much further, as has been said, in interpreting this. Yet to stress these facts, to insist upon the centrality of society, is not deny but to interpret our initial emphasis on religion as personal. The community is based on, as it is integrated to, individual faith. Not only is Muslim society held together (as other societies) by common loyalties and traditions, and by a very carefully worked out system of values and of beliefs. Not only is it the product of a superb ideal. It pulsates with the vitality of a profoundly held and deeply personal conviction, a religious conviction that is warm and meaningful for the individual member.

We may say that this society, this community, is the expression of a religious ideal, using 'religious' in the personal sense earlier proposed. As a creed or theological system may be expression in an intellectual form of a personal faith—as is often the case, particularly with Christians—so a social order and its activities are the expression in a practised form of a Muslim's personal faith.

***Singularity of the Creator :*** This integration, which is an expression of the unity of worship and the Oneness of God, is most precious in Islam. It is the real meaning of Shahadah:

"No God but Allah."

It is the most precious gift that Islam can give to humanity in this age; a humanity perplexed, confused and suffering from anxiety through its loss of the unifying element, whether in its theoretical concepts or in its actual behaviour. It seems uncertain in Toynbee's discussion of the possible future contribution of Islam to new manifestations of religion, whether he was aware of this meaning or not.

Whatever the case may be, this meaning does not present ' a new face of religion' as Toynbee and others thought. It is the true meaning of religion revealed by God to mankind. It is the true meaning which materialised in Islam fourteen centuries ago, and was formulated in a concrete way over a long period and in large areas of the world.

Islam provides us with guidance throughout life from cradle to grave, answering their innate questions that consciously or unconsciously press on man in his journey through this world. What exactly is man? What is his role on the earth? What are the limits of his energies? From where have we come? To where will we go after death? For what purpose do we live? How should we organise our life? These are the questions which demand answers. If no convincing and decisive answer is provided, and if that answer is not that right one, it will undoubtedly affect man's psychological stability and his behaviour.

Man will be in a state of crisis. The present world situation is the most obvious example of the extent of this crisis: no further evidence is needed than modern man's present behaviours. What is man? A simple question, yet how difficult for contemporary mankind to answer, and how far their answer from the truth. Is man really an animal as Darwin suggested, or is he a human being?

Is he a God as portrayed by Julian Huxley? Does man stand alone as his own creator, as suggested by a book with the title Man Makes Himself? Is he a slave as conceived by other doctrines and theories, and if so, a slave to what?

To an exploiting class as suggested by the materialistic theory of history; to his own body and desires; or to the machine as he came to be under technological progress? What are the potentials of man? What are the limits of reason? Is he able by it alone to understand and explain all things? What is his attitude towards those things which he cannot understand or explain? Should he ignore them, or surrender to them reluctantly? Where does man go after death? Is the end of man's limited life on this earth the end of everything, or is there some form of continuation? What is the purpose of human life? Is it to obtain as much material enjoyment as possible, or is there some other objective, and of what kind? Is it to control nature, or to control others? (Or is it perhaps to cooperate with them?) And to what use should this control be put? To enslave others? To destroy? Or merely to assert ourselves?

On the other hand we desire to control others that we may cooperate with them, the same question arises; to what end will we cooperate? the questions are endless. How should man live? Who will decide the question for him? Philosopher, politicians, dictators, the masses, youths, elders? Or should each man decide for himself as Sartre's existentialist philosophy suggests? Clearly the answers to all these questions and more will determine man's behaviours and the kind of life he will lead on earth.

Contemporary mankind whether in the East or the West has provided a variety of answers. For the most part, they are wrong and misleading. The result is the present unprecedented turmoil and chaos, and the misery of the vast majority of mankind is suffering from, despite the technological and scientific progress which was theoretically to provide humanity with spiritual happiness in addition to material prosperity.

***The Role for Man :*** Islam provides humanity with the right guidance for its journey, and right answers to its persistent questions. Thus assured, man is enabled to set out to achieve his objectives in complete harmony of aspiration, thought, and feeling. Man in Islam is simply man. He is neither God nor animal—the two extremes argued by Huxley and Darwin respectively. His role is to be a Vice-regent on earth; to inhabit it in accordance with the will of Allah. Allah has bestowed on man the talents and abilities necessary for this role. Among them is the ability to learn, the ability to know and distinguish between the path or righteousness and the path of evil, and the ability to choose and pursue one of them. It is because of this ability that man's actions acquire moral value. Man cannot, and should not live without moral values.

There is no single human action which does not fall within the scope of morality. We cannot say that morality has no bearing on politics, science or sexual relations. The only acts that have no relation to morality are the acts of an animal:

> "for an animal there is no choice. Man on the contrary had two alternative courses of action open to him, and he is able to follow one of the two. As a result, all his actions have moral value. If he opts out of the moral choice, behaving like an animal, he will pay the price of his action in misery and perplexity."

We came to be by the will of Allah. We will in the end return to Allah. On the day of resurrection, Allah will question us as to what we did in our worldly life. Those who followed the course of Allah and the way revealed by Him, will later see the paradise of Allah. Disbelievers will end up in Hell:

> "And if as is sure come to you guidance from Me, whosoever follows my guidance, on them shall be no fear, nor shall they grieve. But those who reject faith and belie our signs, they shall be companions of the fire, and shall abide therein." (II: 38-39).

The duty of man of earth is to worship Allah:

> "I have only created jinns and men, that they may serve Me." (LI: 56).

The worship meant is the comprehensive worship already indicated, including not only specific acts of worship but everything that man does. Say:

> "Truly my prayer and my service of sacrifice, my life and my death, are (all) for God, the Cherisher of the world. No partner hath He." (VI: 163-164).

If fulfilled in accordance with Allah's purpose, every act becomes an act of worship. The course humanity should pursue is the course of Allah, since Allah is Lord and man is not; He is the Creator and man is not; Allah is Omniscient and man is not. Wherever man creates laws for himself, he sustains harm and introduces disorder and confusion into his life.

Man can only be truly free and truly equal, when he worships Allah alone, complying only with His Shariah. All man-made slogans of freedom and equality will remain illusions with no substance in reality, as long as some men remain the legislators or others.

Such a state of affairs would be consistent with the materialist theory of history. He who owns will be he who rules, while all other people will be his slaves. Feudalists become the rulers and peasants are condemned to servitude; capitalists rule and workers are the slaves; Communism rules, and all people become slaves of the state and are subject to it as their only source for sustenance.

But when Allah is ruler through compliance with Shariah, all people, the rulers and the ruled, will be in the servitude of Allah alone, equal in their servitude to Allah, therefore equal in freedom vis-a-vis each other, since all are bound by Shariah which has not been made by any of them, and none can alter it to defend his own interests at the expense of others.

When man finds this type of guidance on his journey, he will immediately discover the landmarks of the path ahead of him, and will follow this path. His soul then will not be thrown into confusion; his mind will not suffer bewilderment; his footsteps will be firm and steady.

Man should not demean himself. He is a being greatly honoured by Allah, and should not be humiliated or lose his dignity:

> "We have honoured the sons of Adam; provided them with transport on land and sea; given them for sustenance things good and pure; and conferred on them special favours above a great part of our creation." (XVII:70).

On the other hand, man should not imagine himself greater than he is and out of arrogance turn his back on the worship of God:

> "Nay, but man doth transgress all bounds. In that he looketh upon himself as self-sufficient. Verily, to the Lord is the return (of all)." (XCVI:6-8).

Man should not feel that life is an unrepeatable opportunity, a feeling that leads inevitably to over-indulgence in sensual pleasures. Rather he should avail himself of the reasonable share permitted by Allah, and realise that the excessive pleasure he is seeking without permission from Allah, and realise that the excessive pleasure he is seeking without permission from Allah is not good in itself. Allah did not prohibit this excess in order to torture man, but lest it might discourage him from attaining his ultimate aim, and degrade him from human dignity to the level of an animal.

Moreover, every excessive pleasure that man abandons in his worldly life in obedience to Allah, will be compensated for man if old and his return back to Allah. Man should play his role on this earth with clear vision and awareness. He should not build the world of matter while undermining the spiritual world, neither should he create material facilities as ends in themselves, neglecting the ultimate aims of human existence, which will only be attained by establishing divine justice on Earth, and will only be fulfilled by belief in Allah and by following His course.

It is by presenting this concept to humanity, after providing a true meaning of divinity and worship, the Islam gives humanity the guidance it needs instead of the present fumbling in the dark. We return now to a point raised earlier, namely the question of stability and change in human life.

Darwinism has had a immense influence over Western thought. It has suggested that there are no permanent elements in human life, or in any form of life, throughout the entire universe. To regard any value system such as morality or religion as permanent is, therefore, an unscientific way of thinking and a restriction on human life that should be eliminated.

When we think about it outside the context of local and particular conditions in Europe, and the ensuing conflicts between science, religion, learning and other human activities, we realise that it is the extremist rejection of the permanent values in human life that is unscientific, and that it is this which needs a careful scientific examination unconnected with emotional or historical factors.

The economic, political and social aspects of people's lives do change owing to the constant interaction between human reason and the Universe. This reaction constantly generates more knowledge of the mysteries of the Universe; knowledge which is put to use in harnessing its resources in the service of man. This is true. But what has this to do with constant values in human life? What has this to do, for example, with worshipping Allah?

The necessity of this worship is derived from the fact that Allah is the Creator and the Organiser of this Universe with all therein, including mankind. How does man's discovery of the properties of matter, splitting the atom and its molecule, or sending a rocket to the moon, stars or other planets change this necessary relationship?

The story of Prometheus and his rebellion against God when man learned more about the Universe and harnessed its resources, is a myth and not science. We should note, in the age of science, be dominated by unscientific stories. To say that man knows himself and his requirements better than Allah is also an emotional statement which lacks the scientific spirit of enquiry.

This is a result of the situation in mediaeval Europe, when the clergy tyrannized on Earth in the name of God in a way that led people to abandon the God of the church in whose name tyranny was practised, and to invent another God—call it Nature or any other name—who had no church, no priests, and who put people under no kind of obligation.

These circumstances were peculiar to Europe and not universal realities or scientific facts. How can we, in the age of science, cling to a concept derived from a specific historical and geographical base, and turn it into a permanent and universal reality on which our life should be based?

The existence of values in the life of man is objective and derived from the fact that he has more than one course open to him; is able to choose and commit himself to a certain course. How this changed by man's discovery of the secrets of the Universe, or by his harnessing its resources?

The abolition of moral values from the life of man—which means a regression to the level of animals or machines—is based on an unscientific concept, presupposing absolute passivity on the part of man. This is true whether we are talking of the psychic determinism preached by Freud and psycho-analysis, or the economic determinism on which the materialist philosophy of history was based. Freud, for example, has not offered a shred of scientific evidence to proved the existence of the Oedipus complex on which his psychological determinism was based.

In the light of the economic determinism propounded by Marx, England should have been the first country in Europe to experience Communism. England is still not a communist state, while the biggest communist blocks in the world, Russia and China, have moved from feudalism to Communism.

The claim that moral values are not permanent, and that they should keep pace with material development, is based on a supposition incapable of scientific testing or proof, namely that innate entity of man develops with material development. There is no evidence of this. We talk, for food, water, clothes, shelter, sex, ownership of property and self-assertion, and we can say with all certainty that the forms of the these things have developed greatly with the passage of time.

However, who can say in a truly scientific sense, that their substance has changed as well? Moral values are concerned with substance, not form. Though the forms of human activity change, the moral values related to this activity are not changeable; they continue to determine, by virtue of their permanency, all the variable forms of human activity from one generation to another.

The permanency of values does not prevent change in form, nor do changes in form require any change in essence. Contemporary humanity went astray when it removed many things from the realm of permanence and pushed them into the realm of evolution without any valid scientific basis.

The most flagrant example of this was placing the issues of religion and morality within and evolutionary context and claiming that man's behaviour had nothing to do with morality. An illustration of this is the assertion that man's sexual behaviour remains outside the scope of morality since it is a purely biological function.

A strange claim, and stranger still to attribute it to the evolutionary process. Sex as a biological relation unrelated to morality had been for millions of years a fact in the world of animals. What kind of evolution is it which takes man millions of years back to the state of an animal and no more? What scientific spirit is this, Darwinism or other, upon which such a concept and its resulting behaviour can be based?

Islam provides us with a decisive judgment on this topic. It teaches us that human life should develop constantly—scientifically, politically, economically and socially but that in its continuous development it should not abandon the constant values derived from the permanent and unchanging facts related to Allah, in his creation of the Universe, life and man. Life based on this concept will be balanced in its movement. It will not become fixed at any one point, not will it set out irrationally on the path to its own destruction.

By providing humanity with these three major concepts—the unity of divinity and of worship, guidance throughout the human journey, the resolution of what is permanent and what is changeable in human life, Islam gives humanity a radical solution to the chief problem now leading to the disorder and confusion we are witnessing". Having fulfilled its primary mission by re-establishing the right concepts, Islam goes on to provide practical solutions to the problems of every day living. Unfortunately, there is no time to deal with these in detail in the present chapter. The hope is that as here, and elsewhere within this book, a clear model of that solution has been indicated.

## The Perception

Islamic concept of the fundamental rights has been elucidated by scholars to a great extent by the discussion of the Sovereignty of God, man's covenant of service to God, man's dignified position of vicegerency on earth, man's abiding by the code of conduct of life given by God, the accountability for one's deeds in the Hereafter and the abiding reward or punishment according to the good or bad record of these deeds. However, for further elucidation we are now going to take stock of it from historical, legal and moral aspects.

***Historical Aspect :*** Looked at from the historical aspect the concept of fundamental rights in Islam is as old as man himself. The Creator and Master of man, just as He had supplied air, water, food, light and countless other necessities of life, He had also given him a code of conduct for his life right from the beginning of his life. The Quran furnishes a definite evidence of the fact that long before sending man on earth and honouring him with the envied position of vicegerency on earth, he had been given consciousness of rights and obligations, and with the bestowal of the means of life he had been taught the manner and behaviour in life. The first man coming to this world had started his life not in the darkness of ignorance but in the light of knowledge:

> And He taught Adam the names of all things.
>
> (Al Quran 11:31)

Here it has been said he was taught the names of all things which makes it evident that the knowledge given to man was not defective or incomplete. It was perfect. Man had been taught the names of all those things that he had to deal with in the life of this world. Teaching the names of things does not mean that an inventory of these things was given to him. Rather, every thing concerning their characteristics features, properties, beneficial and detrimental aspects, the way they were to be used and the nature of their relationship with man was fully explained. With the evolution of life, man through his fundamental knowledge, and his instinctive search and enquiry, went on extending the sphere of his knowledge of things, and it still continues. Maulana Maudoodi in his commentary of the Quran writes under this verse:

> "The only way man acquires knowledge is through a mental grasp of their names. So we can say all man's knowledge really comprises the names of things. Teaching Adam the names of these things was virtually imparting knowledge of all those things to him."
>
> (Tafheem-al Quran Vol. I.p. 64.)

This knowledge of things also essentially included the consciousness of his rights and obligations with relation to these things. That is why we find that during the life-time of Adam when for the first time the problem of -'right' cropped up, it also became evident along with it that man came to have respect for the rights not merely on the basis of his conjecture or intuition but according to the code of conduct given to him by God. Cain, one of the sons of Adam, when he threatened Habel his brother, with murder after the sacrifice offered by him was rejected, received the following answers from his brother thus threatened:

> If thou dost stretch thy hand against me, to slay me, it is not for me to stretch my hand against thee to slay thee: for I do fear God, the Cherisher of the worlds. For me, I intend to draw on thyself my sin as well as thine. For thou will be among the companions of Fire, and that is the reward of those who do wrong.
>
> (Al Quran V:28:29)

His words amply bear out the fact that Abel had full knowledge of God's injunctions regarding respect for human life. He knew well it was a sinful deed, and the perpetrator of this crime would be consigned to Hell. He lost his life for fear of God but did not lift his hand against his brother.

The code of conduct as regards rights and obligations given to Adam in the context of man's relation with God, the servants of God and other creatives, was given to mankind in various ages and regions of the world through the messengers of God from Adam to Muhammad for their guidance. But in every age it was according to the problems and needs of the times, as human society evolved fresh explanations, elucidations and relative commandments. As the sphere of human relations became wider, there were also rules and regulations revealed to strengthen until by the time of the last prophet, Muhammad (Salam) this arrangement of education and training had reached its stage of perfection, and it was proclaimed:

> This day have I perfected your religion for you, completed My favour upon you and have chosen Islam as your religion. (Al Quran V:3)

This religion, which was perfected when it came to the Prophet Muhammad, had covered long periods of history before that. Let us trace its history with the help of the Quran:

> God did choose Adam and Nuh, the family of Ibrahim and the family of Imran, above all people; offspring one of the other. (Al Quran III-34)

That is to say, the system of guidance for mankind, starting from Adam, continued without break through different messengers of God one after the other. The Quran tells us that it was not only that the revealed guidance continued without break but the more important fact is that all the prophets of God called humanity each in his own time, to the same faith without any basic difference. Their mission was the same and they followed and propagated the same code of conduct for human life. And that code of conduct or the way of life was not their own invention, but conferred on them by the Sovereign Who appointed them to the high office of apostleship.

> The same religion has He established for you as that which He enjoined on Nuh that which We have sent by inspiration to Thee and that which We enjoined on Moses, and Jesus: namely that you should remain steadfast in Religion (establish the Religion of Allah. Tr.) and make no divisions therein: (Al Quran: 13)

This religion was not limited to the reform of beliefs only, but extended from the reform of beliefs to setting right all the affairs of human life, and had detailed instructions for every department of life.

> And We ordained law for him in the Tablets in all matters both commanding and explaining all things, (and said): Take and hold these with firmness, and enjoin thy people to hold fast by the best in the precepts. (Al Quran VII: 145)

Now let us hear in legal terms about the rights and obligations, what was this Religion and what were its details:

> And remember We took a covenant from the children of Israel (to this effect) ; Worship none but God; treat with kindness your parents and kindred, and orphans

> and those in need; speak fair to the people; be steadfast in (establish) prayers; and practise regular charity (Zakat). Then did ye turn back, except a few among you, and ye backslide (even now). And remember We took your covenant (to this effect); Shed no blood amongst you, nor turn out your own people from your homes: (Al Quran 11:83-84)

In the same Surah (II) pointing out the revealed commandments and instruction regarding the individual's relations with the rest of the world, it was said:

> Those who break God's Covenant after it is ratified, and who sunder what God has ordered to be joined, and do mischief on earth: cause loss (only) to themselves. (Al Quran 11:27)

The same thing has been repeated at another place in these words:

> But those who break the covenant of God, after having plighted their word there to, and cut asunder those things that God has commanded to be joined, and work mischief in the London them is the curse; for them is the terrible Home! (Al Quran X111;226)

Explaining these relationships Maulana Maudoodi writes:

> These people sunder those relationships on whose establishment and strengthening depend the collective and individual prosperity, and those that God commanded to be joined. In this short sentence there is such a vast store of meaning that it covers the entire range of man's cultural and moral relationships from that between two individuals to universal international relations of nations. Cutting asunder the relations does not mean only sundering human relationships but all those forms of (unnatural or natural) relations, besides those right and approved by God fall under them since the consequences of unapproved (prohibited) and wrong relation is no different from that of sundering the right ones the corruption of relations between man and the moral and cultural system.
>
> (Tafheem-al-Quran Vol.1, p 60-61)

This history of the human rights presented by the Quran furnishes definite proof of the fact that the concept of fundamental rights in Islam exists from the time the first man was born. And this also makes it clear what the source of these rights is. They did not come into existence as a result of the mutual bickerings and strife between man and the rulers of the state formed by him and the treaties and contracts made between them. They are not the result of the mental exercises of some philosopher or political thinker or legal expert either. Rather they were the endowment of the Creator of man and the true sovereign of His subjects, and are essentially associated with man and his life on earth. They had been determined simultaneously with the creation of man. They have finally been elucidated in the Shariah brought by Muhammad (Salam). These rights transcend the limits of time and space. If man were to take off from this abode of his, the earth, and select the moon or some other heavenly satellite, the nature of these rights shall not change. Just as the change of time and space did not bring about any change in his physical build and his natural necessities, the eternal nature of these rights and obligations shall not change either. These rights are absolutely unchangeable and inalienable. The function of the state is not the determination of these rights but their enforcement only.

The westerners assert that the history of the fundamental rights is three or four centuries old. And whatever they have acquired with great pains and after serious struggle, the whole world is being benefitted by it. But the history presented by the Quran before us proves that the day the first man set foot on this earth the fundamental rights formed part of his feeling and consciousness. And their acquirement was not his own achievement but the Sovereign Himself had conferred these rights on him by degrees. Wherever there is an echo of these rights heard, it was the reflection of the inspired teachings that had awakened the consciousness of the basic rights.

In Norman Cousins' book *In God we Trust* published in New York, in 1958, throwing light on the religious beliefs of the Founding Fathers of the American constitution in detail, it has been stated that Benjamin Franklin, George Washington, John Adams, Thomas Jefferson, James Madison, Allexender Hamilton, Saveel Adam,

John Jay and Thomas Paine were one and all firm believers in the teachings of Christianity, and their thought was deeply impressed by the beliefs. James Madison defining "Right" says:

> Whatever rights man enjoys is an obligation, a duty of other men enjoined by God. (p. 17).

Similarly, if the British and French constitutions are studied in their proper religious perspective, there too, the real source of the Fundamental Rights can be traced to the religious teachings particularly, the powerful impact of Islam on Europe.

Looked at through the mirror of the history presented by the Quran, Islam alone has the right to use the terms Natural Rights and Birth Rights, since the ambiguity relating to these rights found in the western concept of them, is totally absent here. Islam presents a definite answer to the question who determined these rights, when the western supporters of the theory of Natural Rights could not satisfactorily answer the question raised by Bentham and other critics, what they meant by nature, and which is that authority determining these rights. In other words they wanted to know exactly' what was the sanction behind these rights. Islam presenting the "Natural" and "By Birth" aspects of the rights, in great details, left no room for any such objections.

***Legal Aspect :*** Now let us examine the legal aspect of these rights. A common mistake made in all such surveys is that we keep the western concept of the fundamental rights as the norm before us. We select and prepare a list of all such rights from the Quran as came up to the western norm and are in keeping with its limited sphere of application. The logical result of this trend of thought is that the Islamic concept of rights takes a secondary position and its true features do not come out fully in view.

In the west the sphere of the fundamental rights is confined to the relations between the individual and the state. There the rights conferred on an individual by the state armed with very extensive powers, are regarded as basic. Their nature is defensive and protective, and their basic aim is to protect the helpless citizen from the fully authoritative ruler, oppression and tyranny. The constitution incorporating them shows the individual and the state as parties (opponents) and the position of the constitution becomes that of a compromise between the two, in which the limits of the recognized powers for one and those of the recognized rights for the other are determined. As against this in Islam, the common people and the rulers of their state are not parties at cross purposes with each other. Neither the rights of the citizen have been recognized by the rulers nor the powers of the state have been recognized by the citizens. There is no constitutional document either, between them, prepared with mutual consent and consensus, in which the limits of the rights and powers have been detérmined as desired. Both these are bound on equal terms by an oath of allegiance to their Lord and Cherisher and true Sovereign. As vicegerents on earth their position is the same (no superiority for either), since vicegerency was not conferred on any individual or a group but on the Muslim Ummah as a whole.

> God has promised, to those among you who believe and work righteous deeds, that He will of a surety grant them in the land inheritence (of power), as He granted to those before them: (Al Quran XX1V:55)

This verse amply reveals that the delegated authority vested in man as vicegerent on earth is meant for the Muslims as a whole. That is why Abu Bakr, the first caliph of the Prophet had refused to be called "vicegerent of God", since vicegerency had been conferred on the Ummah as a whole and not on him as an individual. His vicegerency lay in that the Muslim Ummah by free option of their own hand delegated these powers of vicegerency to him. It was in view of this concept of the authority of the caliph that Umar, the second caliph of the Prophet, approved of the title "Amir-ul-Muminin" (the person conducting the affairs of the state on behalf of the believers with the powers delegated to him by them). And this term remained in vogue in late times also.

The Amir of the believers and the citizens living within the limits of his Emirate, are bound in their respective spheres by the limits prescribed by Allah. Their powers and rights are not mutually recognized but determined by the Sovereign Himself. Both of them are bound to live according to the dictates of the unchangeable and irrevocable constitution based on the Quran and the Sunnah, not even one article of which is negotiable. There is no clash between their rights and powers. These two are such transgential circles which can never cross each other.

Viewed in this perspective the sphere of the fundamental rights in the Islamic State is very extensive. Like the general run of the constitutions of the world this is not confined to the mutual relations of the individual and the state. The sphere of application of the Quranic constitution extends over the entire life of man. The Quranic injunctions are not limited to the relations of the individual and the state but has so regulated the countless relations in the fields of beliefs, devotional acts, morals, social life, culture, economy, polity, judiciary, war and peace and other departments of life, that there is very little left for the state in the sphere of legislation. And even in this limited field, legislation at will cannot be allowed, but is conditioned that every law must conform to the dictates of the Quran and the Sunnah and their general spirit.

Legislation in the Islamic state is a rare thing not a daily occurrence. The laws of Islam are not passed in a heated assembly by men who ardently desire the legislation in their interest, against men who oppose it for the same reasons. The laws of Islam are firmly based on the Shariah and are therefore in the interest of people as a whole.

Now the rights reserved for the individual by the Divine Law and the Sunnah of the prophet, in as much as they are part of the constitution, above the legislative powers of the state and attainable through the judiciary are one and all without exception, fundamental rights. These rights do not comprise protection of the life, honour, property, attainments of justice, equality, freedom of expression and freedom of belief, alone but from the terms of suckling a new born babe to the right of a woman to her dower are all included in them as determined by God and His Apostle, and which are inviolable. The Quran has used the term the "limits prescribed by Allah" for the limitations set on man's powers of the legislation. These limits apply both to the individual as well as the state. Whatever Allah has approved for man and allowed him to benefit by it, neither an individual nor the Islamic state nor even the Ummah as a whole can make it prohibited. In connection with these limits prescribed by God, the Quran gives us the following instructions. In the Surah Baqrah (II) after enjoining the relevant commandments, Allah says:

> Those are limits (set by) God: approach not might there to. (Al Quran II:187)

Pointing out the characteristics' of the believers Allah says:

> Those that turn (to God) in repentance; that serve Him, and praise Him; that wander in devotion to the cause of God: that bow down and prostrate themselves in prayer: that enjoin good and forbid evil; and observe the limits set by God. (Al Quran IX: 112)

The Quran has said in most clear terms that man has no right of legislation where a law given by God exists. Nor has he any right to declare any thing lawful forbidden. All that is required of him is .to obey God and His Apostle:

> Follow (O men!) the revelation given unto you from your Lord and follow not, as friends or protectors, other than Him. (Al Quran V11:3)

> If any fail to judge by (the light of) what God hath revealed they are (no better than). . . . unbelievers. . . .wrong doers. . . . those who rebel.
> (Al Quran V:47-48-50)

> O ye who believe! make not unlawful the good things which God hath made lawful for you, but commit no excess: (Al Quran V:90)

> Say: See ye what things God hath sent down to you for sustenance? Yet ye hold forbidden (some things) lawful. Say: Hath God permitted you.(Al Quran X:59)

> But say not—for any false things that your tongues may put forth, "This is lawful, and this is forbidden," so as to ascribe false things to God.
> (Al Quran XVI: 116)

Allah did not only put restrictions on legislation by the common people, but did not allow even His Apostle to make any changes where a Divine Law existed:

> Say: "It is not for me, of my own accord, to change it: I follow naught but what is revealed unto me: if I were

> to disobey my Lord, I should myself fear the Penalty of a Great Day (to come)." (Al Quran X: 15)

So when the Prophet took a vow not to taste honey any more to humour certain wives of his. God took serious notice of it;

> O Prophet! why boldest thou to be forbidden that which God has made lawful to thee? Thou seekest to please thy consorts. (Al Quran LXXV1:1)

The Prophet had not declared honey forbidden for the Muslims. He could not even think of declaring forbidden what God had made lawful for them. He had himself decided to abstain from it. But since any act of his could become an argument for the Muslims, the error of this decision of his was pointed out to him, that he had no right to declare forbidden even for himself some thing that was made lawful by God.

On the one side this is the state of affairs of the Prophets powers in matters pertaining to God's commandments. But on the other side the Quran also makes it evident that where no injunctions from God exist on any particular issue or the Divine injunction needs elucidation and explanation the opinion of the Prophet is decisive and final. And it will be regarded equivalent to God's injunctions. Since the Prophet is the manifestation of God's political and legal sovereignty his interpretative and legislative position was defined saying:

> He who obeys the Apostle, obeys God:
> (Al Quran IV:80)

> So take what the Apostle, assigns to you, and deny yourself that which he withholds from you.
> (Al Quran IIX:7)

Keeping in view this position of the Quran and the Sunnah if a list of fundamental human rights based on the Quran and the Sunnah is prepared in an Islamic state, it will comprise all those rights that have been determined by god and his Apostle, no matter which department of life they belong to.

What other difference is there between fundamental rights and legal rights than the fact that the former are unchangeable by any measure except through an extraordinary process provided in the constitution itself. They can be attained through the judiciary, and with its help and support, the executive can be kept back from oppression and tyranny. As against this, the legal rights fall in the sphere of usual legislation (common law) and can be amended or cancelled by the state through its legislative powers.

Keeping in view this difference between the fundamental and legal rights it is noteworthy that no right conferred by Quran and the Sunnah can be kept out of the list of the fundamental rights, which is beyond the legislative powers of the state, which can be attained through judiciary and in connection with which the Quran and the Sunnah themselves have not conferred on the state any extraordinary powers with which it (the state) can usurp, limit or suspend it under pretext of extraordinary circumstances of emergency. Their exclusion from this life cannot be accepted on the plea that the westerners recognize as fundamental only those rights that concern mutual relation of the individual and the state. This argument can be brought forward only in favour of following the west, but has no weight in the light of the well known legal term fundamental rights and the sense it conveys. The right which enjoys a permanent and eternal position, which the state is unable to change or cancel and is attainable through the judiciary, must of necessity be deemed a fundamental right by any interpretation of law.

If a woman is divorced when she is suckling a baby, the Quran lays down the following code of conduct of rights and obligations between the baby, the divorced mother and her husband:

> The mothers shall give suck to their offspring for two whole years, if the father desires to complete the term. But he shall bear the cost of their food and clothing on equitable terms. No soul shall have a burden, on it .greater than it can bear. No mother, shall be treated unfairly on account of her child. Nor father on account of his child, an heir shall be chargeable in the same way. If they both decide on weaning, by mutual consent, ani' after due consultation, there is no blame on them. If ye decide on a foster-mother for your offspring, there is no blame on you, provided ye pay (the mother) what ye offered, on equitable terms. (Al Quran 11:233)

The rights determined for a new barn baby, its mother and father, come under the fundamental rights, since they form part of the constitution of the state, have been determined by the .Sovereign, are attainable through the judiciary, and the state cannot frame any regulation in this matter digressing from the Divine dispensation. The term appointed by the Quran for the suckling of the baby cannot be reduced or increased by the state even by a day. The position of this right of the babe can be gauged by an incident during the time of the Prophet.

> A certain woman, Ghamidiyah by name, came to the Prophet and confessed her guilt of adultery repeatedly (four times it is aid), stating that she was pregnant and wished to be cleansed of this fifth of her sin through stoning to death. The Prophet said to her, "If you insist on your confession, go now and come after delivering the babe". When she returned once again with a babe in her arm, repeating her request to be cleansed, the Prophet told her to suckle the baby and come after weaning. When she came back after weaning the babe, she had brought a piece of bread along, to demonstrate that the suckling period was over and the babe could now subsist on solid food. Thus assured, the Prophet arranged for the care of the child then ordered that she be stoned to death.
>
> (Tafheem-al-Quran Vol III.p.336.)

This incident reveals that the Prophet postponed the limit set by God in the form of her execution, on the first occasion to save a life, and on the second occasion to allow the full term of the suckling of a baby appointed by God, and ordered it only when he was fully satisfied that the baby had been weaned and could now subsist on food other than mother's milk. Two fundamental rights were involved in this case that of the preservation of life, and the other that of the completion of the period of suckling appointed by God. The Prophet through deferring the enforcement of the punishment of a heinous crime like adultery, made it evident that under the Islamic order, not to speak of a citizen, the rights of even an unborn babe and a suckling one cannot be ignored or tampered with. The pronouncement of the Prophet in this case is a legal precedent, and in such a case the Islamic state can never overlook or override it. That is to say, its legislative power is bound to follow this decision of the Prophet. And it is this restriction which brings the right of a babe to be born and to be suckled for definite period, under the fundamental rights.

Yet another right is determined by this decision of the Prophet's court. The child born out of wedlock shall be deemed innocent, and the Islamic state along with the enforcement of the limit set by God on the parents for their prime, shall arrange for the care and upbringing of the child. That is tantamount to allowing a child, along with the right to be born and to be suckled (for two years), the right of maintenance also. And also that he (or she) shall not be looked down upon but shall enjoy the same position with other normal children.

Now take another right which is usually placed in the sphere of moral rights, but is in reality a fundamental right, as determined by God and His Apostle. God says:

> And that ye be kind to parents. Whether one or both of them attain old age in thy life say not to them a word of contempt, nor repel them, but address them in terms of honour And, out of kindness lower to them the wing of humility, and say: "My Lord! bestow on them thy Mercy even as they cherished me in childhood." (Al Quran XVII:23-24)

On the basis of this verse, we now present two decisions, of the Prophet's court which have served as important precedents:

1. Somebody brought case against his parents to the court of the Prophet. He told him that both he and his wealth were his father's. Then the Prophet instructed his father to benefit by his son's 'wealth and in case of resistance he should approach him (the Prophet, and he will be helped against his son.
2. Someone complained to the Prophet of Go-l that his father demanded (his share) of his (son's) wealth. The Prophet asked him to comply and pay him his due. He further explained that his father wanted that he (the son) should surrender every thing he had in his (father's) favour. The

Prophet ordered him to do as he (the father) wished. The reporter of this case goes on to say that the Prophet advised the son not to disobey (and displease) his parents. If they demanded that he should leave this world for them, he must comply with their orders.

In the light of the Divine Injunction and the decisions of the Prophet's court, the legists have determined the rights of the parents in great detail, which is proof enough of the fact that this (kind treatment of the parents) is not a mere moral recommendation but a fundamental right which no (Islamic) government can change through exercise of its legislative powers. It cannot give the offspring the liberty of shirking their responsibility of the support and maintenance of the parents.

Now let us take up the case of dower. It is the wife's right that her husband owes to her according to the contract of the marriage. This right of the wife has been determined by the Quran:

> And give the women (on marriage) their dower as a free gift; but if they, of their own good pleasure, remit any part of it to you, take it and enjoy it with right good cheer. (Al Quran IV:4)
>
> Seeing that ye derive benefit from them, give them their dowers at least) as prescribed.
> (Al Quran IV:24)

That is to say, the Quran has declared dower a right of the woman which a husband must pay at all costs. And also that it a woman, of her own free will, were to surrender this right (in part or full), the Islamic state has no right to cancel or even limit it through legislation. So when Umar, the second Caliph, during his period wanted to limit the right of woman's dower and said in his harangue:

> "Do not exceed forty Oqiah; An old weight equivalent to 40 drachms. The drachm itself was an old Greek weight equivalent to 3.071 gm. So an Oqiah comes to our present day weight of 122.84 'Umar wanted to bring down the dower of women to 40 Oqiah of silver which would weigh 4913.6 grams, and at the present day market rate of Rs. 40 per 10 gms of silver, even

> this lowly dower cost a husband Rs. 19,654.00 or about Rs. 20.000/- Tr. of silver in the payment of dower to women. Those who pay more I shall take the excess of his wealth for Bait-al-Mal (the public treasury)."

Immediately on hearing this a tall woman got up and said in a loud tone: "You have no right to do that". And on Umar's asking her to explain her assertion, she said in reply that God had said otherwise in the Quran:

> Even if ye had given her a whole treasure for dower, take not the least bit of it back: would ye take it by slander and a manifest wrong ? (Al Quran IV;20)

Umar on hearing this argument said, "The woman is right, the man was in the wrong."

And with that remarks he took back his verdict. The moment his attention was invited to the injunction of the Quran, he desisted from limiting that right. This incident is proof of the fact that in the Islamic state even the right of a woman to her dower is a fundamental right, and it (the state) has no right to cancel, limit or suspend it.

Similarly, all those rights relating to Qisas (life for life and equal for equal), blood money, alimony, inheritance, will, marriage and divorce and matters relating to penalties and fighting, that have been determined by the Quran and the Sunnah of the Prophet. It is not only that the Islamic state has no right to amend these rights but because of the injunction of the Sovereign, it is bound to enforce them. Here these rights are not of a defensive and protective nature, but positive rights, and it is the responsibility of the state to ensure their enforcement exercising all its powers and using all its resources in this work.

The state will have the right to legislate only relating to those matters where the Shariah has not given any injunction. For example, the modern state of today can legislate in keeping with the Islamic principle of legislation in connection with elections, the procedure of the legislative and other assemblies, internal and foreign trade, business transactions, public services like railways, electrical energy, transport, gas, water supply, housing, education, industry, wages, welfare of the government and other servants, workers and peasants and such other matters. The rights determined by these laws shall be called legal rights. These laws shall be framed according to the changing time and space problems and the nature of the conditions and resources. They shall differ from country to country and the change of times, and the resulting rights must also differ due to the difference in laws. For example, the laws relating to acquirement of citizenships can be different in Pakistan and Turkey. But where the rights determined by the Quran and the Sunnah are concerned they are eternal, universal and all-pervasive, transcending time and space, inalienable, outside the sphere of the authority of the state. And wherever in the world an Islamic state comes into existence it is bound to enforce them in toto and as such these rights shall be placed under the "Fundamental Rights".

Here a very pertinent question can be raised that this interpretation of the fundamental rights can be acceptable to the believers only, but can those, who do not believe in God, the Quran and the Day of Reckoning, accept it. What will be their fundamental rights then? Is there going to be any difference between their fundamental rights and those of the Believers?

To answer this pertinent question it is necessary that we try to fully understand the position of non-Muslims in the Islamic State. The Islamic, unlike other states to the world is not a national state. The government there is not normed by any particular nation, race or a linguistic or regional group, so much so that the right of sovereignty does not belong to the Muslims. This is an ideological state. It's Sovereign and Ruler is God Himself. He has fully stated in the Quran through very evident commandments and instructions to tell us about the type of the society He wants to bring into existence on this globe of ours. He has, through His Apostle (Muhammad Salam) also presented practically a pattern of His Sovereignty. The government of the Muslims which is termed "Caliphate", is a government through delegated powers that is bound to run the state according to the dictates and limits set by the true Sovereign. The status of the citizens of the Islamic state has two aspects—one as human being and another as Muslims or non-Muslims. The first status is determined by their birth and the other on the basis of belief or unbelief as a result of their own free option. In their capacity as human beings they are all equal in every respect. All distinctions of colour, race, region and tongue are baseless. They have not the least importance in the sight of God. He says:

> He created you (all) from a single Person.
> (Al Quran XXXIX)

In the first verse of Surah Al-Nisa (iv) it has been said:

O mankind! revergence your Guardian-Lord, Who created you from a single Person, created, of like nature, his mate, and from them twain scattered (like seeds) countless men and women,

At another place it has been said:

> Verily, this Brotherhood of yours is a single Brotherhood, and;
>
> I am your Lord and Cherisher: therefore serve Me (and no other) (Al Quran XXI:92)

In the sight of God mankind in its entirety is a single Ummah. Since He is the Creator of them, Muslims and non-Muslims, is their Master and Sustainer in the matter of the rights of all His human creatures. He has conferred equal status. He has enjoined on us (Muslims) the protection of the life, property and honour and dignity of the non-Muslims just as the protection of those of the Muslims. And after declaring this equality on the basis of creation. He divides human being on the basis of their attitude and behaviour, for which they themselves are responsible, into two groups:

> Mankind was one single nation, and God sent Messengers with glad tidings and warnings.
> (Al Quran 11:213.)

> Mankind was but one nation, but differed (later).
> (Al Quran X:19)

That means, the brotherhood of mankind got divided due to its own disobedience and rebellion, some of them, for faking Allah's religion, invented some new creeds for themselves, which resulted in further divisions and sub-divisions of one Ummah. To bring mankind once again to unite by taking to the Religion of Allah, Messengers were sent by God. But due to their own wickedness, they failed to come to this unity. The Divine Message in the form of the Quran is even today calling humanity to unity and integration thus becoming single Ummah. The Quran was not revealed to the guidance of any particular nation and territory but for the guidance of entire humanity. And in the same way, Muhammad (Salam), the Apostle of God, was not commissioned as "Mercy to the believers" but as "Mercy for the worlds" (We sent thee not but as a Mercy for all creatures or people.—Al Quran XXI 107 Tr). The rights determined by the Quran for those believing in God and His Apostle are meant for the entire humanity. The message of the Quran is that every one should become a servant of Allah (by total submission to His Will) and should come to deserve their rights, and benefiting by them should live an honourable life in this world. Muslim is not the title of any race or a nation but of all those people believing in Allah's Religion.

That is why a person in any part of the world of any colour or race, immediately on declaring his belief in and entering the fold of Islam, becomes entitled to all those rights conferred on the believers by God that born Muslims, through generations, enjoy. Now it is evidently against common sense and most illogical that those recognizing God as their true Sovereign, and the Quran as their code of conduct in life and their constitution, be placed on a par with those rejecting both. Do America, Britain, Russia or any other country make no distinction among those loyal to their constitution and those rejecting it? Such rejectors would not even be allowed to live in those countries. Rather, they would be declared rebels and hanged or exiled. Why then expect the Islamic state to recognize the right of those not recognizing its sovereign and constitution to be included among those who do, and give them equal rights with them? Which of the legal or moral code keeps the rebel on a par with the loyal? This confusion is created by the secular trend of thought and erroneously taking Islam to be a religion having nothing to do with the affairs of the state. But after recognizing God as Sovereign of the state and the Quran and the Sunnah its constitution, there is no room left for this absurd question why Muslims and non-Muslims are not guaranteed the same status in an Islamic state and why the believers in God and those rejecting Him or His sovereignty are not brought on a par?

This aspect of Islam that it not only allows those in rebellion against God and traitors to live within the boundaries of its state in peace and tranquility but in the matters of human rights puts them on a par with the believers. Difference between the loyalists and the infidels lies in that the Muslims on account of their recognizing the political sovereignty of God have been made responsible for its enforcement, when the non-Muslims not recognizing this sovereignty, due to their own rejection of it, have been kept out of it. If they come to believe in God, they would automatically be entitled to the highest post in this set up. But as long as they insist on their rejection of Him, how can Sovereign allow them to participate in the responsibilities of enforcing His injunctions and instructions. He says:

> Is then the man who believes no better than the man who is rebellious and wicked? Not equal are they.
> (Al Quran XXXII: 18)

In another verse it has been said:

> O ye who believe! Take not into your intimacy those outside your ranks; they will not fail to corrupt you. They only desire ruin. (Al Quran 111:118)

In a preceding verse of the same Surah it has been said:

> Let not the Believers take for friends or helpers unbelievers rather than Believers:
> (Al Quran 111:28)

The same warning is repeated once again with greater emphasis;

> O ye who believe! Take not for protectors your fathers or your brothers if they love infidelity above Faith: If any of you do so they do wrong. (Al Quran IX:23)

***Line of Demarcation :*** This line of demarcation between the believers and unbelievers was drawn by the Sovereign Himself, and does not involve any territorial, national or religious prejudices on the part of the believers. It is their earnest desire, rather they have been commissioned in this world by the Sovereign to take His Message to every one of His servants that he should rid himself of all sorts of bondage by entering the fold of Islam, and share all those rights that have been granted to the believers. Unlike the westerners their trend of thought is not that the world should accept their religion but need not share their political ascendancy and authority. Here is a glimpse of the Muslim trend of thought in connection with the unbelievers: Rabiah bin' Amir, a companion of the Prophet, addressing Rustam the Persian governor and his courtiers, before the batter or battle of Qadisiyah, said:

> We have been commissioned by God to rid all those servant of His as are anxious to be free men, from, the bondage of men like themselves, and take them away from narrowness of this world to the vast expanse of the life Hereafter and from the excesses of religions to the shade of Justice and Equity under Islam.

If despite this Message of goodwill and glad tidings, an individual or a group persists with its rejection, they themselves are determined to live as Zimmis: literally one living under protection. As a technical term of the Islamic Shariah' the unbeliever who does not accept Islam but is willing to submit to its ideals being enforced in the Muslim state saving only his personal liberty of conscience as regards themselves. Jizya or a kind of poll-tax was levied on-them. There was no amount fixed for it, and in any case, it was symbolical acknowledgment that those whose religion was tolerated would in their turn not interfere with the preaching and progress of Islam. The tax varied in amount and there were exemptions for the poor, for females and the children (according to theorist Abu Hanifa for slaves and monks and hermits. Being a tax on able bodied Zimmis males of military age, it was in a sense a commutation for the military service, when the believers fought in the way of Allah and could be called to arms at a very short notice, and paid Zakat regularly. Moreover, the taxes on Muslims can be enhanced or fresh taxes levied in a national emergency, but not those once levied on Zimmis. However, there should be no misunderstanding that Zimmis have been assigned any lower or secondary position as compared with the believers. As a matter of fact just the reverse is the case. First of all let us consider the word Zimmis itself. It signified those persons safeguards for whose life, property, honour and dignity have been guaranteed. The Islamic state normally takes upon itself the responsibility of the protection of every citizen. But a special term was adopted in connection with non-Muslims in which the element of protection is outstanding. In their case protection and care have been assigned special importance. And it was not a put-up show to impress the world, but the injunctions of God and the Prophet are in fact to this effect. We have quoted above the Quranic verses strictly forbidding Muslims to take into confidence the unbelievers to keep out of harm's way. But here is the other side of the picture. In the matter of justice, emphasizing equality for one and all. God says:

> O ye who believe! Stand out firmly for God, as waitresses to fair dealing, and let not the hatred of others to you make you swerve to wrong and depart from justice. Be just: That is next to piety: and fear God. For God is well-acquainted with all that ye do.
>
> (Al Quran V:9)

> O ye who believe! Stand out firmly for justice, as witnesses to God, even as against yourselves, or your parents or your kin; (Al Quran IV: 131)

A certain member of the Bani Zafar tribe from Ansars, Tamah by name, stole the steel armour belonging to another person from Ansars. And to save himself from the punishment of stealing, he entrusted it to the custody of a Jew, and also charged him with theft. His tribe also with one voice, levelled the charge of theft against the Jew and in presenting the case to the Prophet insisted that the Jew be denied the right of his defence on the ground that Tamah was a believer and the Jew a polytheist. But before the Prophet could pronounce his judgement after hearing the case. God revealed the true position of the case to him. In a severe warning to the believer bringing a false charge against the Jew, God said in His revelation to the Prophet:

> We have sent down to thee the Book in truth, that thou mightiest judge between men, as guided by God: so be not (used) as an advocate by those who betray their trust. But seek the forgiveness of God; for God is oft-forgiving, Most Merciful. Contend not on behalf of such as betray their own souls; for God loveth not one given to perfidy and crime; they may hide (their crimes) from men, but they cannot hide (them) from God, seeing that He is in their midst when they plot

> by night, in words that He cannot approve: and God doth compass round all that they do. Ah! these are the sort of men on whose behalf ye may contend in this world; but who will contend with God on their behalf on the Day of Reckoning, or who will carry their affairs through! If anyone does evil or wrongs his own soul but afterwards seeks God's forgiveness, he will find God Oft-forgiving, Most Merciful. And if any one earns sin, he earns it against his own soul: for God is full of knowledge and wisdom. But if any one earns a fault or a sin and throws it on to one that is innocent, he carries (on himself both) a falsehood and a flagrant sin. But for the Grace of God to thee and His Mercy, a party of them would certainly have plotted to lead thee astray. But in fact they will lead their own souls astray, and to thee they can do no harm in the least. For God hath sent down to thee the Book and Wisdom and taught thee what thou knowest not before: and great is the Grace of God unto thee.
>
> (Al Quran IV: 105-113.)

This topic continues and we are told that there is no good in the secrets of people. These verses give us an idea what a heinous sin it is to charge an innocent person even if he is a non-Muslim and to mete him out punishment for a crime that he never committed, and how by intervening through revelation He managed the honourable acquittal of a Jew against a Muslim and all his supporters.

Now let us see what the Apostle of God has to say about the Zimmis:

> Beware! Whoever wrongs a Zimmi, curtails his rights, or puts him to more and harder work than he is capable of, or takes something from him against his consent, I shall personally stand as a complainant against him on the Day of Reckoning.(Abu Daud-Kitab-al-Jihad.)

The Prophet never said this about the oppressed Muslims that he would stand up to put their case in the Divine court of justice on the Day of Reckoning. But about the Zimmis he said that if they were oppressed by the Muslims he would be a complainant on their (Zimmi's) behalf. Now it is noteworthy that no Muslim worth the name could even think of oppressing those whose cause the Apostle of God would champion in the Hereafter.

During the period of Abu Bakr's caliphate, the teeth of a woman, who sang satiric verses about Muslims, were extracted as punishment for her highly objectionable activity. When the caliph learnt about it he wrote to his governor, Muhajir bin Ummayyah:

> I have been given to understand that you got two front (ubcusir Tr.) teeth of the woman who ridiculed Muslims in her satiric verses that she went about singing. If such a guilty woman be a believer, serious reprimanding her would be enough and corporal punishment should not be meted out or her disfigurement. But in case of her being a Zimmi woman, what weight does her satire of Muslims carry when we are putting up with their most heinous crime of polytheism. . If only 1 had cautioned you about it earlier, you would have been brought to book for that lapse.

The second caliph, Umar even during death pangs, had the problem of the treatment meted out to the Zimmis, upper most in his thoughts. Almost exhausted as a result of ghastly wounds and profuse bleeding he leaves sound advice for his successor:

> "I strongly recommend to my successor in the office of caliphate that those whom the Prophet pledged protection, must be treated sympathetically to honour his pledge to them. They should be protected from harm and they should not be burdened with mor than what they can easily bear."

Not only during the period of the Prophet and the rightly guided caliphs but also during the Umayyid and Abbasid dynasties as well as the Muslim rulers of later days, the protection provided to the non-Muslim minorities with regard to their lives, property and honour and dignity has been recognized by the westerners also. The famous orientalist Montgomery Watt writes:

> In the matter of the benevolent treatment meted out to the non-Muslims the Muslim states have, on the

> whole, the best record. Benevolent treatment to the non-Muslims was a matter of honour and pride to them. During the period of the rightly guided caliphs the protection of the non-Muslim minority paid annual tribute or Jizya in the form of goods or cash according to the agreement. The same amount had to be paid by them in the form of taxes per head. In return for this they were provided protection from foreign aggression and the internal security enjoyed by the Muslims. In those provinces where Zimmis lived, it was the duty of the government to realize Jizya from them and settle the disputes between them and the Muslims. Every minority was perfectly autonomous in their internal affairs. Their religious leader was responsible for the realization of Jizya and it was he who looked after all their internal affairs including the enforcement of their religious laws.

The same author further informs his readers:

> Definite guarantees were provided in all the agreements arrived at during the period of the Prophet of God, that every Zimmi minority would enjoy perfect freedom in its religious affairs. And this freedom was maintained during the later period also. The Christian churches and the Jewish synagogues were projected. Later it was suggested that they should not be allowed to build more places of worship than they already had, but in connection with the Zimmis, this and such other suggested rules and regulations (not included in the earliest agreements) were not put into practice.

This is the position of the Zimmis in an Islamic State. We are going to present in detail the commandments and precedents with regard to the rights of the Zimmis in the following pages; here it was our aim to define the attitude of the Muslim state in connection with them.

Now, where equality of the status of the Muslims and the non-Muslims is concerned, we have the verdict of the Quran before us that the believers and the rejectors are not equal. They are certainly equal with them in as much as they have the common bond of humanity between them, and as human beings they enjoy the same rights that their Muslim compatriots do. And they are equal in this respect too that the rights of both the Muslims and the non-Muslims have been determined by God and His Apostle. Just as the rights of the Muslims are inalienable and irrevocable, so are those of the non-Muslims. If the state cannot tamper with the rights of the Muslims, it cannot amend or cancel the rights of the non-Muslims either. If the Muslims can attain their rights through the judiciary by putting forth the edicts of the Quran and the Sunnah and the precedents of the rightly guided caliphate, the non-Muslims too have the guarantee of attaining their's with reference to the same sources. During the Fatimite regime when some governors wanted to lay hands on the properties of some Christian monks and Jews of Sinai and levied some fresh taxes on them, they approached the government at the centre and presented the documents of the agreements of the past and obtained the court decrees in their favour from Bahram, the vizier of Abdul Majeed Al Hafiz, and Al-Abbas and Talaqi, the viziers of Al-Zafar, in which the governors were directed to respect the old agreements and to strictly abide by the decisions of the rightly guided caliphate. Simultaneously, orders were issued that all new taxes be abolished with immediate effect and the Christians and the Jews be protected and well looked after.

Such examples are found during the Abbasid dynasty and even later period are proof enough of the fact that against the state both Muslims and non-Muslims stand equally protected. And this protection has been provided by Him Whose Entity and Sovereignty the Zimmis do not recognise.

Notwithstanding equality of status from the legal aspect, there is yet a difference between the fundamental rights of the Muslims and non-Muslims. And this difference lies in their political rights. And the reason behind it is neither any discrimination nor religious prejudice, but the peculiar nature of their attitude in the matter of loyalty to the Sovereignty of the Islamic state. The non-Muslims do not recognize the political order of Islam, based on the Sovereignty of God and depending for its constitution on the Quran and the Sunnah, and do not take that oath of allegiance to it which the Muslims do. Since a Muslim believing in God makes a covenant with Him that he will establish His political sovereignty on earth and that he will not only not recognize the sovereignty of any ones else but will efface it even at the cost of his own life, he comes to share the delegated powers conferred by God. Any individual of mankind who makes his covenant with God and takes an oath of allegiance, automatically comes to share these delegated powers. But one who is not prepared to shoulder this responsibility and rejects the sovereignty of God outright, how could he be called to share this authority.

Can any authority delegate its power to an individual or a group that does not recognize its entity and authority? Not withstanding this difference between the Muslims and non-Muslims in principle, Islam has not totally deprived the non-Muslims of the political rights. However, they are not qualified for appointment to the key posts in a Muslim state for which they do not fulfil the essential conditions of taking oath or allegiance to the constitution and its enforcement. In view of this position of non-Muslims, the fundamental rights in a Muslim state will have to be divided into three categories:

1. Those common to the Muslims and non-Muslims.
2. The Relative fundamental rights of the Muslims.
3. The Relative fundamental rights of the non- Muslims.

Among these, the first list will be longest, since God has attached utmost importance to the position of man because of birth. The other two lists shall comprise the rights that accrue to man as a Muslim or a non-Muslim.

***Moral Aspect :*** After taking stock of the history of fundamental rights in Islam and their legal position, let us now take up the moral aspect of these rights. We call only these rights legal which come under the Positive Law, and are enforcible by the executive and attainable through the judiciary, for example the security of life and property and liberty of organization and assembly, and such other rights. But those that are beyond the sphere of the authority of the executive and the judiciary and their enforcement has been left to the conscience and intuition of man, are all moral rights, for example visiting the sick to enquire after their health, aid and support of the needy, entertaining the guests and kind treatment of the neighbours, and the like. That means at the back of the legal rights there exists sanction of the law or the authority of the state, but the enforcement of the moral rights depends on the inner condition of man. Imam Ghazzali defining morality, says:

"Morality is the hidden form of the inner-self."

Since this inner form of man is beyond the grasp of physical observation and transcends the limited circle of man's knowledge and consciousness., the law did not include it in its sphere of action. Legislation and enforcement of law end at the apparent and observable acts of man. But it has nothing to do with the inner motives behind these acts and the ideas, beliefs and tendencies and leanings that take part in shaping and building the intellectual life of an individual. These things can come up for discussion under morality. And the determination of the human rights under this head is not the job of the legislators but the moral teachers. Maulana Hafiz-ur-Rehman of Seohara, explaining the application of the legal and moral spheres, says:

> The positive law is applicable to the observable acts, but the moral law keeps an eye on acts and the motivating forces behind them, and is applicable to both, so much so that some of those acts which apparently bear good results, the verdict of the moral law on them is that of mischievous, because the motive behind is unhealthy. The positive law is enforced through external forces like officials, army, police, the constitution of the state, jails and modern methods of reform. But the moral law is enforced by the hidden force of the inner self or intuition. The positive law compels the individuals only to the extent of those obligations on which depends the survival of the collection or society, like the protection of and respect for the life and property and other things of that sort. But the moral law compels man to take to virtue and excellence as well as obligations at the same time. And it makes men used to it that their efforts should be on the path of virtue, and as far as possible they should strive to attain the highest position they can, on this path."

Our legists, in view of this difference between law and morality, draw a line of demarcation between the legal and moral position of the rights. Allama Syed Sulaiman Nadvi, explaining the Rights due to God and those due to man, says;

The relation between the Creator and the creatures or God and His servants if related to mental exercise and the state of his heart, it is belief or "creed". And if our body and soul and our goods and property are also involved in this relation, it is service or "worship". The relations between man and man, and man and other creatures, also impose on us certain obligations, which if only legal in nature, are "dealings". But, in case they are not legal but spiritual teachings and instructions, it is "morality."

The same classification of legal and moral is met within the books on jurisprudence. But one important aspect of it is usually overlooked, or divorced from its real context, it is placed under some other head. And that is why the mutual relation between the legal and moral rights fails to be fully explained. According to the general run of the legal and moral principles in the world, this division is in order. But in view of the Sovereignty of God and the position of man as vicegerent on earth, the nature of this classification is entirely changed in Islam. Here legal and moral rights have been determined under the commandment of the one and only Sovereign, and as such the difference here is not that of the law framed by a legislative authority and the moral principles presented by a moral teacher. They do not differ even in the matter of being an enforceable and incapable of enforcement. A Muslim under the covenant with his Lord and Cherisher binds himself to total obedience of God and His Apostle.

> Say: Truly, my prayer and my service of Sacrifice, my life and my death, are (all) for God, the Cherisher of the World. (Al Quran VI: 162.)

On the one hand this covenant of loyalty on the part of the servant and on the other the following declaration by God:

> God hath purchased of the Believers their persons and their goods; for theirs (in return) is the Garden (of Paradise): (Al Quran IX : 111)

After this covenant and mutual agreement where is the room left for a believer to discriminate between the legal and moral laws and adopt different attitudes towards them. To him every edict of the Quran is a law by itself. He obeys every order of God with equal sense of responsibility. To him legal rights alone are not due and binding, but all those rights coming under morality are equally due and binding. The moral code of conduct ends on establishing a norm of good and evil. Its enforcement is left to the conscience of man, and is voluntary in nature, and nobody is accountable for it in any way. The greatest sanction that can be afforded to it is in any form of social pressure. However, a revolt against it is neither a cognizable offence nor punishable in any court of law. Is this the plight of moral rights under Islam too? Evidently enough the answer is in the negative. The Muslim has to account for every tiny particle without any distinction of legal or moral.

> Then shall any one who has done an atom's weight of good see it! And anyone who has done an atom's weight of evil, shall see it. (Al Quran XCIX : 7-8)

When such is the case, why do the jurists classify on the basis of moral and legal bases? On what basis do they make this distinction?

This difference, in Islam, lies in this that individually every Muslim is bound to obey every injunction of his Lord and this duty is of a legal nature since he has to account for every act of his before the Sovereign and it is on the basis of these acts that reward or punishment will be decided for him in His court of justice. There he cannot put up the excuse that, where his own life and his powers were concerned, he was unable to abide by the laws given by God and render his due to Him. But an Amir or Imam has been made responsible for the enforcement of only those rights which he can enforce with the help of his limited knowledge, and understanding and observation based on his senses. These are the rights known as "legal". That amounts to saying that the classification has been undertaken from the point of view of the powers of the government, and not from that of the responsibility and accountability of an individual. For the individual all the rights have a legal position. But considering the limitations of the authority and the responsibilities of the Amir or Imam they get divided into legal and moral. The minimum rights which God has deemed inevitable for making the human society balanced, just, peaceful and prosperous and decent. He made them enforceable through His delegated authority. And in this connection he also gave him the necessary instructions and powers. Those rights which He deemed essential for the building up of the society on the highest moral foundations and the best formation of the individuals' characters for this purpose. He made the individuals singly responsible for their enforcement. And accountability in this behalf He reserved exclusively for Himself. Now, to the extent of the enforcement of the legal rights, the individual and the society both together will be held accountable and punishable in the court of sovereign. But the rights that have been kept out of the sphere of the authority of the state, the individual will still be accountable for them, and to this extent there will be no difference between the legal and the moral rights.

That is to say, in the sphere of the mutual relations of the individual and the delegated authority, the rights on the basis of their observable expression and enforcement, they shall be divided into the legal and moral limits. But where it comes to mutual relations of God and His servant, this division disappears, and all the rights come to have a legal position. To ensure enforcement of the legal rights, God has entrusted them to the state so that if an individual fails in his duty concerning these rights, the state with the powers of the executive and the judiciary may enforce them under compulsion, and let no deserving individual suffer usurpation or injury to his rights. But since the state can discharge this duty only to the extent of observable conduct of people, it was not charged with the legal responsibility of the enforcement of the moral rights. But with the individual it persists. He has not been given the slightest allowance in the matter of enforcing the moral rights however petty in appearance.

Where the government is concerned, it cannot but depend on the statements of the plaintiff, the defendant and the witnesses and the report of the police instead of relying on its direct knowledge, in adjudicating a dispute. All the means of information at its command can encompass the external conduct, having no access whatsoever to the inner self of any person. So in view of these frailties of human beings, the government run by them has been made responsible for the enforcement of the legal rights concerning the external conduct. And even in connection with these rights absolute and final justice has been reserved by God His own court on the Day of Reckoning, since it is possible that in spite of honesty and the best of intentions, due to lack of access to the true facts some of those charged with authority might have failed in dispensing justice. Even the Prophet of God who was the most knowledgeable among men, says about himself:

> I am (after all) human. Among those appearing before me for the settlement of their disputes, one party may be more clamorous and clever at exaggeration than the other, and I may decide the case in his favour taking him to be truthful. So if I give somebody what really belongs to his brother, he should not take portion of Hell-fire.

God says:

> They know but the outer (things) in the life of this world: but of the End of things they are heedless.
>
> (Al Quran XXX:7)

Umar, the second caliph, explaining the sphere of action of the government run by men, says:

> During the Prophet's time the Divine revelation always came out with the truth and kept you in your places.

If any one concealed any thing he was exposed and the one who revealed anything against the truth, was also caught. You must exhibit the best in you of morality. God knows what is in your breasts. Whoever shows evil on the outside and claims a wholesome inner-self, we shall not verify it. And whoever shows a good exterior we shall take him to be good.

In another tradition the same theme is met with in these words:

> Hark ye! When reciting the Quran look only for the reward from Allah, and show it in your deeds. When the revelation was current, we could recognize you through that mirror, since the Prophet of God was amongst us then. Now the revelation has come to an

> end and the Prophet has left. Now I can recognize you through only those things (norms) I have told you. Hark! Whoever shows goodness we shall take him to be good and form a good opinion of him. And whoever shows evil, he shall be in our bad books and we shall detest him (for evil deeds).

That amounts to saying that even those rights that we term legal, can be enforced only to the extent of human knowledge and perception. They will be finally decided in the Divine Court. That is why Allah Himself kept all those rights that needed for their enforcement knowledge beyond the ken of senses and observation of the inner-self, beyond man's limited powers and authority. And making man bound individually for them He has reserved the decision for Himself, since the inner-self which is not accessible to human perception is open before God. There are no secrets that are hidden from Him. With His perfect and infallible knowledge He will decide all disputes over rights. And there will be no distinction of moral and legal there (in His court of Justice). He says:

> Know they not that God knoweth what they conceal and what they reveal. (Al Quran II: 77)
>
> But never will they hide a single fact from God. (Al Quran IV:42)
>
> For God is witness of all things.(Al Quran XXII: 17)
>
> God knoweth well all the secrets of the heart. (Al Quran :119)

Since man's motives, aspirations, intentions, thoughts beliefs, in short, nothing is hidden from Him, man's exterior and inner-self are clearly before Him, in His court no right shall remain merely "moral right", but all the rights shall be legal rights, and they will be decided according to all the known legal procedures. He will listen to all the wronged ones.

> When the female (infant), buried alive, is questioned for what crime she was killed.(Al Quran LXXXI:8-9)

He will examine the reports prepared by the guardian angels:

> But verily over you (axe appointed angels) to protect you, kind and honourable, all that ye do. (Al Quran LXXXII: 10-12)

> He will call in evidence the tract of land on which a certain incident occurred:
>
> On that Day will she (the earth) declare her tidings.
> (Al Quran XCIX:4)

He will give hearing to the statement of the culprit and also the evidence of his own hands and feet:

> On the day when their tongues, their feet will bear witness against them as to their actions.
> (Al Quran XXIV:24)

After taking evidence of the prophets and other witnesses He will furnish undeniable proof that -truth had been conveyed to them:

> The Prophets and the witnesses will be brought forward:
> (Al Quran XXXIX:69)

And finally the culprit himself will confess that he had been guilty of the crime on his record:

> They will say: Yes indeed: a Warrer did come to us, but we rejected him and said, 'God never sent down any (Messenger)'. (Al Quran LXVII;9)

And after they have been convincingly indicted. He will pronounce His Judgement:

> And a just decision pronounced between them; and they will not be wronged (in the least). And to every soul will be paid in full (the fruit) of its deeds; and (God) knoweth best all that they do.
> (Al Quran XXXIX:69-70)

Now just imagine, on what basis the rights that are to come up in the greatest and final court of Justice for decision according to all the known conditions of dispensation of justice, can be termed "moral rights". It is also noteworthy how mutually the moral rights will be examined at the time of hearing in this court. The Quran says:

> When a courteous greeting is offered you, meet it with a greeting still more courteous, or (at least) of equal courtesy. God takes careful account of all things.
> (Al Quran IV:86)

The concluding portion of this verse clearly points to the fact that this is not mere moral recommendation but an injunction, a regulation, and the defaulters shall be called to account in the court of the Sovereign. It is very difficult for a court in this world to determine whether the courteous greeting offered was met with properly or not. So they were not charged with the responsibility of the enforcement of this moral right. But in the court of the Sovereign, the tongue and the hands and the feet themselves shall bear witness whether that method was proper or not, and the heart also shall furnish evidence whether it was full of sincerity or brimming over with the filth of contempt, malice and enmity.

Now let us take up the right in some detail from the Quran and the Sunnah:

> Say: "Come, I will rehearse what God hath (really) prohibited you from": join not anything as equal with Him; be good to your parents: kill not your children on a plea of want; We provide sustenance for you and for them; come not nigh shameful deeds, whether open or secret; take not life, which God hath made sacred except by way of justice and law: Thus doth He command you, that ye may learn wisdom. And come not nigh to the orphan's property, except to improve it, until he attain the age of full strength: give measure and weight with (full) justice... no burden do. We place on any soul, but that which it can bear; whenever ye speak, speak justly, even if a near relative is concerned: and fulfil the covenant of God: thus doth He command you that ye may remember. Verily, this is My Way, leading straight: follow it: follow not (other) paths: they will scatter you about from His great path; thus doth He command you, that ye may be righteous.
>
> (Al Quran VI: 151-153)

All those beliefs and deeds are those for which accountability before God is certain. The sphere of the powers and the scope of hearing of this court (of God) has been fully brought out in Surah Zilzal. (The convulsion-XCIX):

> Then shall anyone who has done an atom's weight of good, shall see it ! And any one who has done an atom's weight of evil, shall see it.
>
> (Al Quran XCIX:7-8)

Pondering over these verses (VL151-153), we find that polytheism, kind treatment to parents, killing of children, shameful deeds, respect for human life, misappropriation of the property of orphan, honesty in measure and weight, speaking the truth, the covenant of God and following His Straight Path— all these instructions in succession are being given with equal emphasis.

The first and foremost right stressed here is that of God and it is that we must not take other gods, with Him. Ascribing partners to God is a sin absolutely unpardonable. The Quran pronounces that verdict:

> God 'forgiveth not that Partners should be set up with Him; but He forgiveth any thing else, to whom He pleases, to set up partners with God is to devise a sin most heinous indeed. (Al Quran IV:48)

In the enforcement of this greatest of rights, the courts and the governments of this world can exercise their power only to the extent of the observable conduct. So when Umar, the second caliph of the Prophet, learnt that people came and offered prayers beneath the tree in whose shade the Prophet had taken the covenant of the Believers (Baiat-e-Rizwan at Hudaibiyah), he smelt polytheism in this attitude of people and had it felled leaving no trace of it, and remarked:

> O ye people ! I find that you have started worshipping the god Uzza Hark ! After today I would not tolerate anyone coming this way to offer, prayers. If ever I learn of any one doing it I will have' him executed, just as the apostates are executed.

But where things are not as apparent as that, and Uzza, Lat and Manat have found their way to the deepest recesses of the hearts and are snugly seated there who is going to stop and put an end to such polytheism. And if eradication of such hidden heatheism is not possible for any government, will this right of God be deemed a mere "moral right" and be consigned a secondary position to a "legal right". Never! This right is of primary importance according to the covenant between man and God which is the sacred duty of every man, and the rest of the legal and moral rights entirely depend on the recognition and enforcement of this first and foremost right. This is that one right which when neglected and shirked God did not wait for the Day of Reckoning to settle accounts with the criminals and meted out such horrible punishments to them that served as a warning and an admonition to others.

> Say: Travel through the earth and see what was the End of those before (you): Most of them worshipped others besides God. (Al Quran XXX; 42)

That is to say when the people as a whole were bent on taking gods other than God and did not listen to the Prophets of God that were commissioned to ask them to desist from their heathenic beliefs and practices and to enforce the commandments of God, He took the command directly in His Own hands and bringing down upon them the scourage of punishment for their evil deeds wiped them off from the face of the earth.

Since the perfect enforcement of this right is totally beyond the powers of man and those of the highest executive or judicial institution founded by him, it will be recognized as a legal right in so far as its external manifestations are concerned. But from the point of view of belief and faith, it will be regarded as a legal right in the society. However, in the court of God this will be the first legal right about which people will be questioned. And that leaves no room for a believer to regard it only as a "moral right."

This was about polytheism, the most heinous crime in the sight of God. But the Prophet of God tells us that every right, no-matter what its significance in our sight, has the same importance. The Prophet says:

> Seest thou one who denies the Judgement (to come)? Then such is the (man) who repulses the orphan (with harshness), and encourages not the feeding of the indigent. So woe to the worshippers who are neglectful of their Prayers, those who (want but) to be seen (of men) but refuse to supply even neighbourly needs.
> (Al Quran CVII: 1-7)

Harsh treatment of the orphan, refusing food to the indigent, are all crimes of a moral nature. But those guilty of them are being given warning and illtidings of ruination in the Hereafter, and told to take heed and not to regard them unimportant; it is on their performance in these fields that their ruination or their salvation and felicity depend. Let us now take another example:

> Ann do good to parents, kinsfolk, orphans, those in need, neighbours, who are near, neighbours who are strangers, the companion by your side, the way-farer (ye meet), and what your right hands possess: for God loveth not the arrogant, the vainglorious; (nor) those who are niggardly or enjoin niggardliness on others, or hide the bounties which God has bestowed on them; for we have prepared for those who resist Faith, a Punishment that steeps them in contempt; nor those who spend of their substance, to be seen of men, but have no faith in God and the Last Day: if any take the Evil one for their intimate, what a dreadful intimate he is! And what burden were it on them if they had faith in God and in the Last Day, and they spend out of what God hath given them for sustenance? For God, hath full knowledge of them. God is never unjust in the least degree: if there is any good (done). He doubleth it, and giveth from His Own presence a great reward. Now then if we brought from each people a witness, and we brought thee as a witness against these people! On that day those who reject Faith and disobey the Apostle, will wish that the earth were made one with them but never will they hide a single fact from God;
>
> (Al Quran IV:36-42)

All these verses relate to the "Moral Rights." But ponder a little over those beginning from "God is never unjust in the least degree" to the end, are all those rights for which we will be called to account, and rewards and punishments pronounced on them, witnesses will be called to furnish evidence, and when there is no flaw left in the legal process, pronouncement will be made on the case.

Here the servants of God have been addressed directly. And the rights pointed out here are such as do not permit division into the legal and the moral. Due to the expressed will of the Sovereign, they are all legal in nature. On what basis can we discriminate between one and another of the rights conferred by the Sovereign as legal and moral? What justification is there for such (arbitrary) classification? At the most what can be said about them is that these rights are beyond the grasp of the state. But are they also beyond the grasp of the Sovereign? If it is not so, how could we be free in either living up to them or neglecting them at our own discretion. And when this freedom is non-existent and not leaving it to our conscience and intention, they have been made obligatory, how can they be regarded as moral rights. They are one and all legal rights. Only this reason that they do not permit the intervention of the state due to its limitations of powers, does not in any way make any difference in their being the injunctions of the Sovereign. Even if we somehow manage to escape from the grip of the human courts and executives, how can we save ourselves from the accountability of the Sovereign's own court?

From among the human beings too, those chosen ones elevated to the highest position conferred on man by God, and who are not dominated by the human sovereignty of limited knowledge and powers, but directly under the sovereignty of the All-knowing and Well-acquainted Sovereign, with them even in this world all moral rights are treated as legal rights in the method of enforcement. So we find that the Prophet who stood at an exalted standard of character by the Grace of his Lord (And thou (standest) on an exalted standard of character—Al Quran LXVIIL4), when on one occasion, while conveying the message of God to the tribal chiefs in a select gathering, on the (untimely) interruption by a blind companion of his, Ibne-Umm-e-Maktoom, showed signs of disapproval, God at once took serious notice of it and said in a rather admonitory tone:

> (The Prophet) frowned and turned away; because there came to him (interrupting). But what could tell thee but that perchance he might grow (in spiritual understanding)?—Or that he might receive admonition,

> and the teaching might profit him? As to one who regards himself self-sufficient, to him dost thou attend: though, it is not Thee if he grow not (in spiritual understanding), and but as to him who came to thee striving earnestly, and with fear in his heart, of him wast thou unmindful. (Al Quran LXXX:1-10)

Since God had a direct contact with his Apostle through revelation, for the perfect enforcement of a moral right, he was called to account here in this world. But the procedure for the common people is different. Here they are under the domination of a delegated authority, which has been made responsible for the enforcement of legal rights only because of its limited knowledge and information. But when all of them will be there in the presence of their Lord and Cherisher, directly, without any intermediary, the distinction of the moral and legal rights shall have ended and there will be equal accountability for every right.

The discussion so far must have made it quite clear how important is morality in Islam. And how much different are the rights we call moral rights in their sense from the moral rights of the common political terminology of the modern secular world, and how in the final court of justice, the legal and moral rights acquire the same status.

If this position of the rights in the life Hereafter is kept in view, man can develop the highest moral character, and he obeys every divine commandment, not under any external pressure or compelling force but under the urge of his inner self and sense of responsibility, without any hesitation or reserve and with perfect readiness of mind and with a heart full of fear of God, never dividing these commandments into legal and moral spheres. This classification had really to be made with a view to define the limits of the powers of the state, and not to compel man to perfect compliance with same commandments of God and to permit some allowance or indulgence in the case of some others. In the commandments of God conveyed through the Quran all the instructions in connection with beliefs, devotional acts, dealings and moral issues are often met with in the same continuation, intermingled with one another in such a way that there is no room for making any distinction between the external and the inner aspects of man's conduct. The Quran does not split man into an "external man" and an "inner man", but addresses him as an "undivided person" whose mental, physical, emotional and spiritual life is an integrated unity and totality. That is why it was said:

> O ye who believe! Enter into Islam whole-heartedly:
> (Al Quran 11:208)

Explaining this verse Maulana Syed Abul Ala Maudoodi says'

> Which is the same as to say submit your life in its entirety without any exceptions or reserves. Your ideas, your opinions, your disciplines, your manners and habits, your dealings and the course of your action and struggle, must all be made subservient to Islam. Take heed, lest you should divide your life into various compartments, subordinating some to Islam and keeping others away from its sway.
> (Tafheem al Quran, Vol.I.p.160.)

Allah wants total obedience of the whole person. To the extent this obedience was deemed essential for the prosperity and well-being of the individual and collective life and to check confusion and chaos in the human society, it was managed and ensured through laws and the powers of the state to enforce them. But in the life Hereafer the salvation and felicity everlasting shall be decided on the basis of "moral law", since beliefs, devotional acts and the excellence of deeds all come under this law. Viewed from this angle, moral laws and moral rights in Islam have a superiority over the "legal rights", since the code of the Divine court will be that in which the moral aspect has priority and importance.

There, the quality of our faith and belief and the sincerity of devotional acts and the inner aspect of our observable acts shall be determined by the "moral laws" alone. Here in this earthly life it is just possible that a person despite his hypocrisy, may pass as a Muslim due to his apparent conduct, and may go on all his life deriving all the benefits of rights, from the Muslims that Islam has conferred on them. But after death his case shall not be decided on the external form of his deeds but on the basis of his inner self, and exactly in accordance with the following unambiguous decision of the Quran:

> For God will collect the Hypocrites and those who defy Faith —all in Hell. (Al Quran IV;140)

And in Hell they will be assigned the lowest depths:

> The hypocrites will be in the lowest depths of the Fire: no helper will thou find for them:(Al Quran. IV: 145)

This is the unhappy end of those who had offered prayers observed fasts, participated in the Hajj and Jihad (or striving in the way of Allah,) and were found busy in the remembrance of God. But what was the condition of their hearts:

> The Hypocrites—they think they are over-reaching God, but He will over-reach: when they stand up to prayer, they stand without earnestness, to be seen of men, but little do they hold God in remembrance; (they are) distracted in mind even in the midst of it,—being sincerely for neither one group nor another.
> (Al Quran IV: 142-143)

The hypocrites on account of this inner state of theirs, which is entirely of a moral nature, will be the recipients of the severest punishment from God and their observable conduct and deeds which gave them all the rights in this world, will be of no avail to them there, although it was due to these apparent .deeds here in this world that the Prophet of God did not decide that they were unbelievers and never stopped the leaders of the hypocrites like Abdullah bin-e-Ubai, because of their lip service to Islam and showy deeds, from entering and moving about freely among the ranks of the believers.

In the whole of the Quran and particularly in the verses dealing with the Last Day, God has made the inner life of man as the basis of His decisions, which clearly brings out the fact that our salvation depends on what we call "morality." There, not deeds alone (of any sort) but "righteous deeds," shall be our real assets, and this condition of "righteousness" which is here a purely moral issue, will be entirely legal.

The superiority of morality over law can be estimated by a tradition of the Prophet in which he has pointed out that the real mission of his teaching and preaching was for the purpose of perfecting morality. He says:

> I have been commissioned for perfection of morality.
>
> (Musnad-e-Ahmad, Baihaqi, Ibn-e-Saad)

And this is that morality which is supported by the accountability of the Hereafter and its great power of enforcement.

Explaining this relation of law and morality Maulana Mufti Muhammad Shaft says:

> One of the distinctions of Islam is this that, looked at from a wider perspective, its moral instructions are also legal injunctions, since it is on their basis that the reward and the punishment of the Hereafter are to be decided which is of fundamental importance in the life of a Muslim. This creed of the life Hereafter is that which has not only conferred on morality the status of law, but provided support to those, technically termed laws. If you think over the style of the Quran you will, find that with every legal and moral injunction are associated reminders of the concepts of fear of God and provisions for the life Hereafter.

***All Rights are God's :*** After this much understanding of the mutual relation of the legal and moral rights, we shall now take stock of the moral aspect of the rights. Our legists have classified rights in another way under the heading, the "Rights of God" and the "Rights of His Servants." According to this classification, the belief and the devotional acts like Prayers, Fasting and Hajj and such other practices are the rights of God. And all those rights which are mutually due from the servants of God to their brethren are the rights of the servants of God or men, such as security of life and the rights of inheritance, dower and alimony and the like. Some rights are common to both. For example, Zakat being service to God involving man's goods, is a right of God and from a consideration of those deserving (help with) it, it is a right of the servants of God. Similarly, sacrifice which is a right of God in as much as it is an offering of life to Him but in relation to the giving away of the hide and the flesh of the animal to the deserving men it is also a right of the servants of God.

But the way the difference of moral and legal rights disappears in the life of a Muslim and in the court of God and all the rights, likewise the division of the rights of God and those of the servants of God ends in the final analysis, and the rights all come to belong to God and from the moral point of view attain that highest position which they are not assigned in any legal order and any moral code of the world.

This classification of the rights of God and the rights of men was meant to determine the direction of the fulfillment of these rights. In other words the rights whose recipient is God they fall under the heading rights of God. And those whose recipient are men are included in the list of the rights of the servants of God. But pondering over the fundamental question of the legal and moral position and justification for them, we have to determine whether man came to deserve these rights on grounds of some struggle or his accepted demands or they have been determined by any social contract, an agreement on the basis of consensus between the people and the government, a constitution framed by man or an agreement between man and man. If there is no such thing, what is the basis for these rights of his. Apparently enough, the only basis for it is the injunction of the Sovereign. It is He Who has determined the rights of every deserving one, and decided the priorities between the rights of these deserving people. About Zakat He says:

> Alms (Zakat Tr.) are for the poor and the needy and those employed to administer the (funds); for those whose hearts have been (recently) reconciled (to truth); for those in bondage and in debt; In the cause of God; and for the way-farer: (thus is) ordained by God, and God is full of knowledge and wisdom.
>
> (Al Quran IX:6Q.)

Here, along with pointing out those deserving Zakat, priorities among them have been determined and concluding, it has been said that these rights have been determined by God and their fulfillment has also been ordered by Him. If any one is guilty of a lapse in the matter of these rights he must be aware that none of his deeds is hidden from God.

Similarly, after detailing the rights of various inheritors it has been said.

> These are settled portions ordained by God: and God is All knowing, All wise. (Al Quran IV:11.)

Following this verse the inheritors' portions have been determined and this serial too ends with the following verse:

> Thus it is ordained by God: and God is All-Knowing forbearing. (Al Quran IV:12)

After detailed injunctions regarding which women are allowed to the believers and which not, it is said:

Thus hath God ordained (prohibitions) against you: (and it is binding on you to observe them).

And after determining the rights of men and women in connection with divorce. Allah says:

> These are the limits ordained by God; so do not transgress them If any do transgress the limits ordained by God; such person wrong (themselves as well as others,) (Al Quran 11:229)

In connection with rust and Justice it is ordained:

> God doth command you to render back the Trusts to those to whom they are due; and when ye judge between man, and man that ye judge with justice. (Al Quran IV:58)

The rights of the needy, those who asked and those who failed to get their due, are determined in the wealth of the rich.

> And in their wealth and possessions the right of the (needy) him who asked and him who for some reason was prevented from asking. (Al Quran 1.1:19)

In short, taking any one from the rights of God, or those of His servants, and studying the relevant verses of the Quran and every right takes its sanction from the Divine injunction, and its fulfillment has also been ordained by Him .

God did not only determine the rights, but placed Himself as the recipient of every right, so that the person charged with the fulfillment of it may realise that he is offering it not to any one else but to God All mighty Himself. He says:

> Eat of their fruit in their season, but render the dues that are proper (God's share, Tr.) on the day that the harvest is gathered. (Al Quran VI:41)

Here, while ordaining the share of His servants in yield of fruit, God associated that share with Himself to bring home to man that whatever he gives to his servants is really His right that He will be fulfilling. He also takes upon Himself the reward for such fulfillment and says:

> So give what is due to kindred, the needy, and the way-farer. This is best for those who seek the countenance of God, and it is they who will prosper. (Al Quran XXX:38.)

That means, you may be paying the dues of God or those due to men, the motivating force is the same, and that is obedience to God and seeking His countenance, and through its reward acquiring the facility everlasting. A Muslim offering greeting to his Muslim brother in all sincerity and with love, the motive behind it is never to derive any benefit from him, but through carrying out an order of God he is looking forward to seek His pleasure. And when he is paying out Zakat and Sadqat (charities), he has this end in view. In the collective system of the payment of Zakat, he does not know whom he is going to benefit with his share of Zakat. He entrusts it to the Islamic state as his due to Allah, which in turn spends it on the deserving servants of God. This was the relation in vein between God's and man's rights which prompted Abu Bakr, the first caliph of the Prophet, to declare war in the way of Allah against those who refused to pay Zakat after the passing away of the Prophet.The tribes with holding payment of Zakat were those who subscribed to Islam in all departments, established the (system of) Prayer and were believers in the unity of Allah and the

Prophethood of His Apostle. They had only withheld their goods from the deserving servants of God, thus denying a right ordained by Him. On this occasion many of the Prophet's companions, including even Umar, the great undaunted champion of the Islamic cause and well versed in the finer points of the temperaments of the Faith of God, had expressed his opinion thus:

> We should not lake up arms against those who believe in God and His Apostle, but asking them to join hands with us, we should tackle the problem of the apostates with all the forces at our command.

The dialogue between Abu Bakr, the caliph in saddle, and Umar who became his successor, makes it quite evident that the former made no distinction between the rights of God and those of His servants, while 'Umar' was making such distinction, but was finally in agreement with the latter. When after consulting the companions of the Prophet on this issue, Abu Bakr made the forceful assertion:

> By Allah! If those refusing to pay Zakat withhold even a rope that they paid during the period of the Prophet, I will wage war against them.

On hearing this Hadrat 'Umar' who was of the opinion that 'fighting against those refusing to pay Zakat was not in the interest of the Muslims, hatted up a bit and said;

How can we wage war against them when we know that the Prophet of God has definitely told us that he had been ordered to fight against people only so long as they had not pronounced 'There is no god but God and Muhammad is His servant and Apostle." And one who had once announced his belief in this Kalima, security of his life and property would be the concern of the Muslims, whatever was due from him would be demanded of him. About his intentions only God would call him to account.

Abu-Bakr was not satisfied with the arguments of Umar and said:

> By God! I must fight against those who regard Zakat any the less important than Prayer, since Zakat is the right in goods and the Prophet had said that those

> entering the fold of Islam shall have to pay all that is due from them.

Umar used to say later:

> Abu Bakr's reply convinced me that Allah Himself had conferred clarity of vision on the issue of those refusing to pay Zakat. And the Truth was with Abu Bakr.

This incident reveals the important position of the right of His servants determined by Allah, and how it is realizable like the rights of Allah. Refusal to comply with the demand in this connection is tantamount to disobeying Allah Himself. The Quran says:

> Reverence God through Whom ye demand your mutual (rights), and reverence the woman (that bore you): for God ever watches over you. (Al Quran IV: I.)

Immediately following this verse there is the long series of the rights of the orphans, women, men, the needy, the inheritors and other servants of God. But it has been made very clear in the beginning that every one's right gets its sanction from God, and He is ever watching over you. So fear Him and duly fulfil the rights, or you shall be taken to task in the Hereafter.

To offer a goodly loan is to help a brother in need. But this loan God has taken upon Himself instead of the person helped, and has promised to repay it with manifold increase and also forgive your sins in return for it:

> If ye loan to God a beautiful loan. He will double it to your (credit), and He will grant you Forgiveness:
> (Al Quran LI V: 17)

At another place it has been said.

> And establish regular Prayer and give regular charity (Zakat); and loan to God a beautiful loan.
> (Al Quran LXX1II:20)

Similarly take the case of spending in the way of Allah. God declares the monetary help offered to any servant of His in need as "spending in the way of Allah", Himself becomes its recipient and promises the best return for it:

> Those who spend their substance in the cause of God, and follow not up their gifts with reminder of their generosity or with injury, for them their reward is with their Lord: On them shall be no fear, nor shall they grieve. (Al Quran 11:261)

The same thing has been repeated in LVII:10, 18 and 11:272 and in many other verses of the Quran. If a person enters into an agreement with another, written or oral, and brings in Allah as witness, that agreement he makes with Allah, and He watches over the actions of both the parties involved in it for the protection of their rights.

> And break not your oaths after ye have confirmed them; indeed you have made God your surety; for God knoweth all that ye do. (Al Quran XVI:91)

Similarly, plighting fealty at the hands of the Prophet was declared to be the same as plighting fealty to God:

> Verily those who plight their fealty to thee do no less than plight their fealty to God: The Hand of God is over their hands. (Al Quran XLVIIL-10)

The great exegetist of the Quran, Abdullah bin-Masood says:

> Whenever somebody gives charity (Sadqah), before finding its way to the hands of the needy who asks for it, it touches the hands of Allah and it is He Who remits it to him. Then he recited the following verse:
>
> Know they not that God doth accept repentances from His votaries and receives their gifts of charity. (Al Quran IX: 14)

A study of these verses reveals that Allah associating every right, whether the right of God or that of His servants, has conferred such a lofty moral and legal position to it that for a true Muslim no distinctions are left as regards their obligatory nature and their importance. Whenever there is a right due for fulfillment for us, there, with the recipient of that right, God is always associated. To quote the Traditions of the Prophet:

> The Prophet is reported to have said that God will say on Doomsday, 'O son of Adam! I was sick and thou

> did not visit Me to ask after My health.' He will say: 'O my Lord and Cherisher! How could I visit Thee in Thy sickness? Thou art the Lord of the worlds.' To which God will say: didst thou not know that such and such of My servant was lying in sick bed and thou didst not visit him to ask after his health. Didst thou know that if thou hadst visited him in his sick bed, thou-wouldst have found Me close to him.

Muslim, Reported by Abu Hurayrah

In another Tradition the same theme is met with in these words:

> The Prophet of God said: "God will say on Doomsday 'O son of Adam; I asked thee for food but thou didst not feed Me.' He will say in reply, 'O my Lord and Cherisher; how could I feed Thee when Thou art the Cherisher and Sustainer of all of us? Allah will say, 'Dost thou not know that such and such of My servants asked thee for food but thou didst not feed him. If thou hadst given him food, thou wouldst have found that food here witn Me. O son of Adam! I had asked thee for water but thou didst not give Me water.' To this he will say, 'O my Lord and Cherisher! How could I give thee water to drink when Thou art the Lord and Cherisher of the world. God will say to him, 'Such and such of my servants had asked thee for water but thou did not give him that. If thou hadst given him water thou wouldst have found that water here with Me'."

Muslim, Reported by Abu Hurayrah.

Zakat, Sadqah, giving loans, feeding the hungry, quenching The thirst of the thirsty and entering an agreement with any one, are one and all the rights pertaining to the servants of God. But it is noteworthy how God, associating Himself with every recipient of the right has taken them to the level of the. Rights of God. The famous legist Shatabi says:

> "There are two kinds of rights, 'Rights of God and rights of the servants of God.' The latter includes the Rights of Allah also, and those that we term the 'Rights of God' benefit His servants only."

Going a little further, we can say that all rights belong to Allah, and all of them come under service to God. However, all the benefits are derived by the servants of Allah. When a servant of Allah fulfills the right due to Allah, he himself derives all the benefits, since Allah is far above and Independent to need any benefits from any servant of His. When he worships Him he benefits himself in the form of self purification, moulding of the character and perfection of humanity. And when he fulfills the rights due to the servants of God, this benefit becomes two sided. The person fulfilling these rights, having the best character, he is the recipient of honour and respect, ease of conscience, peace of heart and mind and honour and dignity in the Hereafter. And the recipient of the rights on receiving them lives a life of satisfaction and happiness mutual relations of sincerity and love sacrifice and sympathy get strengthened, and in this way the entire human society becomes the cradle of peace and tranquillity and prosperity and security.

Now let us also find out that along with the priorities of right determined by God in this world, what priorities have been provided in this connection in the Hereafter, Anas, a companion, reports from the Prophet:

> On the Day of Reckoning there will be three lists of the deeds of men. One of them will be from which not a word will be left by God without taking serious notice of. The second will be that of which little or no notice will be taken. And the third list will comprise those deeds of which not an iota can be forgiven.

The list with forgivable sins will comprise polytheistic practices- That of which God will take no notice is the wrong that an individual has done to his own soul and which is between man and his Lord (such as lapses in offering prayers and fasting and the like). God will forgive sins on this list whomsoever He wills, and he will be saved. But the list of which not a word will be passed over without scrutiny and action will comprise wrongs done by one man to another, save in case of the wronged one having forgiven his tormentor.

(Jamaat Fawaid, Muhammad bin-Sulaiman Ahmaghribi, Vol.11, p.527, Loyalpur, with reference to Musnad-e-Bazaz).

The same tradition has been quoted in *Musnad-e-Ahmed* and *Mustadrak-Hakim* as reported by Aishah. The well-known book on Hanafite jurisprudence, entitled *Al Hidayah* under the title Hajj and related mailers, says:

> Hajj became obligatory only when the person concerned is in a Position to provide enough for his defendants to live on during the period of his absence from home, since the rights of the servants to God have priority over those of God, under Hip own injunctions.

Now the question arises why did God give priority to the rights of His servants over His own! The reason is to be found in the fact that by his lapses in fulfilling the rights of God man can do Him no harm, but only wrongs his own Soul and comes to harm. But when he deprives another servant of God, like himself, of a certain right, he injures some interest of his brother which is a factual loss to him. And this is that wrong which is unpardonable in the sight of God, save in case where the wronged persons or groups forgive him of their own free will and choice.

This is the history of rights in Islam, their legal position and their moral status. Unfortunately, this concept is out of the sight of Muslims themselves, and by their own classification of the rights, determined by God, into legal and moral and the Divine and Human rights, have attached greater importance to some and very little or none to others, which is untraceable in any degree in the early period of the Islamic history. In the matter of obedience to God, the unity of character and uniformity was the essence of the lives of the companions of the Prophet.

The care they took of their prayers, fasting, Hajj and Zakat, was also devoted to honesty in weights and measures, keeping agreements, help to the brethren in need and such other matters concerning human life, in which each and every injunction from God and His Apostle was respected and duly complied with. Their personality was not divided into compartments (compliance in some and reservations in others) but was a pattern of total submission to the will of their Lord. Shatibi pointing to this spirit of obedience says:

> The classification of Mustahab: Desirable, Preferable or recommendable, Mandoob, that which creates excellence, obligative and Makrooh: Detestable, abhorrent disgusting and Haram (Illegal):
>
> Strictly prohibited, find no place in the Programme of seeking closeness to Allah and purification of the inner-self, since the real objective is self purification: whatever helps in this programme is important no matter whether it is Mustahab or obligatory; and that which leads to evil is prohibited, irrespective of its being Makrooh or Haram (strictly prohibited)."

The spirit of the creed of the unity of God is that everything should be done under the commandment of Allah, the way it has been prescribed by Allah, and to seek His countenance alone. The same principle holds in the matter of rights, and according to it, every right, in its determination, enforcement and its consequences at every stage, is associated with God.

5

# Protection by Law

## Rights Guaranteed by Law

In an Islamic State, certain rights are conferred on the citizens, which are backed by law. In view of a great scholar, these rights are more extensive than the general human rights which have been described earlier, they need separate treatment.

***Security of Life and Property :*** In the address which the Prophet delivered on the occasion of the Farewell *Hajj,* he said: "Your lives and properties are forbidden to one another till you meet your Lord on the Day of Resurrection." God Almighty has laid down in the Holy Quran: "Anyone who kills a believer deliberately will receive as his reward (a sentence) to live in Hell for ever. God will be angry with him and curse him, and prepare dreadful torment for him" (4:93). The Prophet has also said about the *dhimmis* (the non-Muslim citizens of the Muslim state): " One who kills a man under covenant (i.e. a *dhimmi*) will not even smell the fragrance of Paradise" (Bukhari and Abu Daud). Islam prohibits homicide but allows only one exception, that the killing is done in the due process of law which the Quran refers to as *bil-haqq* (with the truth). Therefore a man can be killed only when the law demands it, and it is obvious that only a court of law can decide whether the execution is being carried out with justice or without justification. In case of war or insurrection a just and righteous government alone, which follows the *Shariah* or the Islamic law, can decide whether a war is just or unjust, whether taking of a life is justified or not; and whether a person is a rebel or not and who can be sentenced to death as a punishment. These weighty decisions cannot be left in the hands of a court which has become heedless to God and is under the influence of the administration. A judiciary like this may miscarry justice. Nor can the crimes of state be justified on the authority of the Holy Quran or Traditions *(Hadith)* when the state murders its citizens openly and secretly without any hesitation or on the slightest pretext, because they are opposed to its unjust policies and actions or criticize it for its misdeed, and also provides protection to its hired assassins who have been guilty of the heinous crime of murder of an innocent person resulting in the fact, that neither the police take any action against such criminals nor can any proof or witnesses against these criminals be produced in the courts of law. The very existence of such a government is a crime and none of the killings carried out by them can be called "execution for the sake of justice" in the phraseology of the Holy Quran.

Along with security of life, Islam has with equal clarity and definiteness conferred the right of security of ownership of property, as mentioned earlier with reference to the address of the Farewell *Hajj.* On the other hand, the Holy Quran goes so far as to declare that the taking of people's possessions or property is completely prohibited unless they are acquired by lawful means as permitted in the laws of God. The law of God categorically declares "Do not devour one another's wealth by false and illegal means" (2:188).

***Protection of Honour :*** The second important right is the right of the citizens to the protection of their honour. In the address delivered on the occasion of the Farewell *Hajj,* the Prophet did not only prohibit the life and property of the Muslims to one another, but also any encroachment upon their honour, respect and chastity was forbidden to one another. The Holy Quran clearly lays down:

(a) "You who believe, do not let one (set of) people make fun of another set.

(b) Do not defame one another.

(c) Do not insult by using nicknames.

(d) And do not backbite or speak ill of one another" (49:11-12).

This is the law of Islam for the protection of honour which is indeed much superior to and better than the western Law of Defamation. According to the Islamic law if it is proved that someone has attacked the honour of another person, then irrespective of the fact whether or not the victim is able to prove himself a respectable and honourable person the culprit will in any case get his due punishment. But the interesting fact about the Western Law of Defamation is that the person who files suit for defamation has first to prove that he is a man of honour and public esteem and during the interrogation he is subjected to the scurrilous attacks, accusations and innuendoes of the defence council to such an extent that he earns more disgrace than the attack on his reputation against which he had knocked the door of the court of law. On top of it he has also to produce such witnesses as would testify in the court that due to the defamatory accusations of the culprit, the accused stands disgraced in their eyes. Good Gracious! what a subtle point of law, and what an adherence to the spirit of law! How can this unfair and unjust law be compared to the Divine law? Islam declares blasphemy as a crime irrespective of the fact whether the accused is a man of honour or not, and whether the words used for blasphemy have actually disgraced the victim and harmed his reputation in the eyes of the public or not. According to the Islamic law the mere proof of the fact that the accused said things which according to common sense could have damaged the reputation and honour of the plaintiff, is enough for the accused to be declared guilty of defamation.

***Sanctity and Security of Privacy :*** Islam recognises the right of every citizen of its state that there should be no undue interference or encroachment on the privacy of his life. The Holy Quran has laid down the injunction: "Do not spy on one another" (49:12). "Do not enter any houses except your own homes unless you are sure of their occupants' consent" (24:27). The Prophet has gone to the extent of instructing his followers that a man should not enter even his own house suddenly or surreptitiously. He should somehow or other inform or indicate to the dwellers of the house that he is entering the house, so that he may not see his mother, sister or daughter in a condition in which they would not like to be seen, nor he would himself like to see them in that condition. Peering into the houses of other people has also been strictly prohibited, so much so that there is the saying of the Prophet that if a man finds another person secretly peering into his house, and he blinds his eye or eyes as a punishment then he cannot be called to question nor will he be liable to prosecution. The Prophet has even prohibited people from reading the letters of others, so much so that if a man is reading his letter and another man casts sidelong glances at it and tries to read it, his conduct becomes reprehensible. This is the sanctity of privacy that Islam grants to individuals. On the other hand in the modern civilized world we find that not only the letters of other people are read and their correspondence censored, but even its photostat copies are retained for future use or blackmail. Even bugging devices are secretly fixed in the houses of the people so that one can hear and tape from a distance the conversation taking place behind closed doors. In other words it means that there is no such thing as privacy and to all practical purposes the private life of an individual does not exist.

This espionage on the life of the individual cannot be justified on moral grounds by the government saying that it is necessary to know the secrets of the dangerous persons. Though, to all intents and purposes, the basis of this policy is the fear and suspicion with which modern governments look at their citizens who are intelligent and dissatisfied with the official policies of the government. This is exactly what Islam has called the root cause of mischief in politics. The injunction of the Prophet is: "When the ruler begins to search for the causes of dissatisfaction amongst his people, he spoils them" (Abu Daud). The Amir Muawiyyah has said that he himself heard the Prophet saying: "If you try to find out the secrets of the people, then you will definitely spoil them or at least you will bring them to the verge of ruin." The meaning of the phrase 'spoil them' is that when spies (C.I.D. or F.B.I, agents) are spread all around the country to find out the affairs of men, then the people begin to look at one another with suspicion, so much so that people are afraid of talking freely in their houses lest some word should escape from the lips of their wives and children which may put them in embarrassing situations. In this manner it becomes difficult for a common citizen to speak freely, even in his own house and society begins to suffer from a state of general distrust and suspicion.

## Individual Liberties

***Personal Freedom :*** Islam has also laid down the principle that no citizen can be imprisoned unless his guilt has been proved in an open court. To arrest a man only on the basis of suspicion and to throw him into a prison without proper court proceedings and without providing him a reasonable opportunity to produce his defence is not permissible in Islam. It is related in the Hadith that once the Prophet was delivering a lecture in the Mosque, when a man rose during the lecture and said: " O Prophet of God, for what crime have my neighbours been arrested?" The Prophet heard the question and continued his speech. The man rose once again and repeated the same question.

The Prophet again did not answer and continued his speech. The man rose for a third time and repeated the same question. Then the Prophet ordered that the man's neighbours be released. The reason why the Prophet had kept quiet when the question was repeated twice earlier was that the police officer was present in the Mosque and if there were proper reasons for the arrest of the neighbours of this man, he would have got up to explain his position. Since the police officer gave no reasons for these arrests the Prophet ordered that the arrested persons should be released. The police officer was aware of the Islamic law and therefore he did not get up to say: "the administration is aware of the charges against the arrested men, but they cannot be disclosed in public. If the Prophet would inquire about their guilt *in camera* I would enlighten him." If the police officer had made such a statement, he would have been dismissed then and there. The fact that the police officer did not give any reasons for the arrests in the open court was sufficient reason for the Prophet to give immediate orders for the release of the arrested men. The injunction of the Holy Quran is very clear on this point. "Whenever you judge between people, you should judge with (a sense of) justice" (4:58). And the Prophet has also been asked by God: "I have been ordered to dispense justice between you." This was the reason why the Caliph Umar said: "In Islam no one can be imprisoned except in pursuance of justice." The words used here clearly indicate that justice means due process of law. What has been prohibited and condemned is that a man be arrested and imprisoned without proof of his guilt in an open court and without providing him an opportunity to defend himself against those charges. If the Government suspects that a particular individual has committed a crime or he is likely to commit an offence in the near future then they should give reasons of their suspicion before a court of law and the culprit or the suspect should be allowed to produce his defence in an open court, so that the court may decide whether the suspicion against him is based on sound grounds or not and if there is good reason for suspicion, then he should be informed of how long he will be in preventive detention. This decision should be taken under all circumstances in an open court, so that the public may hear the charges brought by the government, as well as the defence made by the accused and see that the due process of law is being applied to him and he is not being victimised.

The correct method of dealing with such cases in Islam is exemplified in the famous decision of the Prophet which took place before he conquest of Mecca. The Prophet was making preparations for the attack on Mecca, when one of his Companions, Harib bin Abi Baltaa sent a letter through a woman to the authorities in Mecca informing them about the impending attack. The Prophet came to know of this through a divine inspiration. He ordered Ali and Zubayr: "Go quickly on the route to Mecca, at such and such a place you will find a woman carrying a letter. Recover the letter from her and bring it to me." So they went and found the woman exactly where the Prophet had said. They recovered the letter from her and brought it to the Prophet. This was indeed a clear case of treachery. To inform the enemy about a secret of an army and that too at the time of a war is a very serious offence tantamount to treachery. In fact, one cannot think of a more serious crime during war than giving out a military secret to one's enemy. What could have been a more suitable case for a secret hearing; a military secret had been betrayed and common sense demanded that he should be tried *in camera.* But the Prophet summoned Hatib to the open court of the Mosque of the Prophet and in the presence of hundreds of people asked him to explain his position with regard to his letter addressed to the leaders of Quraish which had been intercepted on its way.

The accused said: " O God's Messenger (may God's blessings

be on you) I have not revolted against Islam, nor have I done this with the intention of betraying a military secret. The truth of the matter is that my wife and children are living in Mecca and I do not have my tribe to protect them there. I had written this letter so that the leaders of Quraish may be indebted to me and may protect my wife and children out of gratitude." Umar rose and respectfully submitted: " O Prophet, please permit me to put this traitor to the sword." The Prophet replied: "He is one of those people who had participated in the battle of Badr, and the explanation he has advanced in his defence would seem to be correct."

Let us look at this decision of the Prophet in perspective. It was a clear case of treachery and betrayal of military secrets. But the Prophet acquitted Hatib on two counts. Firstly, that his past records were very clean and showed that he could not have betrayed the cause of Islam, since on the occasion of the battle of Badr when there were heavy odds against the Muslims, he had risked his life for them. Secondly, his family was in fact in danger at Mecca. Therefore, if he had shown some human weakness for his children and written this letter, then this punishment was quite sufficient for him that his secret offence was divulged in public and he had been disgraced and humiliated in the eyes of the Believers. God has referred to this offence of Hatib in the Holy Quran but did not propose any punishment for him except rebuke and admonition.

The attitude and activities of the Kharjites in the days of the Caliph Ali are well known to the students of Muslim history. They used to abuse the Caliph openly, and threaten him with murder. But whenever they were arrested for these offences, Ali would set them free and tell his officers: "Asiong as they do not actually perpetrate offences against the state, the mere use of abusive Language or the threat of use of force are not such offences for which they can be imprisoned." The Imam Abu Hanifa has recorded the following saying of the Caliph Ali: "As long as they do not set out on armed rebellion, the Caliph of the Faithful will not interfere with them." On another occasion Ali was delivering a lecture in the mosque when the Kharjites raised that special slogan there. Ali Said: "We will not deny you the right to come to the mosques to worship God, nor will we stop to give your share from the wealth of the state, as long as you are with us (and support us in our wars with the unbelievers) and we shall never take military action against you as long as you do not fight with us." One can visualise the opposition which Ali was facing: more violent and vituperative opposition cannot even be imagined in a present day democratic state; but the freedom that he had allowed to the opposition was such that no government has ever been able to give to its opposition. He did not arrest even those who threatened him with murder nor did he imprison them.

***Right to Protest :*** Amongst the rights that Islam has conferred on human beings is the right to protest against government's tyranny. Referring to it the Quran says: "God does not love evil talk in public unless it is by someone who has been injured thereby" (4:148). This means that God strongly disapproves of abusive language or strong words of condemnation, but the person who has been the victim of injustice or tyranny, God gives him the right to openly protest against the injury that has been done to him. This right is not limited only to individuals. The words of the verse are general. Therefore if an individual or a group of people or a party usurps power and after assuming the reins of authority begins to tyrannise individuals or groups of men or the entire population of the country then to raise the voice of protest against it openly is the God-given right of man and no one has the authority to usurp or deny this right. If anyone tries to usurp this right of citizens then he rebels against God. The talisman of Section 144 may protect such a tyrant in this world, but it cannot save him from the hell-fire in the Hereafter.

***Freedom of Expression :*** Islam gives the right of freedom of thought and expression to all citizens of the Islamic state on the condition that it should be used for the propagation of virtue and truth and not for spreading evil and wickedness. This Islamic concept of freedom of expression is much superior to the concept prevalent in the West. Under no circumstances would Islam allow evil and wickedness to be propagated. It also does not give anybody the right to use abusive or offensive language in the name of criticism. The right to freedom of evil and wickedness is made intolerable and hard to bear.

***Freedom of Conscience and Conviction :*** Islam also gives the right to freedom of conscience and conviction to its citizens in an Islamic state. The Holy Quran has laid down the injunction: "There should be no coercion in the matter of faith" (2:256). Though there is no truth and virtue greater than the Religion of Truth—Islam, and Muslims are enjoined to invite people to embrace Islam and advance arguments in favour of it, they are not asked to enforce this faith on them. No force will be applied in order to compel them to accept Islam. Whoever accepts it he does so by his own choice. Muslims will welcome such a convert to Islam with open arms and admit him to their community with equal rights and privileges. But if somebody does not accept Islam, Muslims will have to recognise and respect his decision, and no moral, social or political pressure will be put on him to change his mind.

## Religious Liberties

***Protection of Religious Sentiments :*** Along with the freedom of conviction and freedom of conscience Islam has given the right to the individual that his religious sentiments will be given due respect and nothing will be said or done which may encroach upon this right. It has been ordained by God in the Holy Quran: "Do not abuse those they appeal to instead of God" (6:108). These instructions are not only limited to idols and deities, but they also apply to the leaders or national heroes of the people. If a group of people holds a conviction which according to you is wrong, and holds certain persons in high esteem which according to you is not deserved by them, then it will not be justified in Islam that you use abusive language for them and thus injure their feelings. Islam does not prohibit people from holding debate and discussion on religious matters, but it wants that these discussions should be conducted in decency. "Do not argue with the people of the Book unless it is in the politest manner" (29:46)—says the Quran. This order is not merely limited to the People of the Scriptures, but applies with equal force to those following other faiths.

***Protection from Arbitrary Imprisonment :*** Islam also recognises the right of the individual that he will not be arrested or imprisoned for the offences of others. The Holy Quran has laid down this principle clearly: "No bearer of burdens shall be made to bear the burden of another" (6:164). Islam believes in personal responsibility. We ourselves are responsible for our acts, and the consequence of our actions cannot be transferred to someone else. In other words this means that every man is responsible for his actions. If another man has not shared this action then he cannot be held responsible for it, nor can he be arrested. It is a matter of great regret and shame that we are seeing this just and equitable principle which has not been framed by any human being, but by the Creator and Nourisher of the entire universe, being flouted and violated before our eyes. So much so that a man is guilty of a crime or he is a suspect, but his wife is being arrested for his crime. Things have gone so far that innocent people are being punished for the crimes of others. To give a recent example, in Karachi (Pakistan), a man was suspected of being involved in a bomb throwing incident. In the course of police investigation he was subjected to horrible torture in order to extract a confession from him. When he insisted on his innocence, then the police arrested his mother, his wife, daughter and sister and brought them to the police station. They were all stripped naked in his presence, and he was stripped naked of all his clothes before their eyes so that a confession of the crime could be extracted from him. It appears as if for the sake of investigation of crime it has become proper and legal in our country to strip the innocent women folk of the household in order to bring pressure on the suspect. This is indeed very outrageous and shameful. This is the height of meanness and depravity. This is not a mere hearsay which we are repeating here, but we have full information about this case and can prove our allegations in any court of law. We would here like to ask what right such tyrants who perpetrate these crimes against mankind have to tell us that they are Muslims or that they are conducting the affairs of the state according to the teachings of Islam and their state is an Islamic state. They are breaching and flouting a clear law of the Holy Quran. They are stripping men and women naked which is strictly forbidden in Islam. They disgrace and humiliate humanity and then they claim that they are Muslims.

## Basic Rights

***Right to Basic Necessities :*** Islam has recognised the right of the needy people that help and assistance will be provided to them. "And in their wealth there is acknowledged right for the needy and the destitute" (51:19). In this verse, the Quran has not only conferred a right to every man who asks for assistance in the wealth of the Muslims, but has also laid down that if a Muslim comes to know that a certain man is without the basic necessities of life, then irrespective of the fact whether he asks for assistance or not, it is his duty to reach him and give all the help that he can extend. For this purpose Islam has not depended only on the help and charity that is given voluntarily, but has made compulsory charity, *Zakat* as the third pillar of Islam, next only to profession of faith and worship of God through holding regular prayers. The Prophet has clearly instructed in this respect that: "It will be taken from their rich and given to those in the community in need" (Bukhari and Muslim). In addition to this, it has also been declared that the Islamic state should support those who have nobody to support them. The Prophet has said: "The Head of state is the guardian of him who has nobody to support him" (Abu Daud, Tirmidhi). The word *wali* which has been used by the Prophet is a very comprehensive word and has a wide range of meanings. If there is an orphan or an aged man, if there is a crippled or unemployed person, if one is invalid or poor and has no one else to support him or help him, then it is the duty and the responsibility of the state to support him and assist. If a dead man has no guardian or heir, then it is the duty of the state to arrange for his proper burial. In short the state has been entrusted with the duty and responsibility of looking after all those who need help and assistance. A truly Islamic state is therefore a truly welfare state which will be the guardian and protector of all those in need.

***Equality before Law :*** Islam gives its citizens the right to absolute and complete equality in the eyes of the law. As far as the Muslims are concerned, there are clear instructions in the Holy Quran and *Hadith* that in their rights and obligations they are all equal: "The believers are brothers (to each other)" (49:10). "If they (disbelievers) repent and keep up prayer and pay the welfare due they are your brothers in faith" (9:11). The Prophet has said that: "The life and blood of Muslims are equally precious" (Abu Daud; Ibn Maja). In another *Hadith* he has said: "The protection given by all Muslims are equal. Even an ordinary man of them can grant protection to any man" (Bukhari; Muslim; Abu Daud). In another more detailed Tradition of the Prophet, it has been said that those who accept the Oneness of God, believe in the Prophethood of his Messenger, give up primitive prejudices and join the Muslim community and brotherhood, "then they have the same rights and obligations as other Muslims have" (Bukhari; Nisai). Thus there is absolute equality between the new converts to Islam and the old followers of the faith.

This religious brotherhood and the uniformity of their rights and obligations is the foundation of equality in Islamic society, in which the rights and obligations of any person are neither greater nor lesser in any way than the rights and obligations of other people. As far as the non-Muslim citizens of the Islamic state are concerned, the rule of Islamic *Shariah* (law) about them has been very well expressed by the Caliph Ali in these words: "They have accepted our protection only because their lives may be like our lives and their properties like our properties" (Abu Daud). In other words, their (of the *(dhimmis)* lives and properties are as sacred as the lives and properties of the Muslims. Discrimination of people into different classes was one of the greatest crimes that, according to the Quran, Pharaoh used to indulge in: "He had divided his people into different classes, "... "And he suppressed one group of them (at the cost of others) (28:4).

## Special Rights

***Rulers not Above the Law :*** Islam clearly insists and demands that all officials of the Islamic state, whether' he be the head or an ordinary employee, are equal in the eyes of the law. None of them are above the law or can claim immunity. Even an ordinary citizen in Islam has the right to put forward a claim or file a legal complaint against the highest executive of the country. The Caliph Umar said, "I have myself seen the Prophet, may God's blessings be on him, taking revenge against himself (penalising himself for some shortcoming or failing)." On the occasion of the battle of Badr, when the Prophet was straightening the rows of the Muslim army he hit the belly of a soldier in an attempt to push him back in line. The soldier complained " O Prophet, you have hurt me with your stick." The Prophet immediately bared his belly and said "I am very sorry, you can revenge by doing the same to me. " The soldier came forward and kissed the abdomen of the Prophet and said that this was all that he wanted.

A woman belonging to a high and noble family was arrested in connection with a theft. The case was brought to the Prophet, and it was recommended that she may be spared the punishment of theft. The Prophet replied: "The nations that lived before you were destroyed by God because they punished the common man for their offences and let their dignitaries go unpunished for their crimes; I swear by Him (God) who holds my life in His hand that even if Fatima, the daughter of Muhammad, has committed this crime then I would have amputated her hand." During the Caliphate of Umar, Muhammad the son of Amr bin al-As the Governor of Egypt, whipped an Egyptian. The Egyptian went to Medina and lodged his complaint with the Righteous Caliph, who immediately summoned the Governor and his son to Medina. When they appeared before him in Medina, the Caliph handed a whip to the Egyptian complainant and asked him to whip the son of the Governor in his presence. After taking his revenge when the Egyptian was about to hand over the whip to Umar, he said to the Egyptian: "Give one stroke of the whip to the Honourable Governor as well. His son would certainly have not beaten you were it not for the false pride that he had in his father's high office." The plaintiff submitted: "The person who had beaten me, I have already avenged myself on him." Umar said: "By God, if you had beaten him (the Governor) I would not have checked you from doing so. You have spared him of your own free will." Then he (Umar) angrily turned to Amr bin al-As and said: " O Amr, when did you start to enslave the people, though they were born free of their mothers?" When the Islamic state was flourishing in its pristine glory and splendour, the common people could equally lodge complaints against the Caliph of the time in the court and the Caliph had to appear before the *Qadi* to answer the charges. And if the Caliph had any complaint against any citizen, he could not use his administrative powers and authority to set the matter right, but had to refer the case to the court of law for proper judication.

***Right to avoid Sin :*** Islam also confers this right on every citizen that he will not be ordered to commit a sin, a crime or an offence; and if any government, or the administrator, or the head of department orders an individual to do a wrong, then he has the right to refuse to comply with the order. His refusal to carry out such a crime or unjust instructions would not be regarded as an offence in the eyes of the Islamic law. On the contrary giving orders to one's subordinates to commit a sin or do a wrong is itself an offence and such a serious offence that the officer who gives this sinful order whatever his rank and position may be, is liable to be summarily dismissed. These clear instructions of the Prophet are summarized in the following *Hadith:* "It is not permissible to disobey God in obedience to the orders of any human being" (*Musnad* of Ibn Hanbal). In other words no one has the right to order his subordinates to do anything against the laws of God. If such an order is given, the subordinate has the right to ignore it or openly refuse to carry out such instructions. According to this rule no offender will be able to prove his innocence or escape punishment by saying that this offence was committed on the orders of the government or superior officers. If such a situation arises then the person who commits the offence and the person who orders that such an offence be committed, will both be liable to face criminal proceedings against them. And if an officer takes any improper and unjust measures against a subordinate who refuses to carry out illegal orders, then the subordinate has the right to go to the court of law for the protection of his rights, and he can demand that the officer be punished for his wrong or unjust orders.

***Right to Participate in State Affairs :*** According to Islam, governments in this world are actually representatives *(Khalifa)* of the Creator of the universe, and this responsibility is not entrusted to any individual or family or a particular class or group of people but to the entire Muslim nation. The Holy Quran says: "God has promised to appoint those of you who believe and do good deeds as (His) representatives on earth" (24:55). This clearly indicates that *khalifa* is a collective gift of God in which the right of every individual Muslim is neither more nor less than the right of any other person. The correct method recommended by the Holy Quran for running the affairs of the state is as follows: "And their business is (conducted) through consultation among themselves" (42:38). According to this principle it is the right of every Muslim that either he should have a direct say in the affairs of the state or a representative chosen by him and other Muslims should participate in the consultation of the state. Islam, under no circumstance, permits or tolerates that an individual or a group or party of individuals may deprive the common Muslims of their rights, and usurp powers of the state. Similarly, Islam does not regard it right and proper that an individual may put up a false show of setting up a legislative assembly and by means of underhand tactics such as fraud, persecution, bribery, etc., gets himself and men of his choice elected in the assembly. This is not only a treachery against the people whose rights are usurped by illegal and unfair means, but against the Creator who has entrusted the Muslims to rule on this earth on His behalf, and has prescribed the procedure of an assembly for exercising these powers. The shura or the legislative assembly has no other meaning except that:

(1) The executive head of the government and the members of the assembly should be elected by free and independent choice of the people.

(2) The people and their representatives should have the right to criticize and freely express their opinions.

(3) The real conditions of the country should be brought before the people without suppressing any fact so that they may be able to form their opinion about whether the government is working properly or not.

(4) There should be adequate guarantee that only those people who have the support of the masses should rule over the country and those who fail to win this support should be removed from their position of authority.

***Rights of Enemies :*** After dealing with the rights of the citizens of an Islamic state, we would like to briefly discuss the rights which Islam has conferred on its enemies. In the days when Islam came into focus the world was completely unaware of the concept of humane and decent rules of war. The West became conscious of this concept for the first time through the works of the seventeenth century thinker, Grotius. But the actual codification of the 'international law' in war began in the middle of the nineteenth century. Prior to this no concept of civilized behaviour in war was found in the West. All forms of barbarity and savagery were perpetrated in war, and the rights of those at war were not even recognised, let alone respected. The laws which were framed in this field during the nineteenth century or over the following period up to the present day, cannot be called 'laws' in the real sense of the word. They are only in the nature of conventions and agreements and calling them 'international law' is actually a kind of misnomer, because no nation regards them binding when they are at war, unless, of course, when the adversaries also agree to abide by them. In other words, these civilized laws imply that if our enemies respect them then we shall also abide by them, and if they ignore these human conventions and take recourse to barbaric and cruel ways of waging war, then we shall also adopt the same or similar techniques. It is obvious that such a course which depends on mutual acceptance and agreement cannot be called 'law'. And this is the reason why the provisions of this so-called 'international law' have been flouted and ignored in every way, and every time they have been revised, additions or deletions have been made in them.

***Law of War and Peace in Islam :*** The rules which have been framed by Islam to make war civilized and humane, are in the nature of law, because they are the injunctions of God and His Prophet which are followed by Muslims in all circumstances, irrespective of the behaviour of the enemy. It is now for the scholars to find out how far the West has availed of the laws of war given by Islam thirteen hundred years ago; and even after the adaptation of some of the laws of Islam how far the West attained those heights of civilized and humane methods of warfare which Muslims reached through the blessings of Islam. Western writers have often asserted that the Prophet had borrowed everything in his teachings from the Jews and the Christians. Instead of saying anything in its refutation we will only recommend the reader to refer to the Bible so that he can see which methods of war are recommended by the sacred Book of these Western claimants to civilization and culture.

We have examined in some detail the basic human rights that Islam has conferred on man. Let us now find out what rights and obligations Islam recognises for an enemy.

***The Rights of the Non-combatants :*** Islam has first drawn a clear line of distinction between the combatants and the non-combatants of the enemy country. As far as the non-combatant population is concerned such as women, children, the old and the infirm, etc., the instructions of the Prophet are as follows: "Do not kill any old person, any child or any woman" (Abu Daud). "Do not kill the monks in monasteries" or "Do not kill the people who are sitting in places of worship" (Musnad of Ibn Hanbal).

During a war, the Prophet saw the corpse of a woman lying on the ground and observed: "She was not fighting. How then she came to be killed?" From this statement of the Prophet the exegetists and jurists have drawn the principle that those who are non-combatants should not be killed during or after the war.

***Rights of the Combatants :*** Now let us see what rights Islam has conferred on the combatants.

***Torture with Fire :*** In the Hadith there is a saying of the Prophet that: "Punishment by fire does not behove anyone except the Master of the Fire" (Abu Daud). The injunction deduced from this saying is that the adversary should not be burnt alive.

***Protection of the Wounded :*** "Do not attack a wounded person"—thus said the Prophet. This means that the wounded soldiers who are not fit to fight, nor actually fighting, should not be attacked.

***The Prisoner of War Should not be Slain :*** "No prisoner should be put to the sword"—a very clear and unequivocal instruction given by the Prophet.

***No one Should be Tied to be Killed :*** "The Prophet, has prohibited the killing of anyone who is tied or is in captivity."

***No Looting and Destruction in the Enemy's Country :*** Muslims have also been instructed by the-Prophet that if they should enter the enemy's territory, they should not indulge in pillage or plunder nor destroy the residential areas, nor touch the property of anyone except those who are fighting with them.

It has been narrated in the Hadith: "The Prophet has prohibited the Believers from loot and plunder" (Bukhari; Abu Daud). His injunction is: "The loot is no more lawful than the carrion" (Abu Daud). Abu Bakr Siddiq used to instruct the soldiers while sending them to war, "Do not destroy the villages and towns, do not spoil the cultivated fields and gardens, and do not slaughter the cattle." The booty of war which is acquired from the battleground is altogether different from this. It consists of the wealth, provisions and equipment captured only from the camps and military headquarters of the combatant armies.

***Sanctity of Property :*** The Muslims have also been prohibited from taking anything from the general public of a conquered country without paying for it. If in a war the Muslim army occupies an area of the Enemy country, and is encamped there it does not have the right to use the things belonging to the people without their consent. If they need anything, they should purchase it from the local population or should obtain permission from the owners. Abu Bakr Siddiq, while instructing the Muslim armies being despatched to the battle-front would go to the extent of saying that Muslim soldiers should not even use the milk of the milch cattle without the permission of their owners.

***Sanctity of a Dead Body :*** Islam has categorically prohibited its followers from disgracing or mutilating the corpses of their enemies as was practised in Arabia before the advent of Islam. It has been said in the Hadith: "The Prophet has prohibited us from mutilating the corpses of the enemies" (Bukhari; Abu Daud). The occasion on which this order was given is highly instructive. In the battle of Uhud the disbelievers mutilated the bodies of the Muslims who had fallen on the battlefield and sacrificed their lives for the sake of Islam, by cutting off their ears and noses, and threading them together to put round their necks as trophies of war. The abdomen of Hamzah, the uncle of the Prophet, was ripped open by Quraish, his liver was taken out and chewed by Hinda, the wife of Abu Sufyan, the leader of the Meccan army. The Muslims were naturally enraged by this horrible sight. But the Prophet asked his followers not to mete out similar treatment to the dead bodies of the enemies. This great example of forbearance and restraint is sufficient to convince any reasonable man who is not blinded by prejudice or bias, that Islam is really the religion sent down by the Creator of the universe., and that if human emotions had any admission in Islam, then this horrible sight on the battlefield of Uhud would have provoked the Prophet to order his followers to mutilate the bodies of their enemy in the same manner.

***Return of Corpses :*** In the battle of Ahzab' a very renowned and redoubtable warrior of the enemy was killed and his body fell down in the trench which the Muslims had dug for the defence of Medina. The unbelievers presented ten thousand dinars to the Prophet and requested that the dead body of their fallen warrior may be handed over to them. The Prophet replied "I do not sell dead bodies. You can take away the corpse of your fallen comrade."

***Prohibition of Breach of Treaties :*** Islam has strictly prohibited treachery. One of the instructions that the Prophet used to give to the Muslim warriors while sending them to the battlefront was: "Do not be guilty of breach of faith." This order has been repeated in the Holy Quran and the Hadith again and again, that if the enemy acts treacherously let him do so, you should never go back on your promise. There is a famous incident in the peace treaty of Hudaybiya, when after the settlement of the terms of the treaty, Abu Jandal, the son of the emissary of the unbelievers who had negotiated this treaty with the Muslims, came, fettered and blood stained, rushing to the Muslim camp and crying for help. The Prophet told him, "Since the terms of the treaty have been settled, we are not in a position to help you out. You should go back with your father. God will provide you with some other opportunity to escape this persecution." The entire Muslim army was deeply touched and grieved at the sad plight of Abu Jandal and many of them were moved to tears. But when the Prophet declared that "we cannot break the agreement," not even a single person came forward to help the unfortunate prisoner so the unbelievers forcibly dragged him back to Mecca. This is an unparalleled example of the observance of the terms of agreement by the Muslims, and Islamic history can show many examples of a similar nature.

***Rules about Declaration of War :*** It has been laid down in the Holy Quran: "If you apprehend breach of treaty from a people, then openly throw the treaty at their faces" (8:58). In this verse, Muslims have been prohibited from opening hostilities against their enemies without properly declaring war against them, unless of course, the adversary has already started aggression against them. Otherwise the Quran has clearly given the injunction to Muslims that they should intimate to their enemies that no treaty exists between them, and they are at war with them. The present day "international law" has also laid down that hostilities should not be started without declaration of war, but since it is a man-made rule, they are free to violate it whenever it is convenient. On the other hand, the laws for Muslims have been framed by God, hence they cannot be violated.

This is a brief sketch of those rights which fourteen hundred years ago Islam gave to man, to those who were at war with each other and to the citizens of its state, which every Believer regards as sacred law. On the one hand, it refreshes and strengthens our faith in Islam when we realise that even in this modern age which makes such loud claims of progress and enlightenment, the world has not been able to produce more just and equitable laws than those given 1400 years ago. On the other hand it hurts one's feelings that Muslims are in possession of such a splendid and comprehensive system of law and yet they look forward for guidance to those leaders of the West who could not have dreamed of attaining those heights of truth and justice which were achieved a long time ago. Even more painful than this is the realisation that throughout the world the rulers who claim to be Muslims have made disobedience to their God and the Prophet as the basis and foundation of their government. May God have mercy on them and give them the true guidance.

# 6

# Natural Rights

## Basic Rights

The first thing that we find in Islam in this connection is that it lays down some rights for man as a human being. In other words it means that every man whether he belongs to this country or that, whether he is a believer or unbeliever, whether he lives in some forest or is found in some desert, whatever be the case, he has some basic human rights simply because he is a human being, which should be recognised by every Muslim. In fact it will be his duty to fulfil these obligations.

***Right to Live :*** The first and the foremost basic right is the right to live and respect for human life. The Holy Quran lays down:

> "Whosoever kills a human being (without any reason like) manslaughter, or corruption on earth, it is though he had killed all mankind" (5:32).

As far as the question of taking life in retaliation for murder or the question of punishment for spreading corruption on this earth is concerned, it can be, decided only by a proper and competent court of law. If there is any war with any nation or country, it can be decided only by a properly established government. In any case, no human being has any right by itself to take human life in retaliation or for causing mischief on this earth. Therefore it is incumbent on every human being that under no circumstances should he be guilty of taking a human life. If anyone has murdered a human being, it is as if he has slain the entire human race. These instructions have been repeated in the Holy Quran in another place saying:

> "Do not kill a soul which Allah has made sacred except through the due process of law" (6:151).

Here also homicide has been distinguished from destruction of life carried out in pursuit of justice. Only a proper and competent court will be able to decide whether or not an individual has forfeited his right to life by disregarding the right to life and peace of other human beings. The Prophet, may God's blessings be on him, has declared homicide as the greatest sin only next to polytheism. The Tradition of the Prophet reads: "The greatest sins are to associate something with God and to kill human beings." In all these verses of the Quran and the Traditions of the Prophet the word 'soul' *(nafs)* has been used in general terms without any distinction or particularisation which might have lent itself to the elucidation that the persons belonging to one's nation, the citizens of one's country, the people of a particular race or religion should not be killed. The injunction applies to all human beings and the destruction of human life in itself has been prohibited.

The Right to Life' has been given to man only by Islam. You will observe that the people who talk about human rights if they have ever mentioned them in their Constitutions or Declarations, then it is clearly implied in them that these rights are applicable only to their citizens or they have been framed for the white race alone. This can clearly be gleaned by the fact that human beings were hunted down like animals in Australia and the land was cleared of the aborigines for the white man. Similarly the aboriginal population of America was systematically destroyed and the Red Indians who somehow survived this genocide were confined to specified areas called Reservations. They also penetrated into Africa and hunted down human brings like wild animals. All these instances go to prove that they have no respect for human life as such and if they have, it is only on the basis of their nationality, colour or race. Contrary to this, Islam recognises this right for all human beings. If a man belongs to a primitive or savage tribe, even then Islam regards him as a human being.

***Right to Safety :*** Immediately after the verse of the Holy Quran which has been mentioned in connection with the right to life, God has said: "And whoever saves a life it is as though He had saved the lives of all mankind" (5:32). There can be several forms of saving man from death. A man may be ill or wounded, irrespective of his nationality, race or colour. If you know that he is in need of your help, then it is your duty that you should arrange for his treatment for disease or wound. If he is dying of starvation, then it is your duty to feed him so that he can ward off death. If he is drowning or his life is at stake, then it is your duty to save him. You will be surprised to hear that the *Talmud*, the religious book of the Jews, contains a verse of similar nature, but records it in altogether different form. It says: "Whoever destroyed a life of; the Israelite, in the eyes of the Scripture, it is as if he destroyed the whole world. And whoever protected and saved one life of the Israelite, in the light of the Scripture it is as if he saved the whole world." *Talmud* also contains the view that if a non-Israelite is drowning and you tried to save him then you are a sinner. Can it be given a name other than racialism? We regard it as our duty to save every human life, because it is thus that we have been enjoined in the Holy Quran. On the other hand, if they regard it necessary to save the life of a human being at all, it should be the life of an Israelite. As far as other people are concerned, according to this view, they do not seem to be human enough to deserve protection of their persons. In their literature the concept of 'Goyim' for which the English word 'Gentile' and the Arabic word *Ummi* (illiterate) is used, is that they enjoy no human rights: human rights are reserved only for the children of Israel. The Quran has mentioned this belief of the Israelites and quotes the jews saying: "There is no blame on us (for anything we may do) with regard to the unlettered folk (i.e the *ummi)"* (3:75).

***Respect for the Chastity of Women :*** The third important thing that we find in the Charter of Human Rights granted by Islam is that a woman's chastity has to be respected and protected under all circumstances, whether she belongs to our own nation or to the nation of an enemy, whether we find her in the wild forest or in a conquered city; whether she is our co-religionist or belongs to some other religion or has no religion at all. A Muslim cannot outrage her under any circumstances. All promiscuous relationship has been forbidden to him, irrespective of the status or position of the woman, whether the woman is a willing or an unwilling partner to the act. The words of the Holy Quran in this respect are: "Do not approach (the bounds) of adultery" (17:32). Heavy punishment has been prescribed for this crime, and the order has not been qualified by any conditions. Since the violation of chastity of a woman is forbidden in Islam, a Muslim who perpetrates this crime cannot escape punishment whether he receives it in this world or in the Hereafter. This concept of sanctity of chastity and protection of women can be found nowhere else except in Islam. The armies of the Western powers need the daughters of their nation to satisfy their carnal appetites even in their own countries, and if they happen to occupy another country, the fate of its women folk can better be imagined than described. But the history of the Muslims, apart from a few lapses of the individuals here or there, has been free from this crime against womanhood. It has never happened that after the conquest of a foreign country the Muslim army has gone about raping the women of the conquered people, or in their own country, the government has arranged to provide prostitutes for them. This is also a great blessing which the human race has received afield order. Furthermore this injunction was given in Mecca where there was no Muslim society in existence and where generally the Muslims had to come in contact with the population of the disbelievers. Therefore the clear meaning of this verse is that anyone who asks for help and anyone who is suffering from deprivation has a right in the property and wealth of the Muslims; irrespective of the fact whether he belongs to this nation or to that nation, to this country and to that country, to this race or to that race. If you are in a position to help and a needy person asks you for help or if you come to know that he is in need, then it is your duty to help him. God has established his right over you, which you have to honour as a Muslim.

Anyone who asks for help and anyone who is suffering from deprivation has a right in the property and wealth of the Muslims; irrespective of the fact whether he belongs to this nation or to that nation, to this country and to that country, to this race or to that race. If you are in a position to help and a needy person asks you for help or if you come to know that he is in need, then it is your duty to help him. God has established his right over you, which you have to honour as a Muslim.

***Right to Liberty :*** Islam has clearly and categorically forbidden the primitive practice of capturing a free man, to make him a slave or to sell him into slavery. On this point the clear and unequivocal words of the Prophet are as follows: "There are three categories of people against whom I shall myself be a plaintiff on the Day of Judgement. Of these three, one is he who enslaves a free man, then sells him and eats this money" (Bukhari and Ibn Maja). The words of this Tradition of the Prophet are use general, they have not been qualified or made applicable to a particular nation, race, country or followers of a particular religion. The Europeans take great pride in claiming that they abolished slavery from the world, though they had the decency to do so only in the middle of the last century. Before this, these Western powers had been raiding Africa on a very large scale, capturing their free men, putting them in bondage and transporting them to their new colonies. The treatment which they have meted out to these unfortunate people has been worse than the treatment given to animals. The books written by the Western people themselves bear testimony to this fact.

***The Slave Trade of Western Nations :*** After the occupation of America and the West Indies, for three hundred and fifty years, traffic in slave trade continued. The African coasts where the black skinned captured Africans were brought from the interior of Africa and put on the ships sailing out from those ports, came to be known as the Slave Coast. During only one century (from 1680 to 1786) the total number of free people who were captured and enslaved only for British Colonies amounts, according to the estimate of British authors, to 20 million human beings. Over the period of only one year (1790) we are told that 75,000 human beings were captured and sent for slave labour in the Colonies. The ships which were used for transporting the slaves were small and dirty. These unfortunate Africans were thrust into the holds of these ships like cattle right up to the top and many of them were chained to the wooden shelves on which they could hardly move because these were only eighteen inches apart, kept one on top of the other. They were not provided with suitable food, and if they fell ill or were injured, no attempt was made to provide them with medical treatment. The Western writers themselves state that at least 20% of the total number of people who were captured for slavery and forced labour perished during their transportation from the African coast to America. It has also been estimated that the total number of people who were captured for slavery by the various European nations during the heyday of the slave trade comes to at least one hundred million. This is the record of the people who denounce Muslims day and night for recognising the institution of slavery. It is as if a criminal is holding his finger of blame towards an innocent man.

***Position of Slavery :*** Briefly we would like to tell you about the position and nature of slavery in Islam. Islam tried to solve the problem of the slaves that were in Arabia by encouraging the people in different ways to set their slaves free. The Muslims were ordered that in expiation of some of their sins they should set their slaves free. Freeing a slave by one's own free will was declared to be an act of great merit, so much so that it was said that every limb of the man who manumits a slave will be protected from hell-fire in lieu of the limb of the slave freed by him. The result of this policy was that by the time the period of the Rightly-Guided Caliphs was reached, all the old slaves of Arabia were liberated. The Prophet alone liberated as many as 63 slaves. The number of slaves freed by Aishah was 67, Abbas liberated 70, Abdul Allah bin Umar liberated one thousand, and 'abdur-Rahman purchased thirty thousand and set them free. Similarly other Companions of the Prophet liberated a large number of slaves, the details of which are given in the Traditions and books of history of that period.

Thus the problem of the slaves of Arabia was solved in a short period of thirty or forty years. After this the only form of slavery which was left in Islamic society was the prisoners of war, who were captured on the battlefield. These prisoners of war were retained by the Muslim Government until their Government agreed to receive them back in exchange for Muslim soldiers captured by them, or arranged the payment of ransom on their behalf. If the soldiers they captured were not exchanged with Muslim prisoners of war, or their people did not pay their ransom money to purchase their liberty, then the Muslim Government used to distribute them among the soldiers of the army which had captured them. This was a more humane and proper way of disposing of them than retaining them like cattle in concentration camps and taking forced labour from them and, if their women folk were also captured, setting them aside for prostitution. In place of such a cruel and outrageous way of disposing of the prisoners of war, Islam preferred to spread them in the population and thus brought them in contact with individual human beings. Over and above, their guardians were ordered to treat them well. The result of this humane policy was that most of the men who were captured on foreign battlefields and brought to the Muslim countries as slaves embraced Islam and their descendants produced great scholars, *imams,* jurists, commentators, statesmen and generals of the army. So much so that later on they became the rulers of the Muslim world. The solution of this problem which has been proposed in the present age is that after the cessation of hostilities the prisoners of war of the combatant countries should be exchanged. Whereas Muslims have been practising it from the very beginning and whenever the adversary accepted the exchange of prisoners of war from both sides, it was implemented without the least hesitation or delay.

In modern warfare we also find that if one government is completely routed leaving her in no position of bargaining for the prisoners of war and the winning party gets its prisoners easily, then experience has shown that the prisoners of war of the vanquished army are kept in conditions which are much worse than the conditions of slaves. Can anyone tell us what has been the fate of the thousands of prisoners of war captured by Russia from the defeated armies of Germany and Japan in the Second World War? No one has given their account so far. No one knows how many thousands of them are still alive and how many thousands or them have perished due to the hardship of the Russian concentration-and labour camps. The forced labour which has been taken from them is much worse than the service one can exact from slaves. Even perhaps in the times of ancient Pharaohs of Egypt such harsh labour might not have been exacted from the slaves in building the pyramids of Egypt, as has been exacted from the prisoners of war in Russia in developing Siberia and other backward areas of Russia, or working in coal and other mines in below zero temperatures, ill clad, ill fed and brutally treated by their supervisors.

***Right to Justice :*** This is a very important and valuable right which Islam has given to man as a human being. The Holy Quran has laid down: "Do not let your hatred if a people incite you to aggression" (5:3). "And do not let ill-will towards any folk incite you so that you swerve from dealing justly. Be just; that is nearest to needfulness" (5:8). Stressing this point the Quran again says: "You who believe stand steadfast before God as witness for (truth and) fairplay" (4:135). This makes the point clear that Muslims have to be just not only with ordinary human beings but even with their enemies. In other words, the justice to which Islam invites her followers is not limited only to the citizens of their own country, or the people of their own tribe, nation or race, or the Muslim community as a whole, but it is meant for all the human beings of the world. Muslims, therefore, cannot be unjust to anyone. Their permanent habit and character should be such that no man should ever fear injustice at their hands, and they should treat every human being everywhere with justice and fairness.

## Equality for All

Islam not only recognises absolute equality between men irrespective of any distinction of colour, race or nationality, but makes it an important and significant principle, a reality. The Almighty God has laid down in the Holy Quran: " O mankind, We have created you from a male and female." In other words, all human beings are brothers to one another. They all are the descendants from one father and one mother. "And We set you up as nations and tribes so that you may be able to recognise each other" (49:13). This means that the division of human beings into nations, races, groups and tribes is for the sake of distinction, so that people of one race or tribe may meet and be acquainted with the people belonging to another race or tribe and cooperate with one another. This division of the human race is neither meant for one nation to take pride in its superiority over others nor is it meant for one nation to treat another with contempt or disgrace, or regard them as a mean and degraded race and usurp their rights. "Indeed the noblest among you before God are the most heedful of you" (49:13). In other words the superiority of one man over another is only on the basis of God-consciousness, purity of character and high morals, and not on the basis of colour, race, language or nationality and even this superiority based on piety and pure conduct does not justify that such people should play lord or assume airs of superiority over other human beings. Assuming airs of superiority is in itself a reprehensible vice which no God-fearing and pious man can ever dream of perpetrating. Nor does the righteous have more privileged rights over others, because this runs counter to human equality , which has been laid down in the beginning of this verse as a general principle. From the moral point of view, goodness and virtue is in all cases better than vice and evil.

This has been exemplified by the Prophet in one of his sayings thus: "No Arab has any superiority over a non-Arab, nor does a non-Arab have any superiority over an Arab. Nor does a white man have any superiority over a black man, or the black man any superiority over the white man. You are all the children of Adam, and Adam was created from clay" (Bayhaqi and Bazzaz). In this manner Islam established equality for the entire human race and struck at the very root of all distinctions based on colour, race, language or nationality. According to Islam, God has given man this right of equality as a birthright. Therefore no man should be discriminated against on the ground of the colour of his skin, his place of birth, the race or the nation in which he was born. Malcolm X, the famous leader of African Negroes in America, who had launched a bitter struggle against the white people of America in order to win civil rights for this black compatriots, when he went to perform the pilgrimage, and saw how the Muslims of Asia, Africa, Europe, America and those of different races, languages and colours of skin, were wearing one dress and were hurrying towards God's House—the *Kaaba* and offering prayers standing in one row and there was no distinction of any kind between them, then he realised that this was the solution to the problem of colour and race, and not what he had been trying to seek or achieve in America so far. Today, a number of non-Muslim thinkers, who are free from blind prejudice, openly admit that no other religion or way of life has solved this problem with the same degree of success with which Islam has done so.

***Cooperate or not to Cooperate :*** Islam has prescribed a general principle of paramount importance and universal application saying: "Cooperate with one another for virtue and heedfulness and do not cooperate with one another for the purpose of vice and aggression" (5:2). This means that the man who undertakes a noble and righteous work, irrespective of the fact whether he is living at the North Pole or the South Pole, has the right to expect support and active cooperation from the Muslims. On the contrary he who perpetrates deeds of vice and aggression, even if he is our closest relation or neighbour, does not have the right to win our support and help in the name of race, country, language or nationality, nor should he have the expectation that Muslims will cooperate with him or support him. Nor is it permissible for Muslims to cooperate with him. The wicked and vicious person may be our own brother, but he is not of us, and he can have no help or support from us as long as he does not repent and reform his ways. On the other hand the man who is doing deeds of virtue and righteousness may have no kinship with Muslims, but Muslims will be his companions and supporters or at least his well-wishers.

Every man, whether he belongs to this country or that, whether he is a believer or unbeliever, whether he lives in a forest or in a desert, has certain basic human rights simply because he is a human being. We have seen, too, that it is the duty of every Muslim to recognize these rights. They are:

***I. The Right to Life***

The first and foremost basic right is the right to life. The Holy Quran lays down:

> "Whosoever kills a human being, without any reason like manslaughter, or corruption on earth, it is though he had killed all mankind." (5:32)

The propriety of taking life in retaliation for murder or for spreading corruption can be decided only by a competent court of law. During a war it can be decided only by a properly established government. In any event, no individual has the right to decide such questions by himself. As the Holy Quran makes clear:

> "Do not kill a soul which Allah has made sacred except through the due process of law." (6:151)

Homicide is thus distinguished from destruction of life carried out in the pursuit of justice. The Prophet, blessings of Allah and peace be upon him, has declared homicide as the greatest sin after polytheism. A Tradition of the Prophet reads: "The greatest sins are to associate something with God and to kill human beings."

In all these verses of the Quran and the Traditions of the Prophet the word 'soul' (nafs) has been used in general terms without any indication that citizens belonging to one's own nation or the people of a particular race or religion should not be killed. The injunction applies to all human beings.

The 'Right to Life' has been given to man as a whole only by Islam. You will observe that reference to human rights in constitutions or declarations in many countries clearly implies that these rights are applicable only to the citizens of that country or to the white race. For example, human beings were hunted down like animals in Australia and the land was cleared of the aborigines for the white man. Similarly, the aboriginal population of America was systematically destroyed and the Red Indians who somehow survived this genocide were confined to reservations. In Africa, human beings were also hunted down like wild animals. Contrary to this partial concept of human rights, Islam recognizes such rights for all human beings.

### *II. The Right to the Safety of Life*

Immediately after the verse in the Holy Quran which has been mentioned in connection with the right to life, God says:

> "And whoever saves a life it is as though he had saved the lives of all mankind." (5:32)

There can be several forms of saving man from death. If a man is ill or wounded it is your duty to get him medical help. If he is dying of starvation, it is your duty to feed him. If he is drowning, it is your duty to rescue him. We regard it as our duty to save every human life, because it is thus that we have been enjoined in the Holy Quran.

### *III. Respect for the Chastity of Women*

The third important element in the Charter of Human Rights granted by Islam is that a woman's chastity must be respected and protected at all times, whether she belongs to one's own nation or to the nation of an enemy, whether we find her in a remote forest or in a conquered city, whether she is our co-religionist or belongs to some other religion or has no religion at all. A Muslim may not physically abuse her under any circumstances. All promiscuous relationships are forbidden to him, irrespective of the status or position of the woman or of whether she is a willing partner to the act.

The words of the Holy Quran in this respect are: "Do not approach (the bounds) of adultery" (17:32). Heavy punishment has been prescribed for this crime, and no mitigating circumstances are indicated. Since the violation of the chastity of a woman is forbidden in Islam, a Muslim who perpetrates this crime cannot escape punishment whether he receives it in this world or in the Hereafter.

This concept of the sanctity of chastity and the protection of women can be found nowhere else except in Islam. The armies of the Western powers need the daughters of their own nations to satisfy their carnal appetites even in their own countries, and if they happen to occupy another country, the fate of its womenfolk can better be imagined than described.

But the history of the Muslims, apart from individual lapses, has been free from this crime against womanhood. It has never happened that after the conquest of a foreign country the Muslim army has gone about raping the women of the conquered people, or, in their own country, the government has arranged to provide prostitutes for them.

From the point of view of Islam, not only the woman but also the man possesses chastity. A man who perpetrates rape or adultery spoils not only the chastity of the woman, but his own as well.

### *IV. The Right to A Basic Standard of Life*

Speaking about economic rights, the Holy Quran enjoins its followers:

> "And in their wealth there is acknowledged right for the needy and destitute." (51:12)

The wording of this injunction shows that it is categorical and unqualified. Furthermore, this injunction was given in Mecca where there was no Muslim society in existence and where the Muslims came in contact mostly with disbelievers.

The clear meaning of this verse is that anyone who asks for help and anyone who is suffering from deprivation has a right to share in the property and wealth of a Muslim: irrespective of whether he belongs to this or to that nation, to this or to that country, to this or to that race. If one is in a position to help and a needy person asks for help or if one comes to know that he is in need. Then it is one's duty to help him.

### *V. The Individual's Right to Freedom*

Islam has categorically forbidden the primitive practice of capturing a free man to make him a slave or to sell him into slavery. On this point the unequivocal words of the Prophet (blessings of Allah and peace be upon him) are as follows: "There are three categories of people against whom I shall myself be a plaintiff on the Day of Judgement. Of these three, one is he who enslaves a free man, then sells him and eats this money".

The words of this Tradition of the Prophet have not been qualified or restricted to a particular nation or race, or to followers of a particular religion. The Europeans take great pride in claiming that they abolished slavery from the world, though they had the decency to do so only in the middle of the last century. Before this, the Western powers had been raiding Africa on a very large scale, capturing free men, putting them in bondage and transporting them to their new colonies. The treatment which they meted out to these unfortunate people was worse than that given to animals. Accounts in Western books themselves bear testimony to this fact.

## Slavery Condemned

After the occupation of America and the West Indies, traffic in slave trade continued for three hundred and fifty years. The African ports where the Africans were brought from the interior and put on ships came to be known as the Slave Coast. In the course of only one century (from 1680 to 1786), the total number of free people who were captured and enslaved for the British Colonies amounts, according to the estimate of British authors, to 20 million. We are told that in the year 1790, 75,000 human beings were captured and sent for slave labour in the colonies. The ships which were used for transporting the slaves were small and dirty. These unfortunate Africans were thrust into the holds like cattle and many of them, were chained, one on top of the other, to wooden shelves on which they could hardly move because they were only eighteen inches apart. They were not given proper food, and if they fell ill or were injured, no attempt was made to provide them with medical treatment.

Western writers themselves state that at least 20 per cent of the total number of people who were captured for slavery and forced labour perished while being transported from Africa to America. It has also been estimated that the total number of people who were captured for slavery by the various European nations during the heyday of the slave trade was at least one hundred million. This is the record of the people who denounce Muslims for recognizing the institution of slavery. It is as if a criminal is pointing the finger of blame at an innocent man.

***Slavery in Islam :*** Islam tried to solve the problem of the slaves that were already in Arabia by encouraging people to set them free. Muslims were told that freeing slaves would mean the expiation of some of their sins. Freeing a slave of one's own free will was declared to be an act of such great merit that the limbs of the man who freed a slave would be protected from hell-fire—one for each limb of the slave freed.

The result of this policy was that, by the time the period of the rightly-guided Caliphs was reached, all the old slaves of Arabia had been liberated. The Prophet (blessings of Allah and peace be upon him) alone liberated as many as 63 slaves. The number of slaves freed by Aishah was 67; Abbas liberated 70; Abdullah bin Umar liberated one thousand; and Abdur Rahman purchased thirty thousand and set them free. Other companions of the Prophet liberated a large number of slaves, the details of which are given in the traditions and books of history of that period.

The problem of the slaves of Arabia was thus solved in under 40 years. After this the only slaves left in Islamic society were prisoners of war captured on the battlefield. These were kept by the Muslim government in question until their own government agreed to receive them back in exchange for Muslim soldiers captured by them or arranged the payment of ransom on their behalf. If the soldiers they captured were not exchanged for Muslim prisoners of war, or their people did not pay their ransom money to purchase their liberty, the Muslim government distributed them among the soldiers of the army which had captured them.

This was a more humane way of disposing of them than penning them like cattle in concentration camps and taking forced labour from them and, if their womenfolk were also captured, setting them aside for prostitution. Islam preferred to spread them through the population and thus bring them in contact with individual human beings. Their guardians, in addition, were ordered to treat them well.

The result of this policy was that most of the men who were captured on foreign battlefields and brought to the Muslim countries as slaves embraced Islam and their descendants produced great scholars, imams, jurists, commentators, statesmen and generals. So much so that later they became rulers of the Muslim world.

Today prisoners of war throughout the world are exchanged on the cessation of hostilities. This is a practice which has been learnt from Islam. But treating well prisoners who cannot, for one reason or another, be exchanged, has not been learnt. Can anyone tell us, for example, the fate of the thousands of prisoners of war captured by Russia from the defeated armies of Germany and Japan in the Second World War? No one knows how many thousands of them are still alive and how many thousands of them perished due to the hardships of the Russian concentration and labour camps. It is doubtful if, even in the times of the ancient Pharaohs of Egypt, such harsh labour was exacted from the slaves who built the pyramids as was exacted from the prisoners of war in Russia who developed Siberia and other backward areas of the country.

### *VI. The Right to Justice*

This is a very important and valuable right which Islam has given to man. The Holy Quran has laid down: "Do not let your hatred of a people incite you to aggression" (5:3). "And do not let ill-will towards any folk incite you so that you swerve from dealing justly. Be just: that is nearest to heedfulness" (5:8). Stressing this point the Quran again says: "You who believe stand steadfast before God as witness for (truth and) fair play" (4:135)

The point is thus made clear that Muslims have to be just not only to their friends but also their enemies. In other words, the justice to which Islam invites her followers is not limited to the citizens of one's own country, or the people of one's own tribe, nation or race, or the Muslim community as a whole; it is meant for all human beings.

### *VII. The Equality of Human Beings*

Islam not only recognizes the principle of absolute equality between men irrespective of colour, race or nationality, it makes it an important reality. Almighty God has laid down in the Holy Quran: "O mankind, we have created you from a male and female." In other words, all human beings are brothers. They all are the descendants from one father and one mother. And we set you up as nations and tribes so that you may be able to recognize each other" (49:13). This means that the division of human beings into nations, races, groups and tribes is for the sake of distinction, so that people of one race or tribe may meet and be acquainted with people belonging to another race or tribe and cooperate with one another.

This division of the human race is neither meant for one nation to take pride in its superiority over others nor for one nation to treat another with contempt. "Indeed, the noblest among you before God are the most heedful of you" (49:13). That is, the superiority of one man over another is only on the basis of God-consciousness, purity of character and high morals, and not colour, race, language or nationality. People are therefore not justified in assuming airs of superiority over other human beings. Nor do the righteous have any special privileges over others.

This has been thus exemplified by the Prophet (blessings of Allah and peace be upon him) in one of his sayings: "No Arab has any superiority over a non-Arab, nor does a non-Arab have any superiority over a black man, or the black man any superiority over the white man. You are all the children of Adam, and Adam was created from clay." In this manner Islam established the principle of equality of the entire human race and struck at the very root of all distinctions based on colour, race, language or nationality.

According to Islam, God has given man this right of equality as a birthright. No man should therefore be discriminated against on the grounds of the colour of his skin, his place of birth, the race or the nation in which he was born.

Malcolm X, the leader of African Negroes in America, once launched a bitter struggle against the white people of America in order to win civil rights for his black compatriots. But when he went to perform the pilgrimage, he saw how the Muslims of Asia, Africa, Europe and America were all wearing the same dress and were all hurrying towards the mosque and were offering prayers standing in the same row. He realized that this was the solution to the problem of colour and race, and not what he had been trying to seek or achieve in America. Today, a number of non-Muslim thinkers openly admit that no other religion or way of life has solved this problem with the same degree of success as Islam.

### *VIII. The Right to Cooperate and not to Cooperate*

Islam has prescribed a general principle of paramount importance and universal application. The Holy Quran says: "Cooperate with one another for virtue and heedfulness and do not cooperate with one another for the purpose of vice and aggression" (5:2). This means that the man who undertakes noble and righteous work, irrespective of whether he is living at the North Pole or the South Pole, has the right to expect support and active cooperation from Muslims. But he who practises vice and aggression, even if he is our closest relation or neighbour, does not have the right to our support and help in the name of race, country, language or nationality, nor should he expect Muslims to cooperate with him. The wicked and vicious person may be our own brother, but he is not of us, and he can have no help or support from us as long as he does not repent of his ways. On the other hand, the man who is doing deeds of virtue and righteousness may have no kinship with Muslims, but Muslims will be his companions and supporters, or at least his well-wishers.

***Rights of Citizens :*** We have discussed human rights in general. We turn now specifically to the question of the rights of citizens in an Islamic state. As these rights are more extensive than the general human rights which have been described earlier, they need separate treatment.

### *I. The Security of Life and Property*

In the address which the Prophet (blessings of Allah and peace be upon him) delivered on the occasion of the Farewell Hajj, he said: "Your lives and properties are forbidden to one another till you meet your Lord on the Day of Resurrection." God Almighty has laid down in the Holy Quran: "Anyone who kills a believer deliberately will receive as his reward (a sentence) to live in Hell for ever. God will be angry with him and curse him, and prepare dreadful torment for him" (4:93). The Prophet (blessings of Allah and peace be upon him) has also said about the dhimmis (the non-Muslim citizens of a Muslim state): "One who kills a man under covenant (i.e. a dhimmi) will not even smell the fragrance of Paradise" (Bukhari and Abu Daud).

Islam prohibits all killing except that done in the due process of law. This is referred to in the Quran as bil-haqq ("with the truth"). During wars or insurrections, only a just and righteous government, which follows the sana, can decide whether the taking of a life is justified.

These weighty decisions may not be left in the hands of a court which has become heedless of God's will and is under the influence of the administration. Such judiciary may miscarry justice. Nor can the state seek justification in the Holy Quran or Traditions if it murders citizens because they oppose unjust policies and actions or criticize it for its misdeeds; equally, the state has no right to hire assassins to kill innocent people and then protect the assassins from the just retribution of the courts. The very existence of such a government is a crime and none of the killings carried out by it can be called "execution for the sake of justice", as the Holy Quran puts it.

Along with security of life, Islam has with equal clarity conferred the right of security of ownership of property. The Holy Quran goes so far as to declare that the taking of people's possessions or property is prohibited unless done by lawful means: The law of God categorically declares "Do not devour one another's wealth by false and illegal means" (2:188).

### *II. The Protection of Honour*

The second important right is the right of citizens to the protection of their honour. In the address delivered on the occasion of the Farewell Hajj, the Prophet (blessings of Allah and peace be upon him) not only prohibited Muslims taking the life and property of other Muslims, but also any encroachment on their honour, respect and chastity. The Holy Quran lays down:

(a) "You who believe, do not let one (set of) people make— of another set.

(b) Do not defame one another.

(c) Do not insult by using nicknames.

(d) And do not backbite or speak ill of one another" (49:11-12)

This law is superior to the Western law of defamation- (Jader Islamic law, if it is proved that someone has attacked the honour of a another person then, irrespective of whether the victim is able to prove himself a respectable and honourable person, the culprit will be punished The interesting fact about the Western law of defamation is that the person who files suit for defamation has first to prove that he is a man of honour and public esteem and during the interrogation he may be subjected to scurrilous attacks and accusations by the defence counsel to such an extent that the court hearing may be more damaging than the attack on his reputation which originally led him to the court. In addition, he also has to produce witnesses to testify in court that the defamatory accusations have damaged his reputation in their eyes.

Good gracious! What a subtle point of law and what an adherence to the spirit of law! How can this unfair and unjust law be compared to the Divine law? Islam has declared defamation a came irrespective of whether the accused is a man of honour, or whether the words used have actually disgraced the victim and harmed his reputation. Under Islamic law it is sufficient to prove that the accused said things which according to common sense, could have damaged the reputation and honour of the plaintiff.

### *III. The Sanctity and Security of Private Life*

Islam recognizes the right of every citizen in an Islamic state to no undue encroachment on the privacy of his life. The Holy Quran has laid down the injunction: "Do not spy on one another" (49:12). "Do not enter any house except your own homes unless you are sure of their occupants' consent" (24:27). The Prophet (blessings of Allah and peace be upon him) went to the extent of instructing his followers that a man should not enter even his own house suddenly or surreptitiously. He should somehow indicate to those inside that he is entering so that he may not see his mother, sister or daughter in a condition in which they would not like to be seen, nor in which he himself would like to see them.

Peering into the houses of other people has also been strictly prohibited so much so that there is the saying of the Prophet (blessings of Allah and peace be upon him) that if a man finds another person secretly peering into his house, and he puts out his eye or eyes as a punishment, he will not be liable to prosecution.

The Prophet (blessings of Allah and peace be upon him) has even prohibited people from reading the letters of others; indeed, if a man is reading his letter and another man casts sidelong glances at it and tries to read it, his conduct becomes reprehensible. These are examples of the sanctity of privacy that Islam grants to individuals.

On the other hand, in the so-called modern civilised world we find that not only are the letters of other people read and censored, but even that photostat copies are retained for future use or blackmail. Bugging devices are secretly fixed in houses so that conversations taking place behind closed doors can be taped. In other words, in many spheres of life individuals have no real privacy.

This prying into the life of the individual cannot be justified on moral grounds by a government saying that it needs to know the secrets of potentially dangerous persons. The basis of this philosophy is the fear and suspicion with which modern governments look at those of their citizens who are intelligent and dissatisfied with official policies. This is exactly what Islam has called the root cause of mischief in politics. The injunction of the Prophet (blessings of Allah and peace be upon him) is: "When the ruler begins to search for the causes of dissatisfaction amongst his people, he spoils them" (Abu Daud). The Amir Muawiyyah has said that he himself heard the Prophet saying: "If you try to find out the secrets of the people, then you will definitely spoil them or at least you will bring them to the verge of ruin."

"Spoiling" people is what happens when secret police are spread all around a country looking into their affairs: men begin to look at one another with suspicion, so much so that they are afraid of talking freely in their houses lest some word should escape from the lips of their wives and children which may put them in embarrassing situations. In this manner, it becomes difficult for a common citizen to speak freely, even in his own house: society begins to suffer from mutual distrust and suspicion.

### *IV. The Security of Personal Freedom*

Islam has laid down the principle that no citizen may be imprisoned unless his guilt has been proved in open court. To arrest a man only on the basis of suspicion and to throw him into prison without proper court proceedings and without providing him with a reasonable opportunity to produce his defence is not permissible in Islam.

It is related in the Traditions that the Prophet (blessings of Allah and peace be upon him) was once delivering a lecture in the Mosque, when a man rose and said: "O Prophet of God, for what crime have my neighbours been arrested?" The Prophet appeared not to hear the question and continued his lecture. The man rose again and repeated the question. The Prophet again did not answer and continued his lecture. The man rose for a third time and repeated the question. Then the Prophet ordered the man's neighbours to be released.

The reason why the Prophet had not answered when the question was asked twice earlier was that the police officer who had carried out the arrest was present in the Mosque; if there had been valid reasons for the arrest, he would have got up to give them. Since the police officer did not, the Prophet ordered that the arrested persons should be released. The police officer was aware of Islamic law and therefore he did not get up to say: "The administration is aware of the charges against the arrested men, but they cannot be disclosed in public. If the Prophet inquires about their guilt in camera I will enlighten him." If the police officer had made such a statement, he would have been dismissed then and there. The fact that the police officer did not give any reasons for the arrests in open court was sufficient for the Prophet to give immediate orders for the release of the arrested men.

The injunction of the Holy Quran is very clear on this point. "Whenever you judge between people, you should judge with (a sense of) justice" (4:58). And the Prophet (blessings of Allah and peace be upon him) said: "I have been ordered by God to dispense justice between you." This was the reason why the Caliph Umar said: "In Islam no one can be imprisoned except in pursuance of justice." The words used here clearly indicate that justice means due process of law in open court.

If a government suspects that a particular individual has committed a crime or is likely to commit an offence in the near future, it should give reasons for its suspicion before a court of law and the culprit or the suspect should be allowed to produce his defence. If good reason for suspicion is proved, he should be informed of how long he will be kept in preventive detention.

In all such circumstances, it is essential that the public hear the charges brought by the government, as well as the defence made by the accused, and thus have the opportunity of seeing that the due process of law is being carried out.

The correct method of dealing with such cases in Islam is exemplified in the famous decision the Prophet (blessings of Allah and peace be upon him) made before the conquest of Mecca. The Prophet was making preparations for the attack on the city when one of his companions, Hatib bin Abi Baltaa, sent a letter through a woman to the authorities in Mecca informing them of the impending attack. The Prophet came to know of this through a Divine inspiration. He ordered 'Ati and Zubayr: "Go quickly on the route to Mecca, at such and such a place, you will find a woman carrying a letter. Recover the letter from her and bring it to me." So they went and found the woman exactly where the Prophet had said. They recovered the letter from her and brought it to the Prophet.

This was indeed a clear case of treachery. In fact, one cannot think of a more serious crime during a time of war than giving a military secret to one's enemy. What could have been a more suitable case for a secret hearing than one into the betrayal of a military secret? But the Prophet summoned Hatib to the open court of the Mosque of the Prophet and in the presence of hundreds of people asked him to explain his position with regard to the letter addressed to the leaders of Quraish.

The accused said: "O God's Messenger (may God's blessings be on you) I have not revolted against Islam, nor have I done this with the intention of betraying a military secret. The truth of the matter is that my wife and children are living in Mecca and I do not have my tribe to protect them there. I had written this letter so that the leaders of Quraish may be indebted to me and may protect my wife and children out of gratitude." Umar rose and respectfully submitted: "O Prophet, please permit me to put this traitor to the sword." The Prophet replied: "He is one of those people who took part in the battle of Badr and the explanation he has advanced in his defence would seem to be acceptable."

Let us look at this decision of the Prophet in perspective. It was a clear case of treachery and betrayal of military secrets. But the Prophet acquitted Hatib on two counts. Firstly, that his past record was clean in that he had fought at the battle of Badr when there were heavy odds against the Muslims. Secondly, his family was in fact in danger in Mecca. In such circumstances it was sufficient punishment that his secret offence became public and that he was disgraced and humiliated in the eyes of the Believers.

The attitude and activities of the Kharijites in the days of the Caliph Hadrat Ali are well known to students of Muslim history. They used to abuse the Caliph openly, and threaten him with murder. But whenever they were arrested for these offences, 'ATI would set them free and tell his officers: "As long as they do not actually perpetrate offences against state, the mere use of abusive language or the threat of use of force are not such offences for which they can be imprisoned." The Imam Abu Hanifa has recorded following saying of the Caliph Hadrat Ali, "As long as they do not set out on led rebellion, the Caliph of the Faithful will not interfere with them." On another occasion, 'He was delivering a lecture in the Mosque when Kharijites raised their special slogan there. 'He said: We will not deny the right to come to the mosques to worship God, nor will we stop your share from the wealth of the state, as long as you are with us (and support us in wars against the unbelievers) and we shall never take military action it you as long as you do not fight with us."

One can visualize the opposition which 'All was facing: more violent and vituperative opposition cannot be imagined even in a present-day democratic state, but the freedom that he allowed to the opposition was such that no government has ever since been able to give to its opposition.

### V. The Right to Protest Against Tyranny

Amongst the rights that Islam has conferred on human beings is the right to protest against a government's tyranny. The Quran says: "God does not love evil talk in public unless it is by someone who has been injured thereby" (4:148). This means that God strongly disapproves of abusive language or strong words of condemnation, but that the person who has been the victim of injustice or tyranny has the right to protest strongly against the injury that has been done to him.

This right is not limited to individuals. The words of the verse have general application. If an individual or a group of people or a party usurps power and, after assuming the reins of authority, begins to tyrannize individuals or groups of men or the entire population of the country, then to raise the voice of protest is the God-given right of man. Trying to usurp this right is tantamount to rebellion against God. The talisman of Section 144 may protect such a tyrant in this world, but it cannot save him from hell-fire in the Hereafter.

### VI. Freedom of Expression

Islam gives the right of freedom of thought and expression to all citizens of an Islamic State on condition that it is used for propagating virtue and not for spreading evil. This Islamic concept of freedom of expression is far superior to that of the West. Indeed, the right to freedom of expression to propagate virtue and righteousness is not only a right, but an obligation. Anyone who tries to deny this right to his people is openly at war with God, the All-Powerful. It is equally a right of and an obligation on an individual to attempt to stop evil, whether this evil is perpetrated by an individual or by a group of people or the government of one's own country or the government of some other country. Over and above this, he should openly condemn the evil and point to the morally correct course which should be adopted.

The Holy Quran has described this quality of the faithful in the following words: "They enjoin what is proper and forbid what is improper" (9:71). By contrast, describing the qualities of a hypocrite, the Quran says:

> "They bid what is improper and forbid what is proper" (9:67). The main purpose of an Islamic government has been defined by God in the Quran as follows: "If we give authority to these men on earth they will keep up prayers, and offer welfare due, bid what is proper and forbid what is improper" (22:41). The Prophet has said: "If any one of you comes across an evil, he should try to stop it with his hand (using force): if he is not in a position to stop it with his hand then he should try to stop it by means of his tongue (meaning he should speak against it). If he is not even able to use his tongue then he should at least condemn it in his heart. This is the weakest degree of faith."

The obligation to try to persuade people along the paths of righteousness and away from the paths of evil is incumbent on all true Muslims. Any government which deprives its citizens of this right is in direct conflict with divine injunction. Such a government is then not in conflict with its people, but with God: it is trying to usurp that right of its people which God has conferred not merely as a right but as an obligation.

### *VII. Freedom of Association*

Islam has also given people the right to freedom of association and formation of parties or organizations. This right is subject to certain general rules. It should be exercised for propagating virtue and righteousness and never for spreading evil and mischief. We have not only been given this right to spread righteousness and virtue— we have been ordered to exercise it. Addressing the Muslims, the Holy Quran declares:

> "You are the best community which has been brought forth for mankind. You command what is proper and forbid what is improper and you believe in God" (3:110).

This means that it is the obligation and duty of the entire Muslim community to enjoin people to righteousness and virtue and forbid them to do evil. If the Muslim community as a whole does not perform this duty then "let there be a community among you who will invite (people) to (do) good, command what is proper and forbid what is improper, those will be prosperous" (3:104). This clearly indicates that if the community collectively begins to neglect its obligations, then it is absolutely essential for there to be at least one group within the community prepared to meet them.

It is ironic that in a Muslim country the assembly and association that has been formed for the purpose of spreading evil and mischief should also have the right to rule over the country and the association and party which has been formed for the purpose of propagating righteousness and virtue should live in perpetual fear of harassment and of being declared illegal. Conditions here are the reverse of what has been prescribed by God. The claim is that we are Muslims and that this is an Islamic State, but the work that is being done is directed to spreading evil, to corrupting and morally degrading and debasing people, while there is active and effective hindrance on the work being carried out to reform society and point people to righteousness. Moreover, the lives of those who are engaged in spreading righteousness and checking the spread of evil and wickedness are made intolerable.

### *VIII. Freedom of Conscience and Conviction*

Islam gives the right to freedom of conscience and conviction to the citizens of an Islamic State. The Holy Quran has laid down the injunction:

> "There should be no coercion in the matter of faith" (2:256). Although there is no truth or virtue greater than Islam, and although Muslims are enjoined to invite people to embrace it and advance arguments in favour of it, they are not asked to spread this faith by force. Whoever accepts it does so by his own choice. Muslims welcome such converts to Islam with open arms and admit them to their community with equal rights and privileges. But, equally, Muslims have to recognize and respect the decision of people who do not accept Islam: no moral, social or political pressures may be put on them to change their minds.

## IX. Protection of Religious Sentiments

Along with freedom of conviction and freedom of conscience, Islam guarantees the individual that his religious sentiments will be given due respect and that nothing will be said or done which may encroach on this right. It is ordained by God in the Holy Quran: "Do not abuse those they appeal to instead of God" (6:108). These instructions are not limited to idols and deities—they also apply to the leaders or national heroes of the people. If a group of people hold certain convictions and certain persons in an esteem which you feel is not deserved, then it is not justifiable in Islam for you to use abusive language to them and thus injure their feelings. Islam does not prohibit people holding debate and discussions to be conducted in decency. "Do not argue with the people of the Book unless it is in the politest manner" (29:46), says the Quran. This order is not limited to the people of the Scriptures, but applies with equal force to those following other faiths.

## X. Protection from Arbitrary Imprisonment

Islam recognizes the right of the individual not to be arrested or imprisoned for the offences of others. The Holy Quran has laid down this principle clearly: "No bearer of burdens shall be made to bear the burden of another" (6:164). Islam believes in personal responsibility. We ourselves are responsible for our acts, and their consequences cannot be transferred to someone else.

It is a matter of great regret and shame that we are seeing this just and equitable principle, which has been framed by the Creator and Nourisher of the entire universe, being flouted and violated before our eyes. So much so that if a man is guilty of a crime or if he is a suspect, his wife is also liable to arrest. Indeed, things have gone so far that innocent people are being punished for the crimes of others.

To give a recent example, a man in Karachi was suspected of being involved in a bomb-throwing incident. In the course of police investigations he was subjected to horrible torture to try to extract a confession from him. When he insisted on his innocence, the police arrested his mother, his wife, daughter and sister and brought them to the police station. They were all stripped naked in his presence, and he was stripped naked before their eyes so that a confession of the crime could be extracted from him. It appears as if for the sake of investigation of crime it has become proper and legal to strip innocent womenfolk of a household in order to bring pressure on a suspect.

I would here like to ask what right such tyrants—who perpetrate these crimes against mankind—have to tell us that they are Muslims or that they are conducting the affairs of the state according to the teachings of Islam. They are flouting a clear law of the Holy Quran by stripping men and women naked. They disgrace and humiliate humanity—and then they claim that they are Muslims.

### *XI. The Right to the Basic Necessities of Life*

Islam has recognized the right of the needy to assistance. "And in their wealth there is acknowledged right for the needy and the destitute" (51:19). In this verse, the Quran has not only conferred a right to every man who asks for assistance in the wealth of the Muslims, but has also laid down that if a Muslim comes to know that a certain man is without the basic necessities of life, then, irrespective of whether he asks for assistance or not, it is his duty to give all the help that he can.

For this purpose, Islam does not depend only on voluntary charity, but has made compulsory charity, its third pillar, next only to the profession of faith and worship of God through regular prayers. The Prophet (blessings of Allah and peace be upon him) has clearly instructed us: "It will be taken from their rich and given to those in the community in need."

In addition, it has also been declared that the Islamic State should support those who have nobody to support them. The Prophet has said:

> "The Head of State is the guardian of him who has nobody to support him" (Abu Daud, Tirmidhi). The word which is used by the Prophet has a wide range of meanings. It is the duty and the responsibility of the state to support and assist orphans, the old, the unemployed and the sick if they have no one to help them. If a dead man has no guardian or heir, it is the duty of the state to arrange for his burial. A true Islamic State is therefore a true welfare state.

### *XII. Equality Before the Law*

Islam gives its citizens the right to absolute equality in the eyes of the law. As far as Muslims are concerned, there are clear instructions in the Holy Quran and Hadith that in their rights and obligations they are all equal: "The believers are brothers (to each other)" (49:10). "If they (disbelievers) repent and keep up prayer and pay the welfare due they are your brothers in faith" (9:11), The Prophet has said that: "The life and blood of Muslims are equally precious" (Abu Daud. Ibn Maja). In another Hadith he has said: "The protection given by all Muslims are equal. Even an ordinary man of them can grant protection to any man." In another more detailed Tradition of the Prophet, it has been said that those who accept the Oneness of God, believe in the Prophethood of His Messenger, give up primitive prejudices and join the Muslim community and brotherhood, "then they have the same rights and obligations as other Muslims have." Thus there is absolute equality between converts to Islam and born followers of the Faith.

This religious brotherhood and the uniformity of their rights and obligations is the foundation of equality in Islamic society. The position of non-Muslim citizens in an Islamic State has been well expressed by the Caliph ATI: "They have accepted our protection only because their lives may be like our lives and their properties like our properties" (Abu Daud). In other words, their lives and properties are as sacred as the lives and properties of Muslims. Discrimination based on class was one of the greatest crimes that, according to the Quran, Pharaoh used to indulge in:

> "He had divided his people into different classes," ...
> "And he suppressed one group of them (at the cost of others)" (28:4).

### *XIII. Rulers are not Above the Law*

Islam insists and demands that all officials of an Islamic State, from most senior to most junior, are equal in the eyes of the law. None of them can claim immunity from it. The most humble citizen has the right to file a legal complaint against the highest executive in the land. The Caliph Umar said: "I have myself seen the Prophet, may God's blessings be on him, taking revenge against himself (penalizing himself for some shortcoming or failing)." On the occasion of the battle of Badr. When the Prophet was straightening the rows of the Muslim army, he hit the stomach of a soldier in an attempt to push him back in line. The soldier complained, "O Prophet, you have hurt me with your stick." The Prophet immediately bared his stomach and said, "I am very sorry, you can revenge by doing the same to me." The soldier came forward and kissed the abdomen of the Prophet and said that this was all that he wanted.

A woman belonging to a high and noble family was arrested in connection with a theft. The case was brought to the Prophet and it was recommended that she be spared punishment. The Prophet replied: "The nations that lived before you were destroyed by God because they punished the common man for their offences and let their dignitaries go unpunished for their crimes: I swear by Him (God) who holds my life in His hand that even if Fatima, the daughter of Muhammad, had committed this crime, then I would have amputated her hand."

During the caliphate of Umar, Muhammad the son of Amr bin al-As, the Governor of Egypt, whipped an Egyptian. The Egyptian went to Medina and lodged his complaint with the Caliph, who immediately summoned the Governor and his son. When they appeared before him the Caliph handed a whip to the Egyptian plaintiff and asked him to whip the son of the Governor in his presence. After the Egyptian had taken his revenge, Umar said to him: "Give one stroke of the whip to the Honourable Governor as well. His son would certainly not have beaten you were it not for the false pride that he had in his father's high office." The plaintiff submitted: "The person who had beaten me, I have already avenged myself on him." 'Umar said: "By God, if you had beaten him (the Governor), I would not have checked you from doing so. You have spared him of your own free will." Then he ('Umar) turned to Amr bin al-As and said angrily: "O Amr, when did you start to enslave the people, though they were born free of their mothers?"

When the Islamic State was nourishing in its pristine glory, the common people could equally lodge complaints against the caliph of the time in the court and the caliph had to appear before the Qadi answer the charges. And if the caliph had any complaint against any citizen, he could not act without first referring the case to the court of law.

### *XIV. The Right to Avoid Sin*

Islam confers the right on every citizen to refuse to commit a sin or a crime; if any government or administrator orders an individual to do a wrong, he may refuse to comply. Not only is his refusal not an offence, the giving of an order to one's subordinates to commit a sin or do a wrong is itself an offence and such a serious one that the officer who gives it, whatever his rank, is liable to summary dismissal.

These clear instructions of the Prophet are summarized in the following Hadith. "It is not permissible to disobey God in obedience to the orders of any human being" (Musnad of Ibn Hanbal). In other words, no-one has the right to order his subordinates to act against the laws of God. No offender may seek to prove his innocence or escape punishment by saying that the offence was committed on the orders of a superior. If such a situation arises, the person who commits the offence and the person who orders it are equally liable to criminal proceedings.

### *XV. The Right to Participate in the Affairs of State*

According to Islam, governments are representatives (khalifa) of the Creator of the universe; this responsibility is not entrusted to any individual or family or to any particular class or group of people, but to the entire Muslim community. The Holy Quran says: "God has promised to appoint in which the right of every individual Muslim is neither more nor less than the right of any other person.

The method recommended by the Holy Quran for running the affairs of the state is as follows: "And their business is (conducted) through consultation among themselves" (42:38). According to this principle, it is the right of every Muslim either to have a direct say in the affairs of the state or to have a representative chosen by him and other Muslims to participate in the running of the state.

Under no circumstances does Islam permit an individual or a group or party of individuals to deprive the common Muslims of their rights or usurp powers of the state. Nor does Islam regard it as right and proper for an individual to put on a false show of setting up a legislative assembly and by means of such tactics as fraud, persecution, bribery and so on, get himself and men of his choice elected to the assembly. This is not only treachery against the people whose rights are illegally usurped, but also against the Creator who has entrusted Muslims to rule on earth on His behalf, and has prescribed the procedure of an assembly for exercising these powers.

The shura or legislative assembly should embrace the following principles:

1. The executive head of the government and the members of the assembly should be elected by free and independent choice of the people.
2. The people and their representatives should have the right to criticize and freely express their opinions.
3. The real conditions of the country should be brought before the people without suppression of fact so that they are in a position to judge whether the government is working properly or not.
4. There should be adequate guarantee that only those people who have the support of the masses should rule over the country and those who fail to win this support should be removed from their position of authority.

***Rights of Enemies :*** Before the advent of Islam the world was ignorant of the concept of humane and decent rules of war. The West first began to develop this concept through the works of the seventeenth century thinker, Grotius. But the actual codification of 'international law' in war began in the middle of the nineteenth century. Prior to this, all forms of barbarism and savagery were perpetrated in war, and the rights of those in a war were not even recognized, let alone respected.

The 'laws' which were framed in this field during the nineteenth century or over the following period up to the present day cannot be called laws in the real sense of the word. They are only conventions and agreements, because nations do not regard them as binding unless, of course, their adversaries also agree to abide by them. In other words, these civilized laws imply that if our enemies respect them, we shall also respect them, but if they ignore them then we shall ignore them, too. Arrangements which depend on mutual acceptability cannot be called 'laws'. This is the reason why so-called 'international law' has been constantly flouted and ignored.

***Law of War and Peace :*** The rules which have been framed by Islam to make war civilized and humane are in the nature of law, because they are the injunctions of God and His Prophet (blessings of Allah and peace be upon him) which are followed by Muslims in all circumstances, irrespective of the behaviour of enemy. It would be instructive to research into how well the West has adopted the laws of war given by Islam fourteen hundred years ago; and, even after their adoption, how well the West has managed to attain those heights of civilized and human warfare behaviour which Muslims have reached through the blessings of Islam.

Western writers have often asserted that the Prophet (blessings of Allah and peace be upon him) borrowed his teachings from the Jews and Christians. It is sufficient here to recommend the reader to refer to the Bible so that he can see what methods of war are recommended by the sacred Book of these Western claimants to civilization and culture.

We have examined in some detail the basic human rights that Islam has conferred on man. Let us now look at the rights and obligations Islam recognizes for an enemy.

***Rights of Non-Combatants :*** Islam has drawn a clear distinction between combatants and non combatants in an enemy country. As far as the non-combatant population is concerned— women, children, the old and the infirm - the instructions of the Prophet are as follows: "Do not kill any old person, any child or any woman." "Do not kill the monks in monasteries" and "Do not kill the people who are sitting in places of worship."

During a war, the Prophet saw the corpse of a woman lying on the ground and observed: "She was not fighting. How then came she to be killed?" From this statement of the Prophet, the exegesists and jurists have drawn the principle that those who are non-combatants should not be killed during or after a war.

***Rights of Combatants :*** Now let us see what rights Islam has conferred on the combatants.

### *I. Torture by fire*

In the Hadith, there is a saying of the Prophet that: "Punishment by fire does not behove anyone except the Master of the Fire." The injunction deduced from this saying is that the adversary should not be burnt alive.

### *II. Protection of the wounded*

"Do not attack a wounded person", said the Prophet. This means that wounded soldiers who are not fit to fight, nor actually fighting, should not be attacked.

### *III. Prisoners of war should not be slain*

"No prisoner should be put to the sword" —a very clear and unequivocal instruction given by the Prophet.

### *VI. No one should be tied to be killed*

"The Prophet has prohibited the killing of anyone who is tied or is in captivity.'"

### *V. No looting and destruction in the enemy's country*

Muslims have been instructed by the Prophet not to pillage or plunder or destroy residential areas, nor harm the property of anyone not fighting. It has been narrated in the Hadith: "The Prophet has prohibited the Believers from loot and plunder" His injunction is: "The loot is no more lawful than the carrion". Abu Bakr Siddiq used to tell soldiers on their way to war: "Do not destroy the villages and towns, do not spoil the cultivated fields and gardens, and do not slaughter the cattle."

Booty of war from the battleground is altogether different. It consists of the wealth, provisions and equipment captured from the camps and military headquarters of the combatant armies and may legitimately be appropriated.

### *VI. Sanctity of property*

Muslims have been prohibited from taking anything from the general public of conquered country without paying for it. If the Muslim army occupies an area of the enemy country, it does not have the right to use the things belonging to the people without their consent. If the army needs anything, it should purchase it from the local population or should obtain permission from the owners. Abu Bakr Siddiq used to tell Muslim armies being dispatched to the battle front that they should not even use the milk of the milch cattle without the permission of the owners.

### *VII. Sanctity of a dead body*

Islam has categorically prohibited its followers from mutilating the corpses of their enemies, as was practised in Arabia before the advent of Islam. It is said in the Hadith: "The Prophet has prohibited us from mutilating the corpses of the enemies." The occasion on which this order was given is highly instructive. In the battle of Uhud, the disbelievers mutilated the bodies of the Muslims who had fallen on the battlefield by cutting off their ears and noses and threading them together to put round their necks as trophies of war. The stomach of Hamzah, the uncle of the Prophet, was ripped open by the Quraish and his liver was taken out and chewed by Hinda, the wife of Abu Sufyan, the leader of the Meccan army. The Muslims were naturally enraged by this horrible sight. But the Prophet asked his followers not to mete out similar treatment to the dead bodies of the enemies.

This great example of forebearance and restraint should be sufficient to convince any reasonable man that Islam really is the religion sent down by the Creator of the universe; if Islam allowed human emotions free rein, this horrible sight on the battlefield of Uhud would have provoked the Prophet to order his followers to mutilate the bodies of their enemy in the same manner.

### *VIII. Return of corpses of the enemy*

In the battle of Ahzab a renowned enemy warrior was killed and his body fell into the trench which the Muslims had dug for the defence of Medina. The unbelievers presented ten thousand dinars to the Prophet and requested that the dead body of their fallen warrior be handed ever to them. The Prophet replied: "I do not sell dead bodies. You can take away the corpse of your fallen comrade."

### *IX. Prohibition of breach of treaties*

Islam has strictly prohibited treachery. One of the instruction that the Prophet used to give to Muslim warriors when sending them to the battlefront was: "Do not be guilty of breach of faith."

This order has been repeated in the Holy Quran and the Hadith again and again. There is a famous incident in the peace treaty of Hudaybiya who, after the settlement of the terms of the treaty, Abu Jandal, the son of thee emissary of the unbelievers who had negotiated the treaty with the Muslims came bound and blood-stained to the Muslim camp crying for help. The Prophet told him: "Since the terms of the treaty have been settled, we are not in a position to help you. You should go back with your father. God will provide you with some other opportunity to escape this persecution"

The entire Muslim army was deeply touched and worried at the plight of Abu Jandal and many of them were moved to tear the bonds, when the Prophet declared "we cannot break the agreement." not a single person came forward to help the unfortunate prisoner: so the unbelievers forcibly dragged him back to Mecca. This is an unparralel example of the observance of the terms of agreement by Muslims: Islam can show many similar examples.

### *X. Rules about declaration of war*

It has been laid down in the Holy Quran: "If you apprehend breach of treaty firm a people, then openly throw the treaty at their faces" (8:58). In this verse, Muslims have been prohibited from opening hostilities against their enemies without properly declaring war against them, unless of course, the adversary has already started the aggression. Present-day international law of war, but since this is a man-made rule, it is often disregarded, Muslim laws, on the other hand, have been framed by God and not be disregarded.

This is a brief sketch of those rights which 1400 years ago Islam gave to man, to those who were at war with each other and to the citizens of its state. It reinforce and strengthens our faith in Islam when we realize that even in this modern age, which makes such loud claims of progress and emancipation, the world has not been able to produce more just and equitable laws than those given 1400 years ago. On the other hand, it is saddening to realize that Muslims, nonetheless, often look for guidance to the West. Even more painful is the realization that, throughout the world, rulers who claim to be Muslims have made disobedience to their God and the Prophet, the basis and foundation of their government. May God have mercy on them and give them true guidance.

# 7

# Law and Social Justice

## The Jurisprudence

The *Shariah* is not to be understood in any static sense. The great Muslim political thinker, Ibn-e-Khaldun, in the early 14th century, had said of Muslim Kings that they should "act in accordance with the requirements of the Islamic *Shariah*", and therefore their laws were to be "composed of statutes of the *Shariah,* relation of right conduct, regulations which are natural for political association and other necessary things concerning power". These views were endorsed by Ibn-e-Sina and by Ibn-e-Rushd and indicate beyond question that in the views of these great political philosophers, the integrity of the Muslim State is bound up with adherence to the *Shariah.*

The *Shariah* is not to be understood in any limited sense, in fact, its meaning is almost synonymous with the expression *Fiqh* as appears clearly from the following quotations taken from the Preface to the *Majelle.* The *Majelle* is the work of a learned Commission appointed by the Sultan of Turkey in the last quarter of the 19th century to draw up a Civil Code of contemporaneous character. In the Preface, the members of the Commission spoke of His Imperial Majesty having "entrusted to His humble servants the important work, the production from the practical part of the *Shariah (Fiqh)* of the beneficial work so that it shall be sufficient for application to the transactions of people which happen everyday, according to the wants of the time". In submitting their report to the Sultan, the Committee stated that they had collected the opinions of the *Hanafites* and also "cases from the practical part of the *Shariah* about transactions'. They had submitted their work to the Sheikhul Islam and two other persons who had "sufficient knowledge of the matter and were skilled in the science of the practical *Shariah (Fiqh)"*, and the suggestions which these learned persons had made have been incorporated in their work.

Today we have statutes covering to a very great extent the field of human relationships and transactions on the secular side, we have not paid enough attention to this aspect of legal development. It may be said that if the legislators, the Courts and the lawyers did not care to examine the question whether the laws which are being made and implemented in Pakistan are or are not consistent with the tenants of Islam, then their negligence would give birth to tendencies which would not be consistent with the dictates of Islamic Law and would be injurious to the full development of Muslim society Pakistan as a just society in the way of Islam. We didn't advocate any upheaval of the present system either of legislation or of the Courts. But simply suggest that there should be injected into the system, through the decisions of the Courts, the spirit and the letter of the principles of the *Shariah*. These are dynamic principles, based upon the dictates of Holy Scripture, drawn in accordance with the correct rules of jurisprudence and adapted to meet the changing requirements of the time, in particular the circumstances of each case coming before the Courts. Under our system, the law declared by the superior Courts has a binding effect on all subordinate courts. Inevitably if the superior Courts, care to make use of Islamic jurisprudence, the law they declare will become incorporate in the judicial system of the country.

Any one of you who desires to look into the *Majelle* will find instances of approach to legal matters significantly different from that to which we are accustomed. As an example, there is a law of pre-emption which is dealt with in the *Majelle*. Under a particular Article a demand for pre-emption has to be made immediately and the action to pre-empt must be brought within a month. The right to pre-empt can be destroyed if the pre-emptor delays in making his formal demand. The comparatively lengthy periods of limitation which we observe form no part of this law. And the very short period provided for bringing a suit is another indication that the intention is that the pre-emption should take any steps to his own detriment that could later be raised as a bar. In other branches of secular law too, there are similar differences of a significant nature, which seem to me to operate to minimise litigation, and in particular the abuse of the legal process.

All human activity can, in my submission, be likened to the function of cultivating a garden. In that garden, those plants and trees are most appropriate and therefore most beautiful which grow naturally out of the soil. The duty is to preserve the good and the useful, allowing them to grow to their full size and height, while at the same time discouraging everything in the nature of weeds and other obnoxious growth. We who serve the law and justice also have our garden and it is a great garden indeed. The present condition could perhaps be described somewhat as follows. Instead of maturing and developing the plants and trees of value which are natural to the soil we are engaged in maintaining a garden which is composed almost exclusively of plants and trees which are of exotic growth. We labour incessantly to promote the growth of these foreign forms of vegetation. Many of us find our greatest satisfaction in having created this artificial garden and we require the whole population to take the judicial fruit from these foreign plants and trees and to be satisfied with it. Our own natural growth are allowed to become matters of dusty record in foreign countries, to be buried in libraries and museums, while we diligently and with enormous labour apply ourselves to cultivate and promote the foreign vegetation with which we are seeking to populate our garden. That is why we fail to produce the finest fruit of which our soil and our labour is capable.

The fruit that we produce is a low-level product, compared to that of the gardens where such growth are natural, and it necessarily fails to satisfy the basic sentiments and requirements of our people. Our own plants and trees are relegated to the position of weeds and rough undergrowth in this process. When the master gardeners and their employers were all of foreign origin this was unavoidable. But today we cannot be content with the thought that our laws and our own principles of justice are relegated to a subordinate and indeed an almost irrelevant position, as if they have no place in the garden which we are engaged daily in nourishing. These principles are of the highest validity. The practices of justice based on *Shariah* and *Fiqh* need not give way to any corresponding rules that we found suitable in other countries. Therefore, legislators, Judges and lawyers alike should cultivate this garden with the finest trees and plants which belong to our own history and culture. Then only can the fruit have the true quality which is the basic necessity of the modern society.

There is need for bringing all the processes of justice into the common languages of the people. That indeed is a part of the argument we have just been presenting, for it would be strange indeed if we were to become convinced that unless we use a foreign language, the propagation of our own laws and beliefs as to justice would not be successful. So far it is difficult to see any sign of departure from the course which we have been following, i.e., working for the development of law through the medium of English language. But as time goes on, it is becoming apparent that the substratum necessary to continue that state of affairs is beginning to fail. Interest in the study of, and more so, the mastery of the English language is steadily declining. It no longer approaches the degree of command necessary for the due appreciation and expression of the finer development of the law. Already judgements are appearing from the subordinate Courts whose faulty English clearly indicates that the entire thinking has been in the writers' language and that he would have been greatly assisted in making his meaning clear if he had allowed himself to use that language. That is an unmistakable sign of a change that is inevitable. It may not come in our time but it is certain to come.

***The Conclusion :*** It is well-known that the whole operation of law is a continuous and endless stream in which all of us are merged. Our thoughts and deeds that have gone into the arguments, the judgements that have been written, have become an integral part of that stream. We ourselves are not originators. We have sat at the feet of learned teachers and seniors who in turn have received instruction at the hands of their elders. The whole body of law is a long record whose principles stretch back to the distant past when human beings first became aware of their duty as moral agents in the way of God. The earliest learned writings in law are based on these scriptures. We have used those writings and reports continuously in our work to maintain the steady flow of that great stream. The opportunities of correction within that stream of law are so numerous that the maintenance of its purity is indeed guaranteed. Although active engagement in the process of justice is not open to a Judge after he retires, he has a great satisfaction in knowing that in his time he has been a part of that living and moving stream and perhaps has been fortunate enough to leave a mark here and there which could serve as landmarks of justice. Though not in the mainstream, he may yet assist from the outside by contributions in writing to the better understanding of the laws. Speaking for ourselves we do not feel that we can ever become a stranger to this stream. We owe and hereby tender our very sincere thanks to my learned colleagues who have sat with me, and to the many lawyers whose labours have assisted in the accomplishment of any work that has passed through our hands.

## Cultivation and Evolution

Islamic Law or *Shariah* is the Command of Allah revealed to the Prophet Muhammad (PBUH). Islamic Law, irrespective of the variety of its "sources", emanates from God and aims at discovering and formulating His Will. God's Will is not once and for all defined as a static system; rather it comprehends all spheres of man's life and is progressively unfolded'.

The Islamic concept of law is that God Almighty is the Sovereign. Who is Supreme and in Whom vests all controlling and absolute powers. The very opening Chapter of the Quran says: 'Praise be to God' Lord of the Worlds' (1 : 2). His Sovereignty is repeatedly asserted in various verses of the Holy Book. The Command is for none but Gods' (12:40). 'He is the best to Command' (12:80). His is the Sovereignty of the Heavens and the Earth (57:5). The concept of Sovereignty in Islam is therefore quite different than the one prevalent in a democracy whereby the sovereignty vests in the people. But in Islam He alone is the Creator and the real Ruler and the worldly affairs are to be run according to His Commandments. 'Verily His is the Creation and His is the Command' (7 : 54); And those who do not make their decisions in accordance with that revealed by God, are (in fact) the unjust' (5:47). This follows that the Divine Laws are perfect and are meant for all humanity and for all ages to come and the balance of justice cannot be maintained without obedience to His Commandments.

Islamic Law finds its chief source in the Will of Allah as revealed to the Prophet Muhammad (PBUH). It contemplates one community of the faithful or *Ummah* though they may be of various tribes, colour, caste or creed. Geographical integration is not an essential ingredient for the emergence as one *Ummah.* Islam and not nationalism is the all-prevailing Force which binds them together.

According to Sir John Salmond the legal status of the man-made law depends entirely on the assumption that it enjoys the sanction of the tribal chief or head of the clan, or that a Court has enforced it, or that it has the recognition of a government. If it does not enjoy at least one of the foregoing sanctions it loses its legal status. The Islamic Law on the contrary has no such limitations or sanction behind it for its implementation or recognition of a government. It is Divinely Ordained, Universal in character and for the benefit of mankind not only for this world but for the Hereafter. It does not presuppose the existence of a State rather the State is subservient to it. Its superiority, its legal status is least effected if any court or government does not recognize it. But the court or the government itself would stand indicted for disobedience and rebellion.

> 'Whose judgeth not by that which Allah hath revealed; such are evil livers' (5 : 47).

This position is also supported by the terminology adopted by Islam for its law. One of the words used for Islamic Law is *'Kitab'* or 'the Book by which is meant whatsoever Allah hath written for us. Another name given to it is *"Sunnah"* by which is meant whatsoever the Holy Prophet (PBUH) has determined for us. The third is that well-known word *'Shariah'* by which is meant whatsoever Allah hath appointed for us. Likewise some other terms used for Islamic Law illustrate the same truth'.

> There is uniformity and consistency in Islamic Law as its origin does not lie in the traditions, customs and the habits of the clans and tribes. Identical law was revealed by Allah to all the Prophets. The Holy Quran has elucidated the consistency of the Islamic Law in *Sura Shura.* (42: 13)
>
> 'He had ordained for you that religion which He commanded unto Nuh, and that which We commanded

> unto Abraham and Moses and Jesus saying: Establish the religion and be not divided therein.'

Generally it is said that the Islamic Law originated with the advent of the Holy Prophet (PBUH). This is not the correct estimation. The Islamic Law took its birth with the arrival of Prophet Adam on earth. All the Messengers who preceded the Prophet Muhammad (PBUH) upheld and preached the same law. The distinction of the Holy Prophet (PBUH) in this context is not that this law originated with him, but that it was brought to perfection with him. The development of this law however kept pace with the advancement of society and its needs. Certain changes were made to meet the growing requirements. Islamic terminology for such change is *'Naskh'* (abrogation) or "amendment". But so far as the fundamental principles or basic values are concerned they have remained the same. The difference was in points of detail and not in essentials. *Shariah* remained the same throughout history from the beginning.

The law given to the Holy Prophet (PBUH) was not revealed in a single instalment. This was communicated piecemeal within a period of 23 years. Thus Islamic Law completed after its necessary amendments, came to be compiled finally before the demise of the Prophet (PBUH), 'It was now rich in all the potentialities which were essential to an ideal *Din* or Faith and was now fully equipped to steer mankind through the changing condition of life'.

> 'The development of Islamic Law has proceeded along defined channels and based on certain principles. It does march forward but in doing so it is invariably well anchored to its fundamental principles and basic values. Its track is identified and its boundaries well-known. There is no possibility of its going astray or its being unfaithful to its historic faith'.

There are four main recognised sources of Islamic Law, namely the Holy Quran, the *Sunnah, Ijma* (Consensus), and *Qiyas* (inference through precedent or analogy). The other sources of law are *Istihsan* or Juristic preference, *Al-Masalih al Mursalah* or unrestricted Interests and *Uraf.*

The period of the Prophet commenced with the beginning of his mission in A.D. 610 and came to an end with his demise in

A.D. 632. During this period the Book (The Holy Quran) was the principal source of law. It was revealed by God as a guidance to the right path. The period of revelations extended over a period of 22 years, 1 2 of which were in Mecca before the *Hijra* and the remaining 10 in Medina.

The *Sunnah* is the second source of law after the Holy Quran. It comprises the sayings of the Prophet (PBUH) his deeds and his tacit approval. The Quran and the *Sunnah* are thus the primary sources of law.

The evolution of Islamic Jurisprudence can be divided into the following four periods:

***The Period of the Prophet A.D. 610 to 632 :*** During the period of the Holy Prophet all judicial matters, decisions centered round the personality of the Holy Prophet (PBUH). During this period the foundation of Islamic Jurisprudence was laid on sound footing. Every issue relating to *Aqaid* (beliefs), *Amaal* (conduct or actions) and *Akhlaq* (ethics) was settled in accordance with dictates of Quran and the *Sunnah* and this was termed as *Shariah.*

So long as the Holy Prophet continued his preaching in Mecca, he gave all importance to the Declaration of Oneness of Allah Almighty and eradication of concept of *shirk.* The interpretation of Quranic injunctions started soon after the *Hijra.* The Jurists or *Ulama* during the time of the Holy Prophet (PBUH) were well versed in the Quranic verses and were known as *Qura.* This period was for the development of basic concepts of Islamic society and for the advancement of cause of Islam. The intention of the people was focused on *Jihad* and *Amal* (action). They had no time to give thought to other issues. They had direct guidance from the Prophet (PBUH) for the solution of their day-to-day problems.

The main fountain-heads of the Islamic Jurisprudence in this period were : (i) The Holy Quran, and (ii) The *Sunnah.*

> 'The Quran is the Book which contains the revelations made to the Holy Prophet in his capacity as the Messenger of God. These revelations are in God's own words as communicated from time to time in fragments called *'ayat'* or verses. Many of them laid

down rules of law with reference to cases which actually arose. The other sources of law, the *Sunnah* is not only explanatory of text of the Quran but also complementary to it, for the Prophet 'never spoke of his own will unless it was a revelation revealed to him'.

(Quran 53, 3 : 4)

***The Period of Orthodox Caliphs A.H 11-40 (A. D. 632-661):*** During the lifetime of the Holy Prophet the Companions of the Prophet felt no difficulty as they had the advantage to seek direct guidance from him. After the demise of the Holy Prophet the Caliphs sought guidance from the texts of the Quran and the *Sunnah* and from their own *Ijtihad.* The Muslims subjugated the territories of Qaiser and Kisra. The peoples of Egypt, Syria, Iran and East Africa subdued before the Muslims. The people with different civilizations, castes and creeds gave birth to a number of new and novel political and socio-economic issues. Naturally a guideline had to be sought from the availability of the laws of the First Period for their application in the new spheres of human conduct. The Companions therefore in extracting the rules of law from the main two sources followed the principles of *Qiyas* (analogy) and *Ijma* (consensus). There was a specific indication in the Holy Book and the *Sunnah* to follow the methodology of the two. The Caliphs and the Jurists therefore extended the scope of these two principles to meet the desirability and the requirement of the time. The very first problem that confronted the Companions was the election of their Caliph. The Holy Prophet had asked Abu Bakr to lead prayers before his death. So the Companions decided to accept him as their leader on the analogy that he who is a leader in religious matters can shoulder the responsibilities to run affairs of the state. This election of Abu Bakr was upheld by the general public and thus attained the status of consensus. Analogy and consensus thus were regarded as the primary or original sources of law. 'It may be mentioned that infallibility of *Ijma* is proved by the saying of the Prophet;

'My followers will not agree upon an error.'

An analogical deduction by a qualified person becomes *Ijma* if it is supported by general agreement and analogy is 'an extension of law from the original text to a particular case by means of common cause or *ila'*.

'The period of the Orthodox Caliphs extending over about 30 years was eventful in that there was a revolt against Islamic Faith, which was put down with a heavy hand by Abu Bakr'.

During this period the work of collection of the Holy Quran was completed. Allah has declared that nobody can produce even a single *Surah* like that of the Holy Book.

There are two peculiar characteristics of this period. Firstly, the principles of juristic exercise of the companions *(Ray)* and *Ijma* were followed. This was done because it was the practice of the first two Caliphs Abu Bakr and Umar that whenever a new problem arose, they used to summon the Companions and used to make decisions on their consensus. Secondly, we notice extraordinary juristic capabilities of the second Caliph Umar who made revolutionary decisions confronting him with new victories and domination over new territories. Some of his decisions are as under :

(i) He stopped the share of *Muallafal Qaloob* (those whose hearts were concentrated) whereas this practice was established from the Quranic Nas but Hadrat Umar had his eye not on the *Zahir* of the injunction but on its *ila*. The purpose behind that concession was that it was allowed as a matter of necessity during the early days of Islam with a view to achieve the goodwill of certain sections of people in order to safeguard the Muslims from their *Shar* (ill will). When the Islam was strengthened, the *ila* of this necessity was therefore no more felt.

(ii) Hadrat Umar introduced his *Ijtihad* that suspended the punishment of chopping off the hands of the thieves during the year when the people were dying as a result of famine and instead he awarded punishment by means of *Tazir* because the people indulged in thefts under conditions of *Iztrar.*

(iii) Hadrat Umar allowed a woman to contract a second marriage if the whereabouts of her husband were not known for a period of four years and did not consider it necessary to wait for the news of his death or till the death of the contemporaries of her husband.

(iv) He disbanded the distribution of lands of Iraq and Egypt to the *Mujahidin*. The *Mujahidin* contended that these lands should be distributed to them as a part of enemy property after deduction of *Khamas* but Hadrat Umar declared that these lands were part of *Fai* and *Fai* is that portion of *Baitul-Mal* which is meant for utilization for the welfare of the existing Muslims as well as for their generations to come. And this decision was based on the Quranic text *(Sura Hashar)*. So Hadrat Umar allowed the lands to remain intact with their original owners and levied *Kharaj* on them. The result was that the lands remained under cultivation and everyone benefited out of their produce.

***The Period of the Umayyads A. H. 41-132 (A.D. 661-750):*** This period starts with the rule of Amir Muawiyyah from A.H. 41 to the early period of second century *Hijra*. It was during this period that the political centre was shifted from Medina to Damascus in Syria. The Umayyads were more guided by their mundane considerations than spiritual guidance in the discharge of their functions in all spheres of life with the exception of Umar ibn Abd-al-Aziz who is well-known for his piety and rule strictly in accordance with the Quranic principles and the traditions of the Holy Prophet.

During this period there were two schools of thought amongst the Muslims. One was known as *Hijazi* and the other one as Iraqi. The first group of Scholars had their centre at Medina and of the second at Kufa. The Qadis or Judges enjoyed unrestricted power to decide cases in accordance with their personal opinion *(ray)*. This group of Iraqi *Ulama* was called *Ahal-ur-Ray*. It was because there was less publicity of *Ahadith* in Iraq in the beginning and they were confronted with complicated problems and found no clear *Nas* for their solution. The second school of thought had the advantage that they had direct approach of *Ahadith* at Hijaz and for that reason they did not deem it proper to use their own wisdom or *Ijtihad* in dealing with new matters. This group of *Ulama* was known as *Ahl-e-Hadis*. During this period the Jurists followed the principles of *Qiyas, Istehsan, Istislah*, etc. Some followers of *Ahl-e-Hadis* group however opposed this practice. No schools of *Fiqh* were in existence during this period. Everybody was at liberty to seek guidance from whichever jurist or Mufti he liked. The *Kharjis* and *Shia* sects also progressed during this period.

Hadrat Umar ibn Abdul Aziz emphasised the necessity of collection of *Ahadith*. He wrote to the people of his country to "search for the *Ahadith* of *Rasool Allah* and collect them as there was apprehension of annihilation of knowledge and the *Ulama*". It was also because a practice to introduce false *Ahadith* also started and false stories and sayings were attributed to the Holy Prophet. Divine law was here subjected to reason which only served to deform and distort it. The Umayyads stood condemned as rulers for their disregard of the fundamental principles of law and in consequence the Abbasids came to power in A.H. 132 (A.D. 750).

***The Period of the Abbasids A.H. 132-656 (A.D. 750-1258):*** The foundation of the fourth period had been laid down in the third period as the regular codification of *Fiqh* was undertaken in this period. The renowned *Imams* and Jurists whose followers spread all around the world are the product of this period. It is in this period that a number of schools of law sprang up, outstanding among them being the four *Sunni* schools, named after Imam Abu Hanifa, Imam Malik ibn Abbas, Imam Shafii and Imam Ahmad ibn Hanbal.

***Imam Abu Hanifa :*** Imam Abu Hanifa was born in Kufa (Iraq) in the year A.H. 80/A.D. 699 and died in A.H. 150/A.D. 767. He was a great *Mujtahid* and possessed remarkable qualities of reasoning. He was the propounder of the theory of *Istihsan*. During his time Jurists were, broadly speaking, divided into two classes. Those of Hijaz or Arabia were called the 'upholders of traditions', and those of Iraq were known as the upholders of private opinion.

***Imam Malik :*** Imam Malik ibn Abbas known as Imam Malik was born in A.H. 95/A.D. 713 at Medina. He was a great Jurist and the highest authority in *Hadith*. He is the founder of *Maliki* school and attached great importance to the customs of Medina on the presumptions and belief that they must have been transmitted from the time of the Prophet.

***Imam Shafii :*** Muhammad ibn Idris-al-Shafii, known as Imam Shafii was a pupil of Imam Malik. He was born in Palestine in the year A.H. 150/AD 767 and died in A.H. 204/AD 819. He is considered as the chief architect of Islamic Jurisprudence and his theories are noted for 'moderation of views and balance of judgement'. He discouraged the free use of personal opinion and projected the authority of the Prophet as the law-giver after the Quran.

***Imam Ahmad Ibn Hambal :*** He was born in Baghdad in A.H. 164/AD 780 and died in A.H. 241/AD 855. His full name is Abu Abdullah Ahmad ibn Hambal. He strictly followed the traditions of the Holy Prophet and allowed a little margin to the doctrines of *Ijma* and *Qiyas. Musnad* is his outstanding work which contains more than 40,000 traditions.

After the establishment of the schools of law the period of *Taqlid* (conformity) began. This process was finalised in the fourth century of *Hijra. Ijtihad* within the framework of respective schools started and the process of original *Ijtihad* came to a standstill. In the medieval period a large number of commentaries on the works of the authorities or old masters were written and no original work was done. Consequently *Fiqh* became rigid and stagnant for want of original efforts in this field. A large number of problems have cropped up in the wake of advancement of science and technology. These are to be solved in the light of the Holy Quran and *Sunnah.*

The question arises as to who should exercise *Ijtihad?* This question is important because *Ijma* in the early period seems to be so informal that it is difficult to know whether on a certain point there was *Ijma* or not. We are of the opinion that *Ijtihad* should be exercised by the competent scholars in cooperation with the government so that it can be enacted into legislation; otherwise it would remain purely theoretical and the conflict between the scholars and the Government will continue. In fact collective *Ijtihad* is needed on an international basis by a select committee of Muslim Jurists of the whole world. Most of the problems discussed in the classical *Fiqh* are to be reviewed and up-to-dated. Law is meant for society and not *vice versa.* With the change of society necessary changes in the classical *Fiqh* can be made by mutual consultation to keep pace with the times.

## Laws in Force

***Fiqh and Shariah :*** Here in Muslim society, the duty is to shape the laws in such a way that they become instruments for the manifestation and fulfilment of the will of Almighty, through the lives of the people and the organisation of their State. If that ideal is achieved, the laws would have a natural force to project and sustain them in the same way as its principles are maintained and universally accepted. It will become the delight of the community of Muslims to live according to their laws, and the divine wisdom, as embodied in the laws, will find its delight in providing guidance to the citizens of Muslim countries.

The law in Islam is called *Fiqh;* it is the name given to the whole science of jurisprudence because it implies the exercise of intelligence in deciding a point of law in the absence of a binding command from the Quran or *Sunnah. Fiqh* literally means "intelligence", and *faqih* is a jurist, a person skilled in the law. A *faqih* must possess the quality of independent judgement, *Fiqh* is the soul's cognisance of its rights and obligations. The Turkish Mejelle defines it as the knowledge of practical legal questions.

*Fiqh* is the knowledge of one's rights and obligations derived from the Quran, or the *Sunnah* of the Prophet, or the consensus of opinion among the learned *(ijma),* or analogical deduction *(Qiyas).* The Quran is the first source of *Fiqh, Sunnah,* the second, *Ijma,* the third *Qiyas* and the fourth source of *Fiqh.*

*Fiqh* is divided into two portions: The *Usul* and the *Furu.* The *Usul* are the roots of the law and the *Furu* are the branches. The science of *Usul* deals with the first principles of interpretation and the science of *Furu* deals with particular injunctions which really follow from the science of *Usul.* The science of *Usul* deals with the sources of law and its interpretation: while the science of *Furu* deals with the law as it is actually applicable in the courts of justice; for instance the law of *Waqf* or the law of inheritance.

In Islam the law preceded the state, both logically and in terms of time. The State existed for the purposes of enforcing the law.

Islamic law began with the activities of the jurists; it was not created by State legislation. Law was considered superior to the state, and hence not subject to state legislation.

While Islamic law is assumed to be unchanging, the impact of social change is so profound that it affects legal concepts as well as institutions.

The source of Islamic law is the will of God. Islamic law is an ethical or moral system of rules. There has always been a close connection between Islamic law and theology. Islam is a religion of both belief and action. Islamic law derives its source from the Divine Revelation through the Holy Prophet. Being Divine, these sources are believed to be sacred, final, eternal and hence immutable. Nothing can be qualified as good or bad except in relation to Allah's Will.

Islamic law is not amenable to change through legislation. It is a doctrine of commandments. There is much more emphasis on what one ought to do rather than on what one is entitled to claim as a right. Penalties and sanctions in Islamic law are religious and moral, not civil and legal. The term used for penalty is *Hudud* Allah (the limits fixed by God) which implies that a certain offence has been committed against God and that it is His prerogative to impose the penalty.

In a number of situations, some of the new practices may come into conflict with the teachings of Islamic law. In such cases, the jurists may in their *fatwa* make an attempt to reconcile the new practices with the Islamic law.

The Holy Prophet (peace be upon him) had said that moral values are the criterion of the Islamic law. He emphasised that one who lacked truthfulness and honesty is far from abiding the path of law.

The Holy Prophet brought forth the dawn of a new age—the age of realisation of *Shariah*—the age of emancipation from bonds of lawlessness and despotism—the age of a steady advancement towards perfection. He laid due stress on reasoning. He propounded the idea of social justice. It guaranteed for every individual, social and economic security.

History has never known a person other than Hadrat Muhammad (peace be upon him) to have spent his life fighting tyranny and destroying tyrants. The mission of the Holy Prophet was a complete revolution to liberate humanity, a revolution that encompassed all facets of human life and destroyed tyranny.

Islamic law never became divorced from social realities. For lawyers Islamic law consisted of enforceable legal rules; for traditionists it was a code of moral and religious duties. The concept of *"amal"* in Islamic law emerged as an instrument to modify and adapt the *Shariah* to meet the practical needs of society.

There has been no conflict between theory and practice in Islamic law. The reason for the lack of inconsistency and ambiguity is that the *Shariah* and the *Fiqh* are inseparably connected, *Shariah* being the law, and *Fiqh* the science of knowing the law. *Shariah* is, in the proper sense, the law of Islam. *Fiqh* is the science that deduces rules of law from the *Shariah.* Accordingly, *Shariah* is known through the *Fiqh.*

The *Shariah* is the central core of Islam; no understanding of its civilisation, its social history or its political system is possible without a knowledge and appreciation of its legal system. *Shariah* is the totality of Allah's commandments. *Shariah* embraces all human actions. It contains an infallible guide to ethics. It is a code of obligations. It exhibits a tendency to evaluate all affairs of life. All human activity is embraced in its sovereign domain.

## Laws of Society

*Shariah* is the wider circle, it embraces all human actions; *Fiqh* deals with what are commonly understood as legal acts. *Shariah* reminds us always of revelation, that knowledge which we could never have possessed but for the Quran; in *Fiqh,* the power of reasoning is stressed. The path of *Shariah* is laid down by Allah and His Prophet, the edifice *of Fiqh* is erected by human endeavour.

In the *Fiqh,* an action is either legal or illegal. In the *Shariah,* there are various grades of approval or disapproval. *Fiqh* is the term used for the law as a science; and *Shariah,* for the law as the Divinely ordained path of rectitude. The criterion of human action, however, is the same both in the *Shariah* and the *Fiqh.* The criterion is meant for seeking the approval of Allah by conforming to an ideally perfect code.

*Shariah* is the social code of Islam. It aims at creating a society based on a deep sense of moral responsibility in which every citizen can develop his personality in accordance with his spiritual and moral traits. The main difference between the *Shariah* and the secular law is that the *Shariah* is based on revelation.

The highest religious and juridical office in an Islamic State could be that of *"Qadi-al-Jamaa".* The historians stress that it was the noblest office in the polity of Islam. The evidence is to be found in the generous salaries, the ceremonial investitures, and the lengthy formal decrees of appointment given to the *Qadis.*

The *Fuqaha* may officially be attached to the courts as *Muftis* (jurisconsults) in Pakistan. They may also play the role of *Mushawirs* (consultants) and *Wuth thaq* (formalaries and notaries). The administration of religious and trust properties may be entrusted to them. Whenever the Government makes a donation for a special purpose, a *Faqih* may be appointed to supervise it. The inspection of trade and commerce may be made the responsibility of the *Fuqaha.* They may be given responsibilities for fixing prices and for the quality and weight of commodities in the market. The *Fuqaha* may be required to supervise the minting of coins. The status of *Fuqaha* may be sustained by their control of intellectual life. The institutions of legal learning may be placed under the administrative control of the *Fuqaha.*

On the level of the *Fuqaha* strictly religious matters including those of exegesis and theology may be referred to *Muftis.* On the level of notaries *(Wuth thaq),* the *Faqih* may be applied to register and validate various kinds of contractors and other types of legal documents. These *Wuth thaq* may be appointed also as *Muftis* and *Mushawirs.*

In matters of procedure the litigants may seek the *fatwa* of the *Muftis* in favour of their claims and may present them in the court. The judge may arrive at conclusions after consulting the notables in his court. The notaries could be given limited jurisdictions such as the attestation of a witness or a contract, yet they could not decide a case.

## Great Contributions

The law in Islam is called *Fiqah;* it is the name given to the whole science of jurisprudence because it implies the exercise of intelligence in deciding a point of law in the absence of a binding command from the Quran or *Sunnah. Fiqah* literally means "intelligence", and *faqih* is a jurist, a person skilled in the law. A *faqih* must possess the quality of independent judgement. *Fiqah* is the soul's cognisance of its rights and obligations. The Turkish *Mejelle* defines it as the knowledge of practical legal questions.

*Fiqah* is the knowledge of one's rights and obligations derived from the Quran, or the *Sunnah* of the Prophet, or the consensus of opinion among the learned *(ijma),* or analogical deduction

*(Qiyas).* The Quran is the first source of *Fiqah, Sunnah* the second, *Ijma* the third and *Qiyas* the fourth source of *Fiqah.*

*Fiqah* is divided into two portions : The *Usul* and the *Furu.* The *Usul* are the roots of the law and the *Furu* are the branches. The science of *Usul* deals with the first principles of interpretation and the science of *Furu* deals with particular injunctions which really follow from the science of *Usul.* The science or *Usul* deals with the sources of law and its interpretation, while the science of *Furu* deals with the law as it is actually applicable in the courts of justice; for instance the law of *Waqf* or the law of Inheritance.

In Islam the law preceded the State, both logically and in terms of time. The State existed for the purposes of enforcing the law.

Islamic law began with the activities of the jurists; it was not created by State legislation. Law was considered superior to the State, and hence not subject to State legislation.

The source of Islamic law is the Will of God. Islamic law is an ethical or moral system of rules. There has always been a close connection between Islamic law and theology. Islam is a religion of both belief and action. Islamic law derives its source from the Divine Revelation through the Holy Prophet. Being Divine, these sources are believed to be sacred, final, eternal and hence immutable. Nothing can be qualified as good or bad except in relation to Allah's Will.

Islamic law is not amendable to change through legislation. It is a doctrine of commandments. There is much more emphasis on what one ought to do rather than on what one is entitled to claim as a right. Penalties and sanctions in Islamic law are religious and moral, not civil and legal. The term used for penalty is *hudud* Allah (the limits fixed by God) which implies that a certain offence has been committed against God and that it is His prerogative to impose the penalty.

There has been no conflict between theory and practice in Islamic law. The reason for the lack of inconsistency and ambiguity is that the *Shariah* and the *Fiqah* are inseparably connected, *Shariah* being the law, and *Fiqah* the Science of knowing the law. *Shariah* is, in the proper sense, the law of Islam. *Fiqah* is the science that deduces rules of law from the *Shariah*. Accordingly, *Shariah* is known through the *Fiqah*.

The *Shariah* is the central core of Islam; no understanding of its civilisation, its social history or its political system is possible without a knowledge and appreciation of its legal system. *Shariah* is the totality of Allah's commandments. *Shariah* embraces all human actions. It contains an infallible guide to ethics. It is a code of obligations. It exhibits a tendency to evaluate all affairs of life. All human activity is embraced in its sovereign domain.

*Shariah* is the wider circle, it embraces all human actions; *Fiqah* deals with what are commonly understood as legal acts. *Shariah* reminds us always of revelation, that knowledge which we could never have possessed but for the Quran; in *Fiqah*, the power of reasoning is stressed. The path of *Shariah* is laid down by Allah and His Prophet (PBUH), the edifice of *Fiqah* is erected by human endeavour.

In the *Fiqah*, an action is either legal or illegal. In the *Shariah*, there are various grades of approval or disapproval. *Fiqah* is the term used for the law as a science; and *Shariah*, for the law as the divinely ordained path of rectitude. The criterion of human action, however, is the same both in the *Shariah* and the *Fiqah*. The criterion is meant for seeking the approval of Allah by conforming to an ideally perfect code.

*Shariah* is the social code of Islam. It aims at creating a society based on a deep sense of moral responsibility in which every citizen can develop his personality in accordance with his spiritual and moral traits. The main difference between the *Shariah* and the secular law is that the *Shariah* is based on revelation. That is why Islamic law does not accept the idea that whatever people determine on the basis of what appears useful to them, is good. For example, sexual relations based on free-will are allowed by secular law, while they are held to be a sin under the *Shariah*.

*Usul-ul-Fiqah* are closely related to those of *Shariah*. They have the same relationship to *Shariah* as the *Usul-ud-Din* (the principles of religion) have with *Deen*. *Shariah* is the light of knowledge. The Quran is the totality of *Shariah*, the fountain-head of wisdom. A rule of *Shariah* must essentially conform to the laws of human physical nature. *Shariah* has regularised as legal good what is considered to be good in social experience. The promise is that Allah has instituted the *Shariah* for the benefit of the people. The objective of *Shariah* is to bring *Mukallafin* out of the dictates of their desires so as to make them servants of Allah.

*Fiqah* is supposed to amplify and supplement the *Shariah* but not to supersede it.

Islamic law is the sum and substance of our faith. The purpose of this law is to bend earthly life to the purposes of God. We would interpret this step as signifying our allegiance not only to the Quran as a pure idea but also to the Quran as implemented. Islam is in essence the purposes of God for mankind as expressed in the Quran. Islam for Muslims is not an abstract idea but a system of law in operative practice.

In Islam, the goal of life is to attain eternal felicity through obeying the commands of Allah. Human reason is charged not so much with discovering unknown areas of facts as with uncovering the insights and the directions implied in divine or Prophetic announcements. Islam expects of its followers to demonstrate readiness for subordinating emotional to rationally oriented insights.

Islam is the community that has come into being to transfer into actual living the imperative that is the eternal word of God. Before revelation, the essential law of Islam existed as a transcendent pattern. By revelation, the world has been made incorporated in history with the Muslim community as its keeper. The fundamental religious arguments in Islam have been concerned essentially with what shall be the direction in which the ongoing historical enterprise is to proceed.

The nature of man need be understood only in the light and according to the standard of Quranic revelation. The classical *Ummah* lives under divine law whose protector in the *Ummah* itself; the ruler is neither source nor guarantee of the law; his is only the executive power. The state guarantees the preservation and, if possible, the expansion of religion. Islam's real intellectual bond is the conviction that all believers are brothers. Islam does not reject scientific synthesis. It does not reject free interpretation of facts either. The Islamic legal system has developed from philosophical principles.

Three fundamental values are associated with the Islamic way of life. First, Muslims believe that the goal of life is seen to be other worldly. Any worldly achievement remains valuable only inasmuch as it will be subservient to the life after death. Second, Islam perceives man's existence here and hereafter as an indivisible unit. Third, Islam makes the community the guardian of the road to salvation. By introducing these valued judgements, Islam has introduced at least three fundamental questions: How to live correctly? How to think correctly; How to organise correctly?

The Quran encompasses spiritual and worldly matters and provides the possibility of a Muslim society. This society owes its comparative uniformity to the Islamic law. Grand as may seen to us some of the threads which *Fiqah* has woven around this society, a plausible interpretation can be found for it. To quote Allama Iqbal: "In the evolution of such a society even the immutability of socially harmless rules relating to eating and drinking, purity or impurity, has a life value of its own, inasmuch as it tends to give such society a specific inwardness, and further secures that eternal and internal uniformity which counteracts the forces of heterogeneity always, latent in a society of a composite character".

The Islamic law contains what in theory at least must be considered the most potent means of self-adaptation by recognising the consensus of the competent as one of its foundations. This *Ijma* of the local learned is neither postulative nor formative : it is merely verifying. Theology and law, on the one hand, and the forms of conceptualisation, argument and presentation, on the other provided the most potent means of communicating a sense of cohesion in Islam. Canon law and customary law, canon law and executive law co-exist as an expression of divergent approaches to the social realisation of the ideal Muslim community. The history of the legal rites can to some extent be accounted for through an investigation of their relations to local cultural traditions.

The *Fiqah* covers a large field of human activities in a decisive and methodical way. It shares generously with local customs and discretionary judgement. It includes portions on public law and penal law as well as ethical precepts. The *Fiqah* has been very effective in transmitting the imperatives of Muslim spirituality into the real world.

The development of Islamic law illustrates in a most significant manner the interdependent phenomena of unity and variety in Muslim Civilisation. The essential contribution that Islam made toward the formation of its law emerges from the fundamental attitude that exists in the Quran. It pervades and unites its parts and has made of Islamic law a unique phenomenon suigeneris. Over elements of varied provenance that were retained in Islam, the central core of ideas exerted a strong assimilating power. Permeating them with what is felt to be the true Islamic spirit. This process resulted in the creation of a balance in Islamic law.

The Islamic society created the office of *Mazalim* (Ombudsman) for the redress of abuses. The administrative jurists have held in that the office of *Nazir Fil Mazalim* is of great significance in Islamic law.

The strength of Islamic law is in the extensiveness of approach which at its best is applicable to all situations. It does mean universality. It does imply immediacy in relation to the world of thought and perception which lends so much colour to it. The Islamic law possesses a quality of repose, of dignity and poise, which has developed as a result of the dynamic conception of an ideal society. Islamic law carves good life for Muslims and better life for posterity. It recognizes the supreme value of morality.

The Islamic law is at rest, and the Muslim is at rest within it. His immediacy to Allah and his acceptance of the divine order are not disturbed. A genuine submission to the Will of Allah is rewarded by the consciousness of fitting naturally into the great preordained scheme of things that embraces mankind. The Muslim finds happiness in attuning himself to the wishes of the *Rabbul Alameen.* Allah has revealed to him enough of the truth to understand what needs understanding and to trust divine wisdom where understanding ends.

The Islamic law asserts that man has been created for a purpose. His value is high and his dignity great. His body is temporal but his mind is divine. All wisdom consists in the divine law delivered to human beings. The Muslim stands secure in the centre of a wisely ordained system of law. The law teaches him his duties and his rewards.

Islamic legal system is omnipotent. It has qualities that can keep its identity under changed conditions. It continues to broaden its base within the framework of the Quranic text. It cultivates mental habits that promote legal research and the ability to discuss problems according to the categories of formal logic. It incorporates universal skills. The legal system of Islam maintained its liberal traditions of accepting information, techniques, objects and customs that are supported by logic.

Through emphasis on Quran as the primary bond between people, Islamic law and jurisprudence are capable of maintaining the intellectual unity of the area. A highly educated Muslim jurist is acceptable everywhere in Muslim territory. The dynamism of the Islamic legal institutions are responsible for the presence of component elements which makes Islamic system look like a great civilization. Abounding in its growth during the past fourteen centuries, it has appeared in the 15th Century *Hijra* as a system full of promises for the future. It has mobilized power of organizing the innumerable elements to an organizing idea more comprehensive than the desire for individual liberty.

The Islamic law showed its power in molding the forms and ethics of civic life. It is sympathetic to speculation *(Qiyas)* and it has furnished the Muslim mind with a great deal of imaginative and moralistic subject matter. This feature certainly adds a decisive trait to the cultural profile of Islam.

The originality of Islamic law consists exactly in the capacity of adapting the Quranic inspiration to its needs. Most of its conceptual contribution is either new or unique. Its style of interpretation is without a real precedent. Consequently, to understand the spirit of Islamic law, it is necessary to appraise its effectiveness. This effectiveness can be measured by the extent to which Islamic jurisprudence contributes to the welfare of Muslims.

It is fair to judge Muslim legal achievement by the outstanding accomplishments of Muslim jurists. It is fair because the unusual contribution remains to influence future generations. It is because the Islamic law is fundamentally a stable system of formal and material truths communicated to man.

We are inclined to admire Muslim jurists who broke the limitations imposed on the rational investigation of the universe. They should be accorded due respect for their intellectual boldness. These innovators have established their right to departure from the pre-Islamic system. The habit of *Ijtihad* encouraged the putting forward of opinions which are true and can be proved as facts properly integrated in a system which would assign them their proper significance.

The Islamic legal research continues what might be called an authoritarian tradition. The standards of credibility have been consciously evolved. A significant portion of the work is stimulated by Quranic revelations. The system has accorded recognition to observational and experimental methods of truth finding. To appreciate the Islamic outlook, it must be realized that the art of observation has all along been reasonable and whatever positive knowledge they have contributed is very reliable. The legal constructions are also based on deduction. No amount of logic can impugn them. The lawyers in an Islamic setting had developed precision in the observation and description of symptoms. The system enjoins empirical study. Its experimental spirit has been exceedingly sharp. Its importance as a method of a reorientation of the investigating mind is very considerable. It is necessarily sophisticated. The methods devised for experimental truth finding and some of the problems they are expected to solve are well chosen and soft.

With all the keenness of observation displayed in social studies, it is quite obvious that, on the whole, Muslim scholarship is superior in what is now called jurisprudence. There is infinitely more mental initiative in Muslim jurisprudence than in its obsequious refurbishing of ancient law. One cannot help the impression that the Muslim jurist's mastery of facts was solid and his presentation rational. He was prepared to register the minutest detail when it came to describe legal opinion, and he controlled a superb machinery of concepts and terms to help him organize his results. He can proceed with complete self-assurance: the technique is tested, and his sensitivity to shades of thought is delicately developed. The research acumen of Muslim jurists has always appeared at its best.

To appraise the effect of Islamic civilization on the development of law, three sets of facts must be taken into consideration. Firstly, during the past fourteen centuries Muslim legal scholarship is widely acknowledged. It has never stagnated intellectually. The present state of our knowledge regarding law permits a final judgement on the contribution of Islam to each branch of legal learning. It can be asserted with a fair degree of certainty that, by and large, Muslim jurists have consolidated the conceptual background of the material they took over. They have definitely surpassed their ancient predecessors. Scientific work in the field of law has maintained its vigour, and a great numbers of teachers and students are engaged in its promotion.

Secondly, legal scholarship as transmitter of Quranic thought has been a powerful inspiration for the entire world. And at times the west accepted avidly the concepts offered by the Muslim *Fuqaha.* Leading Muslim jurists are regarded with awe and might in non-Muslim settings.

Thirdly, when Islamic *Fiqah* as it has crystallized through the past fourteen centuries is analyzed for its main components, the extensive effect of its scientific influence is clearly felt. Islamic Civilization, one might say, contributed a good deal of detail, acted as a catalyzer and it did influence the fundamental structure of the legal institutions. There is hardly an area of legal reasoning where Islam has not enriched the universal norms. The concepts of *Ijtihad, Qiyas, Istehsan, Ijma Ibada, Ummah* and many others indicative of the full measure of Islamic contribution would take up many a pages without being even remotely complete.

Mastery of nature, public morality, and the condition of the common man have been suggested as measures of achievement of a civilization. It does not require elaborate demonstration that, by these standards, the Islamic legal system has a definite contribution to make. There has always been a concerted effort in Islam to put *Fiqah* and *Shariah* to such use as would ensure progressive control of the social conditions of life. The Muslim lawyers have paid attention to the problems of poverty. Islamic *Shariah* has encouraged individual charity and religious equality. The finest accomplishments of Islamic *Shariah* have spread to a wide circle. Legal consciousness has grown sufficiently strong to raise the value of human life.

Islamic legal system embodied in the concepts of *Fiqah* and *Shariah* have shown that overflowing abundance of ideas, that boundless fertility that is greatness of the vicegerents of Allah. It manifests itself in exuberant advance to all fields relevant to human life. This system is realistic. The mental effort of the jurists is directed toward ever subtler understanding of the cultural heritage, and toward ever more perfect expression of the familiar. Expansion of the range of control entails the use of proved varieties and procedures. The *Shariah* acts as an authoritative guide to progress. Quranic wisdom is trusted. *Shariah* is the fortress under whose protection Islamic life unfolds itself.

From the viewpoint of what they set out to do, Islamic *Fiqah* and *Shariah* have succeeded in making good their universalistic appeal. They have succeeded in providing the believer with a civilized and dignified form of life. Having been blessed with a divine origin, the achievements of Islamic *Fiqah* are extraordinary, and the great vitality of Islamic civilization emanates from the potentialities of *Shariah* to provide satisfactory answers to the basic questions that have been besetting the humanity on the face of globe.

The Islamic *Fiqah* promotes purpose—directedness of human existence. The *Shariah* pervades every sphere of man's activity, the technological or the economic as well as the political or the interpretative. Man is encouraged to strive for ends that have an objectively valid Orientation. No insight is considered scientific unless it is part of a context and unless this context is structured in accordance with a rational principle. The *Shariah* caters to the needs of the inner and the outer world. It promotes cultural self-understanding which is pragmatic and directly purposive. The Muslim *Faqih* would always determine the rank of his subject within the hierarchy of values by its relatedness to divinity.

The Muslim *Faqih* is aware of the need for mutual respect and for self-respect in matters cultural. The Quran projects the "exceptional value of man" as the most noble creature. The Quranic revelation tends to render man more truly human and encourages him to use the forces of the physical universe as instruments of self-liberation. Islamic humanism is based on the notion that man is destined for a transcendent life of eternal felicity whose attainment presupposes an earthly existence lived in communion with Allah.

Islamic society emphasizes legal continuity. There is a strong correlation between Islamic law and ethics, between law and society, between law and political structure. The cultural achievements develop either from definite legal situations or they may be viewed as responses to them. The very survival of Islam as an organized community under Allah depends on the existence of an adequate body of *Fuqaha* and *Ulama*. Also, integration in that community is indispensable if the individual believer desires to lead the correct life as enjoined by Quran and defined by the *Ijma*.

The science of law is an endeavour to collect and systematise what information the *Ummah* requires to realize its values. It is an effort to widen man's insight into the ways of Allah. Its ethical value depends on the area to which the law relates and on the intention *(Niyya)* of the *Faqih* who attends to it. To be fully relevant, therefore, the science of law must inquire into the data of revelation and of the *Sunna;* and it must adjust the believer systematically to this world. The law provides the hard core of the intellectual life by whose requirements the nature of legal scholarship and of the nature and function of the scholar are formed. The *Ummah* cannot continue without cultivating legal scholarship because it has its roots in fundamental needs. The science of law is directed to reorganizing, adjusting and to the initiation of exploration.

The methods of legal doctrinal utilization in Islam showed a tendency to cover the vital areas of learning as well. The *Faqih* is ever aware of the service of Allah. He demonstrates an element of civic virtue. The legal scholar sustains the framework in which the correct life can be lived. It is left to the canon lawyers *(Fuqaha)* to see to it that the government does not deviate too far from the essential demands of the *Ummah*.

The problem of the relation between co-existing lawyers of law is culturally identified with a civilization of universal "out-reach". This civilization is characteristically associated with legal aspirations. It is largely developed from Quranic message claiming universal validity. The realization of this rationality presupposes the existence of a Muslim identification. Its resolution is attempted within the framework of universal culture.

The legal culture in Islam does not exhibit any conflict. It does not reflect any contradiction between the social forms of existence and the social forms prescribed by Quranic revelation. The *Fiqah* in Islam promotes the universal Islamic culture with which it is intimately affiliated.

A series of objective criteria borrowed from Islamic *Fiqah* can be discovered to form a leading civilization. It provides analytically obtained evidence. It is based on factual knowledge of concrete beliefs and mores. The *Faqih* demonstrates an adequate comprehension of the Islamic way of life. This phenomenon has facilitated the trans-cultural effectiveness of the Muslim mission. It permits the cultural patterns of Muslim life to exist in different parts of the world. These cultural patterns are sufficiently in tune with the ideal represented by the Quran and the *Sunna.* This factor is responsible for strong cohesiveness of the Muslim community.

The Islamic *Fiqah* devises methods of reaching solutions to practical problems. This gives the community a sense of structural permanence.

The Islamic *Fiqah* and *Shariah* speak of the equality with which Allah causes tolerance, freedom and love to prevail. They promote the devotion of Muslims to the essence of truth, virtue and beauty. They provide a rational guide to humanity. They keep the Muslims away from self-seeking *(Ananiyiya)* and lead them to service *(Ubudiyya).* They put every individual in human society in his proper place. They give hope to man and have developed the mood of humanity into active optimism.

The Islamic *Fiqah* steeps itself in the sciences to gain mastery of technology and commerce, and also of defence. Thus the Islamic *Fiqah* has established a tendency to integrate without a break in basic structure the social reformer and his contribution which is perhaps an important pre-requisite of an extended developmental continuity without loss of cultural identity. In this fundamental legal attitude there lie infinite possibilities of advancement of Muslim society.

# Bibliography

Acquinas, St. Thomas : *The Political Ideas of Islam,* Hafner Publishing Company, New York, 1953.

Ahmed, Hasanuddin : *A Brief History of Islam,* Goodword Books Pvt. Ltd., New Delhi, 1998.

Ahmad, Ilyas : *Sovereignty, Islamic and Modern,* Allies Book Corporation, Karachi, 1965.

Ahmad, Moinuddin : *Religions of Mankind,* Kitab Bhavan, New Delhi, 1994.

Amery, Reeves : *The Anatomy of Peace,* Oxford, New York, 2001.

Andre, Beaufre : *General Introduction to Strategy,* Oxford, New York, 2001.

Antony, G.N. Flew : *Wants or Needs : Choices or Commands,* Allen & Co., Paris, 1953.

Arnold, Sir Thomas : *The Caliphate,* MacMillan, London, 1965.

Arnold, Thomas : *The Legacy of Islam,* Oxford University Press, New York, 2000.

Asad, Muhammad : *The Principles of State and Government in Islam,* University of California Press, California, 1961.

Ballard, Robert D.: *Exploring our Living Planet,* National Geographic Society, Washington, 1989.

Barkatullah, M. : *Khilafat,* MacMillan, London,1924.

Batty and Morgan : *War its Conduct and Legal Results,* Feroz Pub., Lahore, 2000.

Berger, M. : *Islam in World Today : Social and Political Aspects of Popular Religion,* MacMillan, London, 1970.

Broun, Daniel : *A New Introduction to Islam,* Atlantic Publishers, New Delhi, 2004.

Bukhsh, S. K. : *Contribution to the History of Islamic Civilization,* Kitab Bhavan, New Delhi, 2000.

Cajori, F. : *A History of Muslims,* Oxford, New York, 1954.

Carre, Olivier : *Islam and the State in the World Today,* Manohar Publisher, New Delhi, 1989.

Clothey, W. : *Images of Man : Religious and Historical Process in South Asia,* New Era Publications, Madras, 1984.

Corbin, H. : *Avicenna and the Visionary Recital,* MacMillan, London, 1960.

De, Laet :*The Political Systems of Empire,* Oxford, New York, 1963.

Divine, Epiphany : *Man and Transformation,* MacMillan, London, 1964.

Edward, Mortimer : *Faith and Power, the Politics of Islam,* Oxford, New York, 2002.

Emil, Brunner : *Justice and the Social Order,* Oxford, New York, 2000.

Engineer, Asghar Ali :*A Rational Approach to Islam,* Gyan Books Pvt. Ltd., New Delhi, 2001.

Faris, Nabith A. : *The Foundations of the Articles of Faith,* Feroz Pub., Lahore, 1963.

Faruqi, Ziya-ul Hasan : *The Deoband School and the Demand for Pakistan,* Popular Prakashan, Bombay, 1963.

Field, Cland H. : *Al-Ghazali : the Alchemy of Happiness,*Macmillan, London, 1910.

Fordon, S. : *The Origin of Malay Shair,* Kuala Lumpur, 1968.

Herklots G. A. and Jafar Sharif : *Islam in India,* Atlantic Publishers, New Delhi, 1999.

Gare, Frederic : *Political Islam in the Indian Subcontinent : the Jannat-i-Islam,* Manohar Publishers, New Delhi, 2001.

Gibb, H.A.R : *Studies in the Civilization of Islam,* Beacon Press, Boston,1962.

Gibran, Khalil : *The Prophet,* Jaico Publishing House, New Delhi, 1995.

Grunebaum, G.E. : *Islam : Essays in the Nature and Growth of a Cultural Tradition,* American Anthropological Association, 1955.

Guillaume, A. : *The Traditions of Islam,* Khayats, Beirut, 1966.

Haji, Khalifah : *Kashf-al-Zunan,* Faiz-a-Islam Pub., Istanbul, 1943.

Hans, Morgenthu : *Politics : Among Nations,* Oxford, New York, 1954.

Hardy, P. : *The Muslims of British India,* Cambridge University Press, New Delhi, 1998.

Hasan, Mushirul : *Islam and Indian Nationalism : Refection on Abdul Kalam Azad,* Manohar Publishers, New Delhi, 1992.

Hassan, M. : *Hadrat Abu Bakr Siddique (R.A.A.),* Kitab Bhavan, New Delhi, 2004.

Helminski : *Women of Sufism : a Hidden Treasure,* New Academic Publishers, New Delhi, 1990.

Hourani, Albert : *Thought in the Liberal Age,* Oxford, New York, 1962.

Hughes, T.P. : *Dictionary of Islam,* Allen & Co., London, 1935,

Husaini, S.A.Q : *The Constitution of the Arab Empire,* Feroz Pub., Lahore, 1954.

Hussain, S. Saukat, : *Human Rights in Islam,* Kitab Bhavan, New Delhi, 2001.

Ikram, S.M. : *Muslim Civilization in India,* Oxford, New York, 1981.

Imtiaz Ahmed, Helmut Reifeld : *Islam in South Asia : Adaptation, Accommodation and Conflict,* Social Science Press, New Delhi, 1999.

Iqbal, Muhammad : *Six Lectures on the Reconstruction of Religious Thought in Islam,* Royal Pub., Lahore, 1930.

Isaac, Asimove : *Exploring the Earth & the Cosmos,* Crown Publishers, New York, 1989.

Jansen, G.H. : *Militant Islam,* Pan Books, London, 1979.

Joshua : *The Chronicle of Joshua the Stylite,* Cambridge, New York, 1882.

Kalim, M. Siddiq : *Studies in Pakistan Culture : an International Perspective,* Manohar Publications, New Delhi, 1993.

Kaur, R. : *Islamic Co-operation and Unity,* Deep & Deep Publications, New Delhi, 1993.

Khab, Qamaruddin : *The Political Thought of Ibn Taimiyah,* Islamic Book Foundation, Lahore, 1983.

Schacht, Joseph, and Bosworth, C.E. : *The Legacy of Islam,* Oxford University Press, New York, 1979.

Seervai, H. : *Constitutional Law of India,* N.M. Tripathi & Co., Bombay, 1967.

Sharma, R.S. and Jha, V. : *Indian Society: Historical Probings,* Rawat Pub., Delhi, 1974.

Shaukat, Ali : *Masters of Muslim Thought,* Deep & Deep Pub., New Delhi, 1992.

Sherfuddin, Mohd. : *Muslim Faith and Practice,* Kitab Bhavan. New Delhi, 1982.

Sherwani, H.R.K. : *Studies in Muslim Thought and Administration,* University of Hyderbad, Hyderabad, 1945.

Siddiqi, M.Z. : *Six Lectures on the Reconstruction of Religious Thought in Islam*, Feroz Pub., Lahore, 1930.

Singh, Nagendar : *Human Rights and International Cooperation,* S. Chand & Co., New Delhi, 1969.

Smith, M. : *Readings from the Mystics of Islam*, MacMillan & Co.. London, 1950.

Smith, V.A : *Early History of India*, Oxford, New York, 1914.

Som, Tamarci : *A Brief History of Islam,* Blackwell, New York, 1992.

Stern, S.M. : *Fatimid Decrees,* Faber and Faber, London, 1964.

Subhan, J.A. : *Sufism : its Saints and Shrines*, Kitabiyat Pub., Lucknow, 1960.

Syed, M. H. : *Islam and Science,* Anmol Publications, New Delhi, 2003.

—— : *History of Muslims in India,* Anmol Publications, New Delhi, 2003.

Tarachand : *Influence of Islam on Indian Culture*, Adam Pub., Allahabad, 1963.

Temple, R.C. : *The Sufi Path of Love,* MacMillan & Co., London, 1954.

Tritton, A.S. : *The Caliphs and their Non-Muslim Subjects*, Oxford, New York, 1930.

Ullah, M. : *Administration of Justice in Islam,* Kitab Bhavan, New Delhi, 1990.

Usmani, J.M. Tariq : *The Authority of Sunnah,* Kitab Bhavan, New Delhi, 1998.

Walker, Benjamin : *Foundation of Islam : the Making of World Faith,* Rupa & Co., New Delhi, 2001.

Wasiti, Hakim Nayyar : *Muslim Contribution to Medicine,* Deep & Deep Pub., New Delhi, 1993.

Watt, W.M. : *Islamic Surveys,* Edinburgh University Press, Edinburgh, 1999.

Watt, W.M.: *Muhammad at Medina,* Oxford University Press, New York, 1956.

Winer, L. : *Contributions towards a History of Arabico-Gothic Culture,* Oxford, New York, 1917.

Yusuf, S.M.: *Economic Justice in Islam,* Kitab Bhavan, New Delhi, 1988.

Zahid, Malik : *Subjects of Quran,* Kitab Bhavan, New Delhi, 1998.

Zaydan, Jurji : *Umayyads and Abbasides,* Luzac & Co., London,1907.